Cognition and Exploratory Learning in the Digital Age

Series Editors

Dirk Ifenthaler, Learning, Design and Technology, University of Mannheim, Mannheim, Baden-Württemberg, Germany
Demetrios G. Sampson, Department of Digital Systems, University of Piraeus, Bentley, Perth, WA, Australia
Pedro Isaías, Institute for Teaching & Learning Innovation
University of Queensland, St. Lucia, QLD, Australia

Editorial Board

David C. Gibson, Curtin University, Perth, WA, Australia
Ronghuai Huang, Faculty of Education Research, Beijing Normal University, Beijing, Beijing, China
Kinshuk, College of Information, University of North Texas, Denton, TX, USA
J. Michael Spector, Department of Learning Technologies, University of North Texas, Denton, TX, USA

This book series focuses on the implications of digital technologies for educators and educational decision makers. Taking an interdisciplinary and visionary perspective on cognition and exploratory learning in the digital age, the series examines how digital technologies can or should be exploited to address the needs and propel the benefits of large-scale teaching, learning and assessment. It includes the newest technical advances and applications, and explicitly addresses digital technologies and educational innovations.

The series incorporates volumes stemming from the Cognition and Exploratory Learning in the Digital Age (CELDA) conference. Since 2004 the CELDA conference has focused on discussing and addressing the challenges pertaining to the evolution of the learning process, the role of pedagogical approaches and the progress of technological innovation, in the context of the digital age. Some of CELDA's main topics include: assessment of exploratory learning approaches and technologies, educational psychology, learning paradigms in academia and the corporate sector, student-centred learning and lifelong learning. In line with and in addition to these CELDA conference volumes, this series publishes monographs and edited volumes covering the following subject areas:

- K-12, Higher Education, Vocational Education, Business Education, Health Education
- Learning Design, Instructional Design
- Change Management, Technology Adoption, Learning Organization
- Data analytics
- Learning, Teaching, Assessment

The book series represents the most recent work in the area where cognitive psychology, information and communications technology and instructional design intersect.

More information about this series at http://www.springer.com/series/16424

Pedro Isaias • Demetrios G. Sampson
Dirk Ifenthaler
Editors

Technology Supported Innovations in School Education

Editors
Pedro Isaias
Information Systems and Technology
Management (ISTM) School
UNSW Sydney, Kensington Campus
Sydney, NSW, Australia

Demetrios G. Sampson
Department of Digital Systems
University of Piraeus
Bentley, Perth, WA, Australia

Dirk Ifenthaler
Learning, Design and Technology
University of Mannheim
Mannheim, Baden-Württemberg, Germany

ISSN 2662-5628   ISSN 2662-5636   (electronic)
Cognition and Exploratory Learning in the Digital Age
ISBN 978-3-030-48193-3   ISBN 978-3-030-48194-0   (eBook)
https://doi.org/10.1007/978-3-030-48194-0

© Springer Nature Switzerland AG 2020
This work is subject to copyright. All rights are reserved by the Publisher, whether the whole or part of the material is concerned, specifically the rights of translation, reprinting, reuse of illustrations, recitation, broadcasting, reproduction on microfilms or in any other physical way, and transmission or information storage and retrieval, electronic adaptation, computer software, or by similar or dissimilar methodology now known or hereafter developed.
The use of general descriptive names, registered names, trademarks, service marks, etc. in this publication does not imply, even in the absence of a specific statement, that such names are exempt from the relevant protective laws and regulations and therefore free for general use.
The publisher, the authors, and the editors are safe to assume that the advice and information in this book are believed to be true and accurate at the date of publication. Neither the publisher nor the authors or the editors give a warranty, expressed or implied, with respect to the material contained herein or for any errors or omissions that may have been made. The publisher remains neutral with regard to jurisdictional claims in published maps and institutional affiliations.

This Springer imprint is published by the registered company Springer Nature Switzerland AG
The registered company address is: Gewerbestrasse 11, 6330 Cham, Switzerland

Preface

This edited volume compiles a selection of extended papers from the 2017 and 2018 edition of the CELDA (Cognition and Exploratory Learning in the Digital Age) Conference (www.celda-conf.org). Research and practice have evolved from questioning if technology should be used for the support of education, to examining its impact for teaching and learning, and exploring the elements that contribute to its successful implementation. Learning technologies in general are at a stage of their evolution that demands a deeper examination of their real learning value. Some technologies have been present in education for decades, while others are just now reaching mainstream education. Nonetheless, the fast pace at which technologies change requires researchers and educators to remain current on the latest technological developments and how these impact educational environments.

The use of digital technologies for teaching and learning is nowadays a mainstream practice for school education worldwide with students, teachers, parents and school leaders being engaged in exploring technology supported innovations at several areas of school life. In this context, embracing the culture of sharing data-driven evidence from school-based action research is important for the sustainability and the wider take up of such innovations. To this end, this volume entitled *Technology Supported Innovations in School Education* presents studies from school education innovations that are supported by digital technologies, including STEM education and teachers' professional development. The chapters in this volume were organized into three parts: (a) exploring the use of digital technologies in school education; (b) technology supported STEM school education; and (c) teachers' professional development.

In Part I, "Exploring the use of digital technologies in school education, various themes emerged from different areas of expertise". In the chapter "Digital ethnicity: Social belonging in the internet age", Adams and DeVaney highlight the impact that the interaction between people and digital media is having on social values. The authors present a set of ethnicity aspects that can be affected by a premature and prolonged interaction with digital communication channels. The chapter posits that the digital ethnicity scale is a valuable instrument and that it assists the identification of digital profiles, which offer insight into the shifting educational and social demands of evolving societal groups. "The use of virtual reality at lower secondary schools", a chapter by Keller, Brucker-Kley, and Ebert, explores the use of virtual reality in the context of Swiss secondary schools. The authors developed a learning unit, which resorted to the use of virtual reality to test its effectiveness in terms of learning benefits. Although the learning unit did result in learning success, their results show that no substantial learning improvements were registered in comparison with the traditional teaching method.

Radi, in the chapter entitled "Language and electronic medium skills development through autonomous and ideological practices", argues that young generations face important challenges deriving from their use of digital technologies. While these technologies constitute a vital resource and offer diverse learning opportunities, students need to learn how to use them not only in terms of simple operation but with concern to appropriate practices, attitudes and values. The author examines how students in two private schools develop their language and computer literacy in the specific domains of language and computers. Couland, Hamon and George in the chapter "Technology enhanced learning of motions based on a clustering approach" present a new approach concerning the analysis of 3D motions. Motion capture is becoming progressively deployed in various sectors (video games, medicine, industry and education). The approach portrayed in this study aims to offer a method to examine the motion via explainable descriptors extracted from it, resulting on the provision of personalized feedback. With this feedback the student can improve their motion. The chapter "Comparing face-to-face to online instruction in secondary education: Findings of a repetitive factoral experiment", authored by Poelmans, Goeman and Wautelet, posits that some limitations remain in understanding the determining factors behind students' performance in online learning. The authors describe a repetitive factoral experiment with 151 secondary school students to assess the antecedents of perceived and observed advantages of online learning in comparison with the conventional face-to-face education delivery. The results reported in this chapter reveal that e-learning is less effective when compared with face-to-face instruction.

In Part II, technology supported STEM school education, the authors examine several educational settings that adopt technology to enhance the many dimensions of the learning process. Rossano, Rosell and Quercia in their chapter titled "Coding and computational thinking – using Arduino to acquire problem solving skills" emphasize the importance of developing elementary coding and computational thinking skills from childhood, not only for programming, but to assist students to perfect problem solving competences and to gain a more comprehensive operational knowledge. This study designed eight learning activities for middle school students, with no coding experience featuring several real life problems that they had to solve. The results revealed an improvement of the students' knowledge and programming. "Learning through a 'route planner'– Human-computer information retrieval for automatic assessment", a chapter by Fioravera, Marchisio, Di Caro and Rabellino, underlines value of using methodologies for the organization of automatic assessment resources resting on natural language metadata. The authors argue that learning management systems convey various benefits for instructors to extend their teaching strategies in collaborative online communities of practice. The features that they offer can assist teachers to support their students' autonomous learning.

The chapter "Orchestrating outdoor location-based learning activities", by Mettis and Väljataga, reports on two pedagogical experiences using a location-based application Avastusrada. During 1 year, a teacher created and assessed different learning scenarios, where the students were to follow outdoor tracks and complete various tasks in different locations. To compare the outcomes in another parallel experiment the students acted as co-creator of the scenarios. The two experiences were assessed via focus group interviews with the participating teachers.

In Part III, teachers' professional development, the emphasis is placed on strategies, tools and technology that can enhance the professional development of teachers. The chapter "Online professional learning communities for developing teachers' digital competences", by Seufert, Guggemos and Tarantini, highlights the impact that the digitalization of education is causing on teachers and their capacity to perform their work. The authors argue that it is necessary not only to determine which digital competences are vital for teachers but also to search for strategies to promote them. This study proposes a framework to outline the core digital skills that teachers require and suggests the creation of online professional learning communities to develop those skills. Lameras and Papageorgiou in their chapter titled "Experiences of multimodal teaching through a serious game: meanings, practices and discourses" focuses on the perceptions and approaches that schoolteachers have towards multimodality via the deployment of a serious game. The authors describe the use of a game (STEAM) that was created with the purpose of assisting schoolteachers to gain insight into the benefits of using multimodality to improve the learning experience of their students. This study examines the results of the game's playtest and the ensuing semi-structured online questionnaires.

Mansor, Yunus and Yuet's chapter titled "The development of teacher leadership inventory in Malaysian educational context" describes and examines the creation of a Teacher Leadership Inventory. The authors propose a new and improved version of the inventory with items to measure teacher leadership within Malaysia's education sector. Their chapter highlights three important factors: knowledge, skill and value. This inventory aims to measure secondary teachers' self-assessment.

Learning Technologies are at the forefront of innovation in education. While the Education sector is advised to distance itself from an excessive technological determinism, it is important to examine the tools that are being deployed in instructional contexts. Their characteristics and affordances are key reasons for their inclusion as a support of both teaching and learning and as such they need to be closely explored and assessed in terms of their pedagogical value. As educators and researchers experiment with technology in education, their findings become central for the advancement of learning technologies, not only in terms of what technologies are more valuable, but also with regards to creating guidelines for their implementation.

Previous editions of the CELDA conference have originated various published volumes. In their first publication, Spector, Ifenthaler, Isaias, Kinshuk and Sampson (2010) approach the general developments and challenges of learning and instruction in the digital age. More specifically, the editors gathered contributions that examined cognitive approaches to learning and instruction, knowledge representation and mental models technology, facilitated tools and techniques, communications and methods and integrative methods and online learning. In Ifenthaler, Spector, Kinshuk, Isaias and Sampson (2011), the editors compiled research initiatives that emphasize multiple perspectives on problem solving and learning in the context of the digital age by exploring related topics such as pedagogical usability issues in web-based learning objects, automated measurement of critical thinking for discussion forum participants, expanding global awareness with virtual collaboration and simulation games as learning experience.

In Isaias, Ifenthaler, Kinshuk, Sampson and Spector (2012), the editors intended to assess the impact of web 3.0 in learning and instruction, by focusing on student-centred learning, collaborative learning and exploratory technologies, and addressing educational precepts such just-in-time learning, constructivism and web 3.0's adoption in education. Following the tendency for the adoption of mobile devices in education, Sampson, Isaias, Ifenthaler and Spector (2013) compiled the most relevant contributions pertaining to ubiquitous and mobile learning in the digital age and all its fundamental ramifications, such as formal and informal learning environments, social web technologies, virtual worlds and game-based learning, and location-based and context-aware environments. On a later publication Sampson, Ifenthaler, Spector and Isaias (2014) emphasized the importance of digital systems for open access in the context of both formal and informal learning and gathered contributions that covered the theoretical and practical aspects of open access, as well as different methods and technologies used to support it. In Isaias, Spector, Ifenthaler and Sampson (2015) the focus was placed on e-learning systems, which were scrutinized from different perspectives: exploratory learning technologies, e-learning social web design, learner communities through e-learning implementations, and collaborative and student-centred e-learning design.

In the following year, Spector, Ifenthaler, Sampson and Isaias (2016) gathered contributions about the competencies, challenges and transformation that stem from the deployment of digital technologies. The publication introduces this subject, reflects about the changes in learning and instructional paradigms, debates assessments and analytics for teachers and decision makers, and examines the changing tools and environments teachers and learners must face. In Sampson, Ifenthaler, Spector and Isaias (2018), digital technologies were explored from the perspective of their role as promoters of sustainable educational innovations for the enhancement of teaching, learning and assessment in all educational levels. The research depicted in this publication addressed the importance of digital technologies in transforming the learning environment, enriching the student learning experiences, measuring and assessing teaching and learning, and cultivating student competences for the digital smart society. In their last publication, Sampson, Spector, Ifenthaler, Isaias and Sergis (2019) focused on the transformational potential that learning technologies have for large-scale teaching, learning and assessment. The editors gathered the outcomes of research efforts featuring state-of-the-art case studies examining the innovative influence of learning technologies, such as Massive Open Online Courses and educational data analytics.

Sydney, Australia Pedro Isaías
Mannheim, Germany Dirk Ifenthaler
Piraeus, Greece Demetrios G. Sampson

References

Ifenthaler, D., Spector, J. M., Kinshuk, Isaias, P., & Sampson, D. (Eds.) (2011). Multiple perspectives on problem solving and learning in the digital age. New York, NY: Springer.

Isaias, P., Ifenthaler, D., Kinshuk, Sampson, D. G., & Spector, J. M. (Eds.). (2012). Towards learning and instruction in Web 3.0: Advances in cognitive and educational psychology. New York, NY: Springer.

Isaias, P., Spector, J. M., Ifenthaler, D., & Sampson, D. G. (Eds.) (2015). E-learning systems, environments and approaches: Theory and implementation. Switzerland: Springer International Publishing.

Sampson, D. G., Ifenthaler, D., Spector, J. M., & Isaias, P. (Eds.). (2018). Digital technologies: Sustainable innovations for improving teaching and learning. New York, NY: Springer.

Sampson, D. G., Ifenthaler, D., Spector, J. M. & Isaias, P. (Eds.) (2014). Digital systems for open access to formal and informal learning. Switzerland: Springer

Sampson, D. G., Isaias, P., Ifenthaler, D., & Spector, J. M. (Eds.). (2013). Ubiquitous and mobile learning in the digital age. New York, NY: Springer.

Sampson, D. G., Spector, J. M., Ifenthaler, D., Isaias, P., & Sergis, S. (Eds.). (2019). Learning technologies for transforming large-scale teaching, learning and assessment. New York, NY: Springer.

Spector, M., Ifenthaler, D., Kinshuk (Eds.) (2010). Learning and instruction in the digital age. Boston, MA: Springer.

Spector, J. M., Ifenthaler, D., Sampson, D. G., & Isaias, P. (Eds.). (2016). Competencies in teaching, learning and educational leadership in the digital age. New York, NY: Springer.

Acknowledgements

We acknowledge the support of the International Association for Development of the Information Society (http://www.iadisportal.org/) and its continuing sponsorship of the ***International Conference on Cognition and Exploratory Learning in Digital Age (CELDA)***. In addition, we wish to express our gratitude to all the members of the CELDA 2017 and 2018 international program committees for their timely and thoughtful reviews of all papers submitted to the conferences. We also would like to acknowledge the support of Springer Science + Business Media and Springer's education editor, Melissa James. Springer has been very supportive of CELDA for many years by supporting the publication of an edited volume based on expanded and edited versions of the best CELDA papers. Finally, we would like to acknowledge the support provided by Sandra Santos and Sara Pífano, our editorial assistants, who were instrumental in formatting the papers for electronic presentation, facilitating this edited volume's publication.

Sydney, Australia Pedro Isaías
Mannheim, Germany Dirk Ifenthaler
Piraeus, Greece Demetrios G. Sampson

Contents

Part I Exploring the Use of Digital Technologies in School Education

1. Digital Ethnicity: Social Belonging in the Internet Age 3
   Nan B. Adams and Thomas A. DeVaney

2. The Use of Virtual Reality at Lower Secondary Schools........... 15
   Thomas Keller, Elke Brucker-Kley, and Nico Ebert

3. Language and Electronic Medium Skills Development Through Autonomous and Ideological Practices 33
   Odette Bourjaili-Radi

4. Technology-Enhanced Learning of Motions Based on a Clustering Approach....................................... 51
   Quentin Couland, Ludovic Hamon, and Sébastien George

5. Comparing Face-to-Face to Online Instruction in Secondary Education: Findings of a Repetitive Factoral Experiment 71
   Stephan Poelmans, Katie Goeman, and Yves Wautelet

Part II Technology Supported STEM School Education

6. Coding and Computational Thinking: Using Arduino to Acquire Problem-Solving Skills 91
   Veronica Rossano, Teresa Roselli, and Gaetano Quercia

7. Learning Through a "Route Planner": Human-Computer Information Retrieval for Automatic Assessment 115
   Michele Fioravera, Marina Marchisio, Luigi Di Caro, and Sergio Rabellino

8. Orchestrating Outdoor Location-Based Learning Activities 143
   Kadri Mettis and Terje Väljataga

Part III Teachers' Professional Development

9 **Online Professional Learning Communities for Developing Teachers' Digital Competences** 159
Sabine Seufert, Josef Guggemos, and Eric Tarantini

10 **Experiences of Multimodal Teaching Through a Serious Game: Meanings, Practices and Discourses** 175
Petros Lameras and Vasiliki Papageorgiou

11 **The Development of Teacher Leadership Inventory in Malaysian Educational Context** 195
Mahaliza Mansor, Jamal Nordin Yunus, and Fanny Kho

Index 213

Contributors

Nan B. Adams Southeastern Louisiana University, Hammond, LA, USA

Odette Bourjaili-Radi La Trobe University, Bundoora, VIC, Australia

Elke Brucker-Kley ZHAW School of Management and Law, Winterthur, Switzerland

ZHAW, Institute of Business Information Technology, Winterthur, Switzerland

Luigi Di Caro Department of Computer Science, University of Turin, Turin (TO), Italy

Quentin Couland Le Mans Université, Le Mans, France

Thomas A. DeVaney Southeastern Louisiana University, Hammond, LA, USA

Nico Ebert ZHAW School of Management and Law, Winterthur, Switzerland

ZHAW, Institute of Business Information Technology, Winterthur, Switzerland

Michele Fioravera Department of Mathematics, University of Pisa, Turin (TO), Italy

Sébastien George Le Mans Université, Le Mans, France

Katie Goeman Research Centre for Information Systems Engineering (LIRIS Brussels), University of Leuven (KU Leuven), Brussels, Belgium

Josef Guggemos Institute of Business Education and Educational Management, University of St. Gallen, St. Gallen, Switzerland

Ludovic Hamon Le Mans Université, Le Mans, France

Thomas Keller ZHAW School of Management and Law, Winterthur, Switzerland

ZHAW, Institute of Business Information Technology, Winterthur, Switzerland

Petros Lameras School of Computing, Electronics and Mathematics, Coventry University, Coventry, UK

Mahaliza Mansor Faculty Management and Economics, Sultan Idris Education University, Tanjung Malim, Perak, Malaysia

Marina Marchisio Department of Mathematics, University of Pisa, Turin (TO), Italy

Kadri Mettis Tallinn University, Tallinn, Estonia

Vasiliki Papageorgiou Centre for Higher Education Research and Scholarship, Imperial College London, London, UK

Stephan Poelmans Research Centre for Information Systems Engineering (LIRIS Brussels), University of Leuven (KU Leuven), Brussels, Belgium

Gaetano Quercia Department of Computer Science, University of Bari, Bari, Italy

Sergio Rabellino Department of Computer Science, University of Turin, Turin (TO), Italy

Teresa Roselli Department of Computer Science, University of Bari, Bari, Italy

Veronica Rossano Department of Computer Science, University of Bari, Bari, Italy

Sabine Seufert Institute of Business Education and Educational Management, University of St. Gallen, St. Gallen, Switzerland

Eric Tarantini Institute of Business Education and Educational Management, University of St. Gallen, St. Gallen, Switzerland

Terje Väljataga Tallinn University, Tallinn, Estonia

Yves Wautelet Research Centre for Information Systems Engineering (LIRIS Brussels), University of Leuven (KU Leuven), Brussels, Belgium

Fanny Kho Chee Yuet Faculty Management and Economics, Sultan Idris Education University, Tanjung Malim, Perak, Malaysia

Jamal Nordin Yunus Faculty Management and Economics, Sultan Idris Education University, Tanjung Malim, Perak, Malaysia

About the Authors

Nan B. Adams (Southeastern Louisiana University) is Professor of Educational Leadership and Technology at Southeastern Louisiana University. She has published numerous articles on topics that surround leadership and the social aspects of technological change. Her past experience as Director of Academic Computing at two large higher education institutions along with over 20 years of teaching graduate level leadership and technology seminars have allowed her to be actively engaged with her research agenda. She has chaired more than 30 dissertation committees in her academic career and has several doctoral students actively working toward graduation.

Odette Bourjaili-Radi (until 2019 La Trobe University, at the present – independent researcher) was born and raised in Lebanon. She was educated in Australia and taught ICT and Humanities in secondary colleges for 24 years and completed her MEd and PhD degrees researching the education sector besides studying other courses. Her PhD thesis investigated the relationship between selected secondary school students' use of computer tools (spelling and grammar checkers) and their English writing. Her thesis was published by Lambert Academic Publishing services. Similarly, in her current study, she is investigating a comparison between two private schools: one is only for girls, referred to as G school, and the other is co-educational, referred to as BG school. The main focus is comparing the students' performance and use of the electronic medium at school and at home. The G school students handwrite their notes and assignments in their workbooks, while the BG students use their electronic medium 7 to 9 hours a day. She presented and published refereed and non-refereed papers based on her findings in Canada, Hungary, Denmark, Cyprus, England, Portugal, Australia, and Budapest.

Elke Brucker-Kley (ZHAW) is an information scientist and has been researching and teaching at the ZHAW School of Management and Law since 2011. Her focus is on interdisciplinary projects dealing with the human-centric design of innovative solutions and the social impact of technologies. Her main research interest currently lies in the effect of mixed reality technologies on learning success and the application of mixed reality for the visualization of future scenarios for human–machine interaction. During and after completing her studies in information science at the University of Konstanz (MSc 1995), she worked for Helvetia Insurance from 1994 to 1998 as a project manager in the Knowledge Management department and in the Technology & Innovation incubator. From 1998 to 2008 she was a Practice Specialist for international consulting projects in the Business Technology Office of McKinsey & Company, where she was responsible for the management of the global Enterprise Architecture practice. From 1998 to 2011, she was a member of the management team in the COO's office of the Presidential Department of the City of Zurich, where she drove forward technology-enabled change in the areas of process management, collaboration and management information.

Quentin Couland (Le Mans University) is a PhD student and junior lecturer at the LIUM (IEIAH team) since 1st September 2015. He studied machine learning (supervised/unsupervised learning), signal and data processing (advanced signal processing, data compression, image compression), and documents processing. His thesis' goal is to develop a Technology Enhanced Learning (TEL) environment allowing a student to improve their motion learning, by using their motion data, with machine learning techniques (clustering).

Thomas A. DeVaney (Southeastern Louisiana University) is Professor of Educational Leadership and Technology, Southeastern Louisiana University. He has numerous published articles on the topics that surround educational leadership and statistical significance. He is currently Department Head of Educational Leadership and Technology at Southeastern Louisiana University, USA. He has served as methodologist on more than 30 dissertation committees in his academic career and has several doctoral students actively working toward graduation.

Nico Ebert (ZHAW) is a senior lecturer and research scientist in the Process Management group at the ZHAW School of Management and Law. He is teaching at bachelor and master's level as well as in continuous education in the area of business analysis and requirements engineering. He holds a PhD in Information Systems and is the author of currently 21 publications in peer-reviewed journals and conference proceedings.

Luigi Di Caro (University of Turin) is a researcher in the Department of Computer Science of the University of Torino since October 2014. He has a Master's degree and a PhD in Computer Science. His main interests include Artificial Intelligence (AI), Natural Language Processing (NLP), Data Mining, Machine Learning, Legal Informatics and related interdisciplinary interactions with Cognitive Sciences and social-impact applications. Luigi Di Caro started working on Data Mining techniques applied on text sources since his master's thesis in 2007. Luigi Di Caro currently works within the Social Computing research group of the Department of Computer Science, where he leads all projects and activities related to Natural Language Processing and Legal Informatics.

Michele Fioravera (University of Turin) is a PhD in Pure and Applied Mathematics from the Turin Doctoral School of Mathematical Sciences. With the aim of facilitating learning and teaching in virtual communities, he studied and developed techniques for automatically generating "routes" of resources shared by instructors. He also collaborated in local and transnational research projects on digital education: training teachers and students, online tutoring, creating open online courses, developing materials and managing virtual learning environments.

Sébastien George (Le Mans University) is Full Professor of Computer Science since 2013 at Le Mans University in France. He teaches at the Institute of Technology of Laval. He is head of the team IEIAH (working in the field of Technology Enhanced Learning) at LIUM Laboratory. He received the PhD degree in computer science in 2001. Then he did a postdoctoral fellowship at the TeleUniversity of Quebec in Canada, before joining INSA Lyon in 2002. He is the co-author of more than 180 publications in scientific books, journals and conferences. He is the editor-in-chief of the journal *STICEF* (Sciences and Technologies of Information and Communication for Education and Training). His major fields of interest are computer supported collaborative learning, authoring tools and assistance to human tutoring. He is particularly interested in applications integrating innovative Human Machine Interactions in the context of education and training (serious games, mixed reality).

Katie Goeman (KU Leuven) holds a PhD in Social Sciences. She was appointed Assistant Professor at the Faculty of Economics and Business of the KU Leuven (Campus Brussels). She investigates design and implementation issues regarding blended learning and training, and monitoring of ICT in education. To this end, she is also affiliated as a researcher with the Centre for Instructional Psychology and Technology at the Faculty of Psychology and Educational Sciences of the same university.

Josef Guggemos (University of St. Gallen) is a postdoctoral researcher at the University of St. Gallen, Switzerland. He received a master's degree in Business Research (MBR) and a PhD in Business Education Science from Ludwig-Maximilians-University Munich. His current research focus is on Computational Thinking, Social Robots in Education and Competencies of Teachers in the Context of Digital Transformation.

Ludovic Hamon (Le Mans University) is an associate professor at "IUT de Laval", Le Mans Université, France, since 2014. In July 2011, he received his PhD in automation and applied computer science from the LARIS laboratory (EA 7315). He currently conducts his research at the LIUM laboratory (computer science laboratory of Le Mans Université). His main fields of interest are: the manual or automatic analysis of data coming from new interaction paradigms in VEHL (Virtual Environment for Human Learning), modelling and analysis of human motions in learning situations, and contributions of virtual and augmented environments in the same context.

Thomas Keller (ZHAW) studied electrical engineering at the Swiss Federal Institute of Technology (ETH) Zurich between 1987 and 1993. Later on, he successfully completed a degree program in information technology at University of Zurich, where he also obtained his PhD. Thomas Keller is an expert in the definition of complex tool systems, business process automation and emerging technologies. Since 2003, he has been a senior lecturer at the ZHAW School of Management and Law, since 2007 as a professor of information technology. From 2008 till end of 2015, he acted as the head of the Institute which he founded. His field of expertise is business process management, modeling and automation, the application of new technologies, e.g., mixed reality and blockchain, in entrepreneurial contexts and scenarios about our future digital lives.

Petros Lameras (Coventry University) is Assistant Professor at the Faculty of Engineering, Environment and Computing, Coventry University, an associate researcher at the Post-Digital Cultures Research Centre and a Visiting Scientist at the Massachusetts Institute of Technology – Media Lab for doing research on games for STEM and games for science teacher training. He is currently the principal investigator of research projects funded by the European Commission such as the H2020 Magellan and Beaconning, the Erasmus + STEAM, Gate:Vet, Rhythm4All and GOAL and a co-investigator on the NEWTON ESRC project CreativeCulture. His interests span the areas of serious games, game-based learning, deep learning and artificial intelligence in teaching and learning, information science, STEM teaching, technology-enhanced learning in general and within the research strand of mapping pedagogical models and principles to game design. He has been awarded the prestigious Society for Research into Higher Education (SRHE) award in the UK for carrying out research on features of serious games design encompassing an attempt to match game categories/mechanics with learning attributes.

Mahaliza Mansor (Universiti Pendidikan Sultan Idris) is a Senior Lecturer in Educational Management Department, Faculty of Management and Economic, Sultan Idris Education University. She holds a Bachelor's Degree in Business Administration from Western Michigan University, USA, as well as Master of Education in Business Administration and Doctorate in Human Resource Development degrees from Sultan Idris Education University. She has served as a teacher at SMK Sungkai, Perak (1996–2013); a lecturer at the Teacher Training Institute, Sultan Abdul Halim Campus, Sg Petani, Kedah (2013–2014); and a lecturer at Sultan Idris Education University (2014 until now). In addition, as a lecturer, she is very active in presenting academic papers at both domestic and international conferences.

Marina Marchisio (University of Turin) is Professor of Mathematics at the University of Turin, Department of Molecular Biotechnology and Health Sciences. Her research domain is Digital Education, in particular teaching and learning STEM disciplines with new technologies. She is the scientist-in-charge of the Italian Ministry of Education's Project Problem Posing and Solving and the coordinator of several projects of the University of Turin for digital university guidance, e-learning, school and academic success.

Kadri Mettis (Tallinn University) is a PhD student in Information Society Technologies in the School of Digital Technologies at Tallinn University (Estonia) and a teacher of natural sciences at Audentes Gymnasium. Her research focuses on learning design and orchestration of mobile outdoor learning.

Vasiliki Papageorgiou (Imperial College London) is currently a Doctoral Researcher at Imperial College London, United Kingdom. Her research focuses on digital pedagogy, design for learning, decision-making in multidisciplinary university design teams and the intersectionality between online and face-to-face teaching and learning approaches. She has worked on FP7 and Erasmus+ European projects in the domain of Technology- Enhanced Learning as well as on educational projects with industry partners. She has also been the principal investigator of individual research projects on the use of technologies to enhance learning and teaching in K-12 Education with a focus on collaborative and social learning. Vasiliki is a qualified teacher and has international experience in teaching nursery and primary school students.

Stephan Poelmans (KU Leuven) is professor of Information Management at the University of Leuven (KU Leuven). He holds a PhD in Business Economics, with a focus on Information Management. His research interests include the usability, implementation and deployment of workflow management systems and enterprise information systems. More recently, his research is focused on e-learning systems and their use in the field of software engineering, as well as software modeling. Stephan is a member of the LIRIS research (campus Brussels) and teaches courses in data management, data mining and software engineering.

Gaetano Quercia (University of Bari) has a bachelor's degree in Informatics and Digital Communication. He defended the thesis entitled "Arduino and scratch: definition and experimentation of a training path for Computational Thinking". Currently, he is working for a software house.

Sergio Rabellino (University of Turin) is the head of the ICT technical staff office of the Department of Computer Science, University of Turin. He co-operates with the research groups in Security, Eidomatics, High Performance Computing, Artificial Intelligence and E-learning. He is a Moodle Developer and hardware/software architect of e-learning platforms. As technical head and architect of the Moodle based projects Start@Unito, Orient@amente, iLearn and at the University, he has more than 40 publications on e-learning tools and methods.

Teresa Roselli (Univeristy of Bari) is Associate Professor in the Department of Computer Science at the University of Bari. She is the coordinator of the TELL laboratory (Technology Enhanced Learning Lab) in the Computer Science

Department of the University of Bari. Currently, she is the coordinator of the degree courses in Computer Science, president of the e-learning services of University of Bari and member of the academic senate. Her research activities are focused on Educational Technology to advance the state-of-the-art and practical use of computation and communication technologies for learning and teaching as well as defining and validating new methods and techniques for the design and implementation of innovative learning environments. She has been supervisor for different PhD students and Research Fellows. She has served as a PC member of several national and international conferences and workshops in the Educational Technology field.

Veronica Rossano (Univeristy of Bari) is Assistant Professor in the Department of Computer Science at the University of Bari. Her research activities are focused on Educational Technology, in particular, the main aim of her research is to advance the state-of-the-art and practical use of computation and communication technologies for learning and teaching as well as defining and validating new methods and techniques for the design and implementation of innovative learning environments. She is part of the editorial staff of *Journal of e-Learning and Knowledge Society* and she is co-organizer of different workshops and special sessions on Educational Technology in different international conferences. She has served as a PC member of several conferences or workshops, including ICALT, CELDA, ICEIT, DMS, IV and T4E. She also serves as a reviewer for the most important journals in the field of Educational Technology, such as *Computers and Education, Journal of Distance Education Technologies, Journal of Visual Languages, Multimedia Tools and Applications, Computing*, and *IEEE Multimedia*.

Sabine Seufert (University of St. Gallen) is a full professor and director of the Institute of Business Education and Educational Management at the University of St. Gallen, Switzerland. She is member of the editorial board of the *International Journal of Learning Technology* and the *International Journal of Advanced Corporate Learning*. Her research interests lie in educational management and digital transformation of education.

Eric Tarantini (University of St. Gallen) is a research and teaching assistant at the Institute of Business Education and Educational Management at the University of St. Gallen, Switzerland. He received a master's degree in Business Innovation. His current research focus is on social video learning and digital transformation of education.

Terje Väljataga (Tallinn University) is a Senior Researcher in the School of Educational Sciences at Tallinn University (Estonia). Her research interests focus on learning designs, orchestration and teacher support in outdoor mobile learning settings as well as students' conceptual change and transformative learning.

Yves Wautelet (KU Leuven) is Professor in Information Systems at KU Leuven, Belgium, and visiting Professor at Université de Namur, Belgium. He formerly has been an IT project manager and a Postdoc Fellow at Université Catholique de Louvain, Belgium. He completed a PhD thesis focusing on project and risk management issues in large enterprise software design. Yves also is a Master of Management Sciences as well as a Master of Information Systems. His research interests include various aspects of software engineering and enterprise information systems such as life-cycle management, requirements engineering, IT governance, agent-oriented development and e-learning. He also focuses on the application of his research into industrial environments.

Fanny Kho Chee Yuet (Universiti Pendidikan Sultan Idris) specializes in educational management for her publication, research and lecture. She is a pioneer in the study of Teacher Leadership in Malaysia. She obtained her Doctor of Philosophy degree in Educational Management at Sultan Idris Education University, the only education university in Malaysia. Fanny currently serves as Senior Lecturer in the Department of Educational Management, Faculty of Management and Economics, Sultan Idris Education University, Malaysia. Recently, she has been awarded the Excellent Service Award 2019. Over the last few years, Fanny has also worked in the Sarawak State Education Department as Deputy Director of English Unit prior to her experience as trained teacher for 18 years. She has also trained hundreds of preschool teachers in making learning fun. Similarly, Fanny has also conducted workshops in Crafting Literature Review for postgraduate students at Sultan Idris Education University. In terms of academic research, Fanny had conducted some research in the area of teacher leadership and edutainment.

Jamal Nordin Yunus (Universiti Pendidikan Sultan Idris) graduated in Geography with education at the Universiti Sains Malaysia in 1990. He went again to the same university in 1994 and completed MEd in Educational Planning. Jamal received a PhD in Educational Management from Universiti Utara Malaysia 2008. He has been Lecturer since 2000 at Sultan Idris Education University. He was appointed Senior Lecturer in 1992 and as an associate professor in educational management in 2016. Jamal has been a Visiting Scholar at the University of Glasgow School of Education. He has the experience of teaching several courses in Management and Educational Leadership. Amongst these courses are: action research, supervision and instruction, research methodology, applied statistics, learning organization in education, curriculum and instructional design, administration and management education, and critical and creative Thinking.

About the Editors

Pedro Isaias is an Associate Professor at the Information Systems & Technology Management School of The University of New South Wales (UNSW – Sydney), Australia. Previously he was an Associate Professor at The University of Queensland, Brisbane, Australia. Before moving to Australia, he was also an Associate Professor at Universidade Aberta (Portuguese Open University) in Lisbon, Portugal, where he was responsible for several courses and director of the master's degree program in Management / MBA. He was also director of the master's degree program in Electronic Commerce and Internet for 10 years. Associate Professor Pedro Isaias holds a PhD in Information Management (in the specialty of information and decision systems) from the New University of Lisbon. Author of several books, book chapters, papers and research reports, all in the information systems area, he has headed several conferences and workshops within the mentioned area. He has also been responsible for the scientific coordination of several EU funded research projects. He is also a member of the editorial board of several journals and program committee member of several conferences and workshops. In the past 20 years, he has developed expertise in Learning Technologies and e-Learning, as part of his roles. Currently, he conducts research activity related to MIS in general and more specifically Learning Technologies, Data Analytics, Business Intelligence, Digital Transformation, e-Business and WWW related areas.

Demetrios G. Sampson is Professor of Learning Technologies at the University of Piraeus, Greece. He is the co-author of 350 articles in scientific books, journals and conferences and the editor of 17 books, 35 special issues in academic journals and 40 international conference proceedings. He has received 10 times Best Paper Award in International Conferences on Learning Technologies. He has been a Keynote/Invited Speaker in 90 International/National Conferences. He has been director, principal investigator and/or research consultant in 70 Research and Innovation projects with external funding at the range of 16 Million€. He has supervised 155 honours and postgraduate students to successful completion. He has developed and delivers the first Massive Online Open Course (MOOC) on the use of Educational Data Analytics by School Teachers (Analytics for the Classroom

Teacher), offered by the edX platform (a Harvard and MIT led global initiative) which has attracted more than 16.000 participants from 160 countries around the world since October 2016. He is the recipient of the IEEE Computer Society Distinguished Service Award (July 2012) and named a Golden Core Member of IEEE Computer Society in recognition of his contribution to the field of Learning Technologies. He is also the recipient of the Golden Nikola Tesla Chain Award of the International Society for Engineering Pedagogy (IGIP) for "International outstanding achievements in the field of Engineering Pedagogy" (September 2018).

Dirk Ifenthaler is Professor and Chair of Learning Design and Technology at the University of Mannheim, Germany, and UNESCO Deputy Chair of Data Science in Higher Education Learning and Teaching at Curtin University, Australia. His previous roles include Professor and Director at Centre for Research in Digital Learning at Deakin University, Australia, Manager of Applied Research and Learning Analytics at Open Universities Australia and Professor for Applied Teaching and Learning Research at the University of Potsdam, Germany. He was a 2012 Fulbright Scholar-in-Residence at the Jeannine Rainbolt College of Education at the University of Oklahoma, USA. Dirk's research focuses on the intersection of cognitive psychology, educational technology, data analytics and organizational learning. His research outcomes include numerous co-authored books, book series, book chapters, journal articles and international conference papers as well as successful grant funding in Australia Germany and the USA. He is the Editor-in-Chief of *Technology, Knowledge and Learning*, Senior Editor of *Journal of Applied Research in Higher Education* and Deputy Editor-in-Chief of *International Journal of Learning Analytics and Artificial Intelligence for Education*.

Part I
Exploring the Use of Digital Technologies in School Education

Chapter 1
Digital Ethnicity: Social Belonging in the Internet Age

Nan B. Adams and Thomas A. DeVaney

1.1 Introduction

Much of current literature focuses on various effects the rapid and pervasive emergence of social media has on our everyday lives. Ethnographies, how to interact with the Internet of Things (IoT), and casting the future as no longer human seem to dominate the discussion. This de facto conversation is interesting but often misses cohesion and reflects an observation or response to some undefined phenomenon rather than an attempt to organize these effects to guide action. The reality is that the influence of these digital communication technologies referred to as social media is changing human actions and beliefs. The construction of our social reality is in flux. For over a decade, the majority of the world's population "text" rather than "talk"; couples fall in love online and meet after the fact; gender identity is becoming a choice made not by biology but by a screen name or the physical appearance of an avatar. Pew Research Center (2019) reported 2/3 of Americans get at least some of their news from social media – and for the first time, 55% of these Americans are ages 50 or older. For the under 50 demographic, 74% of Americans of all races get news on social media sites. Facebook is the most commonly cited social media site, but Twitter, YouTube, and Snapchat are sites on the rise. Growth on each of these social media sites is bolstered by the investments the companies have made of the last year to increase their news usability. As a result of this phenomenal use of social media, social groups are formed in these virtual spaces that provide new kinds of common identity to previously disparate individuals. The digital ethnicity model has yielded digital profiles based on certain demographic characteristics. These emerging digital profiles may provide insight into understanding into how society is changing under the influence of digital tools.

N. B. Adams (✉) · T. A. DeVaney
Southeastern Louisiana University, Hammond, LA, USA
e-mail: Nan.Adams@southeastern.edu; Thomas.DeVaney@southeastern.edu

1.2 Literature Review

Aiken (2017) wrote about the "cyber effect" and discussed "when humans and technology collide." She discussed that "some changes have occurred so quickly that it has become difficult to tell the difference between passing trends, still evolving behavior, and somethings that's already become an acceptable social norm (p. 4)." She observed the significant need to study the cyber effect along with the challenges this poses for systematic academic study of this phenomenon and terms this an accelerated form of socialization. As the concept of digital ethnicity is explored, differences in gender use of computers and social media are of interest to development of digital ethnic profiles.

In a meta-analysis of 71 studies utilizing 644 different measures, Kay concluded that "actual computer behaviour has been studied far less than frequency of computer use, yet it is specific behaviour that can help uncover clues and nuances with respect to gender differences" (2008, p. 19). In 2015, different computer activities were found to be used by different genders, with males performing more gaming and surfing the net and females more email and communication-type activities (Fairlie, 2015).

The rapid increase in the use of social media over the past 15 years reveals similar complexities. The difference between genders consistently reveals that females are more engaged with social media than males.

According to Pew Research, in 2010, 39% of males were engaged with at least one social media site compared to 46% of females. This trend has held. The same longitudinal study by Pew indicates that in 2019, 65% of males are engaged regularly on at least one social media site, compared to 78% of females (https://www.pewinternet.org/chart/social- media-use-by-gender/).

Differences of computer and social media use by age have also been documented. According to the Pew Research Center surveys of social media use, there are substantial differences in social media use by age. 88% of 18- to 29-year-olds indicate that they use any form of social media. That share falls to 78% among those ages 30 to 49, to 64% among those ages 50 to 64, and to 37% among Americans 65 and older. Statista publishes similar statistics, listing 100% of 18–19-year-olds having Internet access. That number falls to 97% of 30–49-year-olds and then 88% of 50–64-year-olds and reveals that 73% of those over the age of 65 have Internet access (https://www.statista.com/statistics/266587/percentage-of-internet-users-by-age-groups-in-the-us/).

The question arises – how does increased use of computers and social media that has developed a level of seamless interconnectedness influence the development of our society – more specifically, how does it impact how people belong to that society? Restated – How does interaction with computers and other digital communication technologies, commonly called social media, influence ethnicity? What ethnic profiles may be developed using the digital ethnicity model?

1.2.1 Varying Definitions for the Term Ethnicity

For most, the word "ethnicity" conjures both abstract and concrete meanings, which are often contextual. In the concrete uses of government and institutions, ethnicity usually denotes race. In the more abstract, it often means a group of humans who are identified through shared characteristics that may be real or assumed. This ambiguity seems to track the lack of agreement among scholars that has ebbed and flowed along with interest in the endeavor of building a consensus for meaning. Isajiw (1974) analyzed 65 sociological and anthropological studies and found that only 13 had definitions for the term ethnicity, with the remaining 52 having no explicit definition at all. With no real resolution in sight, the term has been defined as needed by institutions and individuals to gather data or describe groups of people.

Two major viewpoints guide the issue: objectivists, who regard ethnic groups as cultural and social entities with distinct boundaries that are characterized by lack of interaction and relative isolation, and subjectivists, who describe ethnic groups as culturally constructed categorizations that guide social behavior and interaction and define these groups by subjective self-categorizations (Jones, 1997). This begs the question of whether ethnic groups are based on shared, objective cultural practices that exist independently or the more subjective notion that ethnic groups are constructed by the processes of perception and derived social organization of their members.

Longstreet (1978), unlike other scholars, provides the only constructed model for describing identified aspects of ethnicity. This model provides the sociobiological definition of ethnicity as being "that portion of cultural development that occurs before the individual is in complete command of his or her abstract intellectual powers and that is formed primarily through the individual's early contacts with family, neighbors, friends, teachers, and others as well as with his or her immediate environment of the home and neighborhood" (p. 19). This construction of the concept of ethnicity, originally developed to describe patterns that may exist among members of a social group, provides an appropriate and useful framework for investigating the impact digital communication tools are having on educational practices of cultures and societies.

Our children are interacting with computers very young, even as early as 2 or 3 years of age, which puts them into the age when they are powerful learners of languages of all kinds – including the operational languages of computing. Longstreet's aspects of ethnicity are helpful in describing children growing up engaged and often surrounded by digital environments that encompass their early childhood. They are engaged in interactive video and computer games and other forms of digital communication at a time when biological development and ethnic understandings are most influenced, and yet these young children are not yet in command of their full abstract and intellectual powers, and there is a lack of conceptual awareness of what is happening to them. The ultimate goal for the development of the Digital Ethnicity Scale is to describe those aspects of ethnicity using a digital lens and collect these descriptions along with demographic data to develop profiles of various digital ethnicities. These digital ethnic profiles are intended to provide guidance for effective educational practices to serve the needs of a rapidly changing digital world.

1.2.2 Aspects of Ethnicity: The Underlying Theory and Working Model

Longstreet developed a functional model for the five aspects that may be used to describe her concept of ethnicity. These aspects are (a) social value patterns, (b) intellectual mode, (c) orientation mode, (d) verbal communication, and (e) nonverbal communication. A brief description of each is as follows:

1. Verbal communication may be described as the structure a person uses when communicating orally. The rules or patterns for this oral communication are learned by children prior to the development of their abstract intellectual abilities. The ability to learn language seems to be a universal capacity of humankind (Longstreet, 1978, p. 42).
2. Nonverbal communication may be described as a system of facial expression, body movements, and spatial arrangements that communicate meaning to others (Longstreet, 1978, p. 59).
3. Orientation mode refers to patterns of behavior used, regardless of the presence of others, as ways of orienting oneself to the differing contexts of one's usual environment. It may be described as the way one communicates with themselves (Longstreet, 1978, p. 74). The orientation mode may be the most complex of the described modes. This mode is influenced by the social environment but ultimately becomes the ways one becomes comfortable in their own environment when no communication takes place.
4. Social value patterns are based on the sets of persistent behaviors that a group expects from its members and upon which it places certain values and upholds with certain beliefs (Longstreet, 1978, p. 89).
5. Intellectual modes are described by Longstreet as the most emotionally charged aspect of ethnicity. This mode is not intended to deal with human innate intelligence but rather reflect the way we externalize our thoughts, how we approach a problem, what gets our full attention, and what details we are most likely to recall. Intellectual modes link intellectual performance to past experiences (Longstreet, 1978, pp. 106–107).

When seeking a model to describe human development through social interaction, and especially social interaction in digital communication environments, the notion of identity often emerges. The authors wish to acknowledge that identity focuses on the individual's definition of self (Erikson, 1968), whereas ethnicity describes an individual's place or believed inclusion within a cultural group. This inquiry focuses on the individuals as they relate to a group.

Digital Ethnicity as a Specialized Form of Ethnicity
When constructing a scale to describe those aspects of ethnicity that may be influenced by early and pervasive interaction with digital communication technologies, consideration of which aspects to investigate was a challenging task. Longstreet predicted a variety of contextual ethnicities that may be distinct ethnicities. These distinct and specialized ethnicities were described as being grounded in one or more of the identified five aspects of ethnicity. For example, scholastic ethnicity may be a distinct form of ethnicity grounded in intellectual mode but still related to and having impact upon the other modes identified within this construction of ethnicity. National ethnicity may be a distinct form of social value patterns and communication modes. Gender ethnicity may be a distinct form of orientation mode. In this vein, the current research has sought to describe digital ethnicity as a distinct form of the combined communication mode, which is a combination of verbal and nonverbal communication mode.

1.2.3 The Digital Ethnicity Scale

Over a period of 2 years, the Digital Ethnicity Scale (DES) was developed and refined to test the construct of digital ethnicity using Longstreet's aspects of ethnicity model. The final version of the Digital Ethnicity Scale includes a two-section structure. The first section contains 12 Likert-type items that were retained from the previous analyses. The second section of the survey consists of 16 semantic differentials designed to measure communication mode.

Final analysis in the development process was based on an initial sample of 850 participants. Seven respondents reported an age that was less than 18 and were removed from the analyses. Additionally, 14 respondents did not report an age and were removed from the analyses. Of the remaining 829 respondents, the majority were female (72.3%) and reported their race as White (69.7%). The age of the respondents ranged from 18 to 80 with a mean of 36.71. The majority of respondents reported using the computer everyday (84.7%) and using the computer for a combination of work and recreation.

1.2.3.1 Intellectual Mode, Orientation Mode, and Social Value Pattern

The final version of the Digital Ethnicity Scale contained 12 items designed to measure the three aspects of intellectual mode, orientation mode, and social value pattern. Consistent with the previous revision, the scale was analyzed using exploratory factor analysis. The final analysis was conducted by specifying a three-factor solution with a varimax rotation. Because of previous refinements to the items, the suppression level for the factor loadings was increased to .50.

The results of the three-factor solution from the factor analysis are presented in Table 1.1a. The results indicate that the items loaded as predicted with all items

Table 1.1a Factor loadings for revised 15-item Digital Ethnicity Scale

Item	Factor 1	Factor 2	Factor 3
I respond to emails immediately	0.694		
I would rather send email than talk on the phone	0.675		
I leave my computer on all of the time just in case I need to get online	0.652		
I am usually on the Internet at the same time every day	0.600		
Posting pictures, even misleading ones, on the web doesn't hurt anyone		0.775	
It is okay if I pretend to be someone else online		0.736	
It is okay to talk about my private life online with people I do not know		0.590	
It is okay to download or copy music for free		0.571	
Using a computer makes me smarter			0.701
Because of the Internet I am able to solve problems myself that I would not be able to do otherwise			0.693
Computers make us question what we know			0.656
The Internet helps me make good decisions			0.584
Proportion of variance explained	17.87	15.82	15.57
Reliability	0.634	0.570	0.648
Identified aspect of ethnicity	Orientation mode	Social value pattern	Intellectual mode

loading above the .50 criterion. The first factor contained the four items related to orientation mode and accounted to 17.87% of the variance. Factor 2 contained the social value pattern items and accounted to 15.82% of the variance. The final factor contained the four items related to intellectual mode and accounted for 15.57% of variance. Finally, the reliability estimates ranged from .570 to .648.

1.2.3.2 Semantic Differentials to Measure Communication Mode

The initial analyses of the semantic pairs identified a three-factor structure consistent with the findings of Osgood, Suci, and Tannenbaum (1957). For the final phase of the development, 13 semantic pairs were retained, and biased/fair was replaced because it did not load on any factor during initial analyses. Additionally, two pairs were added to the set for a total of 16 semantic pairs. The structure of the 16-item set was examined using a factor analysis with an eigenvalue greater than 1 extraction criterion, varimax rotation, and .50 display criterion for factor loadings. The results of the analysis are presented in Table 1.1b.

The results of the factor analysis of the 16 pairs indicated a four-factor solution that accounted for 57.08% of the variance. The first three factors corresponded to the dimensions of evaluation, potency, and activity, respectively, and accounted for 48.88% of the variance. The fourth factor only contained one pair, choice-need, and represented an additional unique dimension. Osgood et al. (1957) acknowledged

Table 1.1b Factor loadings for 16 semantic pair set

Pair	Factor 1	Factor 2	Factor 3	Factor 4
Hard-easy	−0.833			
Easy to understand-confusing	0.795			
Fluent-awkward	0.776			
Comfortable-anxious	0.743			
Chaotic-ordered	−0.613			
Wholly engaging-insufficient	0.515			
Trustworthy-bogus		0.777		
Ethical-corrupt		0.702		
Personal-impersonal		0.566		
Part of a community-isolated		0.522		
Informative-entertaining			0.682	
Public-privacy			0.608	
Influential-inconsequential			0.558	
Interesting-boring			0.534	
Choice-need				0.762
Text intensive-highly graphic				
Proportion of variance explained	22.28	15.79	10.81	8.20
Semantic space dimension	Evaluation	Potency	Activity	

that semantic spaces would likely have more than the three dominant dimensions. Therefore, the structure of this set of semantic pairs is consistent with the common structure proposed by Osgood et al. Additionally, the failure of the text intensive-highly graphic pair to load on any of the factors suggests that it also represents a unique dimension. However, the variance accounted for by the dimension is not large enough to be extracted as a factor in the solution.

1.2.4 Digital Ethnic Profiles

To explore the data for possible profiles related to age and gender, a series of two-way analyses of variance was conducted. Each analysis identified statistically significant differences based on age (IM: p = .009; SVP: $p < .001$; IM: $p < .001$). The results further indicated that agreement increased as the age category increased which suggests different perceptions within each domain based on age. Concerning gender, the analysis of variance results indicated statistically significant differences between male and female respondents for SVP and OM and no statistically significant differences with respect to IM. However, unlike the consistency identified in the results for age, the results indicated higher SVP values among females, while females had lower values concerning OM. Finally, the results indicated there was not a statistically significant interaction between age and gender for any of the domains (IM: $p = 783$; SVP: $p = .380$; OM: $p = .923$). These results are illustrated in the figures below.

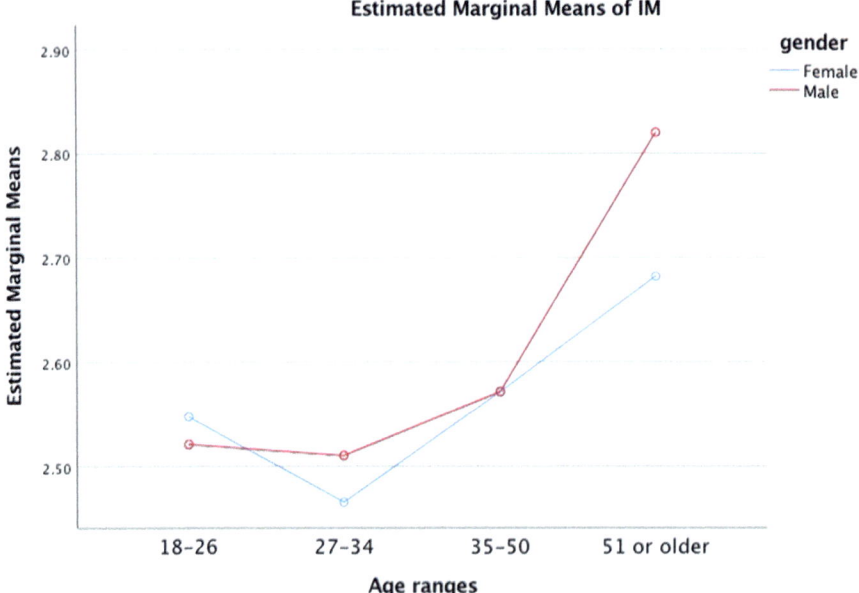
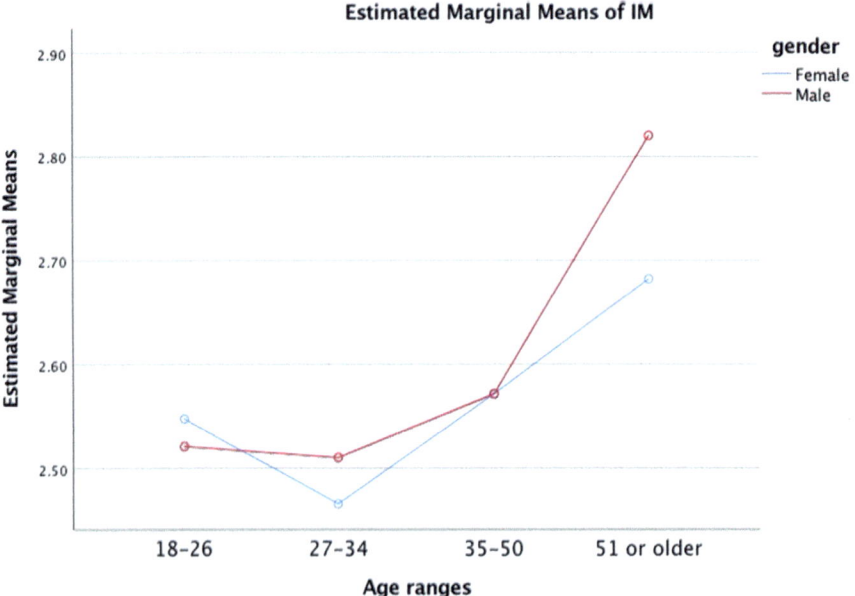

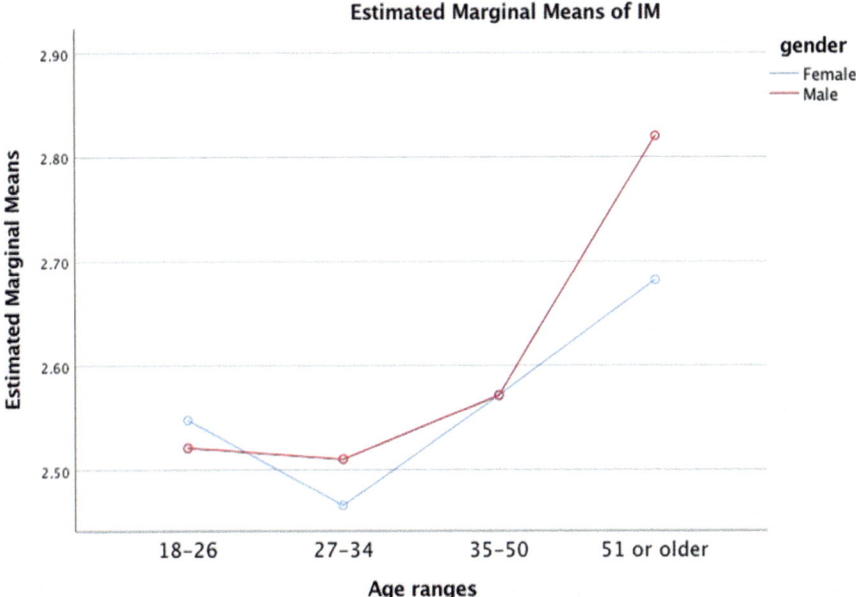

Analysis of survey data reveals that significant differences by gender exist with regard to orientation mode and social value patterns. There is little variation within intellectual mode with regard to gender, which may be interpreted as an indication that we are all part of the same society or national ethnic group, and therefore our intellectual mode has been shaped by our surroundings – schools that share standardized planned development programs, television, and other media sources with synchronized information presented in somewhat standard formats. The differences by orientation mode and social value patterns may reflect the individual in relationship to the group and reveal relationships to (1) personal preferences and how we comfort ourselves (orientation mode) and (2) those values held as a result of our relationship to our surroundings (social value patterns).

Females returned higher means for social value patterns, which indicates they have stronger agreement with the statements, which reflect stronger ties to the societal norms reflected by the survey. For example, posting private information is not acceptable, downloading music without paying for it is not acceptable, etc. Males have stronger agreement with orientation mode items, which indicates more set patterns of behavior and less flexibility for changes in preferred orientations. Because there are apparent differences and they swap for SVP and OM, it gives evidence that there are different profiles based on the three areas for male and female.

With regard to differences by age, the patterns are consistent with each age group returning similar results across the three identified aspects of intellectual mode, orientation mode, and social value patterns. This bodes well for the development of digital ethnic profiles. The largest difference by age occurs with those less than 50 years old and those older than 50 years, with three age ranges of 18–26, 27–34, and

35–50 somewhat combined with less variability to each other and more variability with those over 50 years of age. This tracks previous research (Adams, 2004) that suggested a difference in ways of knowing may exist between those born before or after 1970.

1.2.5 Discussion of Results

As digital communication technologies increasingly replace face-to- face communication and interactions, the experiences that construct human perceptions of reality are altered. Marshall McLuhan (1964) observed that "Everybody experiences far more than he understands. Yet it is experience, rather than understanding, that influences behavior" (p. 277). The Digital Ethnicity Scale seeks to describe those aspects of ethnicity that are influenced by immersive experience with digital communication tools.

When constructing a scale to describe those aspects of ethnicity that may be influenced by early and pervasive interaction with digital communication technologies, consideration of which aspects to investigate was challenging. We were unable to obtain consistent separate sets of data for the aspects of verbal and nonverbal communication. It appears that the digital media, not television but all other digital communication environments, has impacted the verbal forms of communication in ways that cannot be tested separately from nonverbal communication and in ways that do not exist in other environments. This fusion may well be a major characteristic of digital ethnicity, but not one that can as yet be characterized by the instrument we have developed. However, digital influences on those ethnic aspects of social value patterns, orientation mode, and intellectual mode provided distinct descriptions of digital ethnic behavior that appear to be useful for the development of digital ethnic profiles. Gender emerged as having significant differences within the aspects of orientation mode and social value patterns. When investigating profiles by age, consistencies within each age group emerged. Together, gender and age differences by the different aspects of digital ethnicity suggest that further research with this instrument might provide even greater description of digital profiles.

1.3 Conclusion

The pervasive use of social media in the forms of Facebook, Twitter, Instagram, and other digital communication platforms coupled with the current lack of guidelines or policy to ensure the ethical and truthful dissemination of information through these digital social media communication platforms underpin the central need for utilizing the identified aspects of digital ethnicity model as a tool describe phenomena to guide our futures.

The ability to understand and accommodate changing orientation and intellectual modes along with an understanding of changing social value patterns that result from interaction with digital media will inform educators and other social scientists as we work to understand this emerging digital society.

There exists a large amount of interaction between the world around us and the digital environment – we are currently experiencing multiple environments that the individual is negotiating. The investigation of this negotiation of a variety of digital and non-digital communication environments is not studied with this current inquiry but should be part of further study and may be informed by the development of digital ethnic profiles utilizing the aspects of digital ethnicity. The ability to understand and accommodate changing orientation and intellectual modes along with an understanding of changing social value patterns that result from interaction with digital media will inform policy-makers, educators, and other social scientists as we work to understand this emerging digital society.

Just because this research did not find a description of the changes occurring to communication modes does not mean that these changes are not occurring. McLuhan's (1967) conception that *the medium is the message* provides insight into this media-induced change and is probably more relevant now than when it was originally discussed. Even more relevant may be pursuing the impact of the digital environment on the construction of meaning and even of reality.

References

Adams, N. (Spring 2004). Digital Intelligence Fostered by Technology. *Journal of Technology Studies, 30*, 93–98.
Aiken, M. (2017). *The cyber effect*. New York, NY: Spiegel & Grau.
Erikson, E. (1968). *Identity: Youth and crisis*. New York, NY: W. W. Norton.
Fairlie, R.W. (2015). Do boys and girls use computers differently, and does it contribute to why boys do worse in school than girls? Discussion paper no. 9302 August 2015 IZA DP No. 9302.
Isajiw, W. (1974). Definitions of ethnicity. *Ethnicity, 1*, 111–124.
Jones, S. (1997). *The archeology of ethnicity*. London: Routledge.
Kay, R. H. (2008). Exploring gender differences in computer-related behaviour: Past, present, and future. https://doi.org/10.4018/978-1-59904-774-4.ch002.
Longstreet, W. S. (1978). *Aspects of ethnicity*. New York, NY: Teachers College Press.
McLuhan, M. (1964). *Understanding media: The extensions of man*. New York, NY: McGraw-Hill.
McLuhan, M. (1967). *The medium is the message*. New York, NY: Bantam Book.
Osgood, C., Suci, G., & Tannenbaum, P. (1957). *The measurement of meaning*. Urbana, IL: University of Illinois Press.
Pew Research. (2019). https://www.pewinternet.org/chart/social-media-use-by-gender/

Chapter 2
The Use of Virtual Reality at Lower Secondary Schools

Thomas Keller, Elke Brucker-Kley, and Nico Ebert

2.1 Introduction

VR has received a great deal of media attention as a result of the technological developments over the last few years. Currently, it is mainly utilized by private consumers for personal entertainment. In the future, however, the technology could increasingly be used by companies and public institutions. According to technology analysts, VR will become part of the classroom environment within the next 5 to 10 years.

This chapter examines the practical application of VR at a Swiss elementary school (Keller, Glauser, Ebert, & Brucker-Kley, 2018; Keller, Hagen, & Brucker-Kley, 2019). For this purpose, a prototype of a VR learning environment has been developed for the competence area "Nature and Technology (3.3)" by Curriculum 21 (Lehrplan.ch., 2018), a Swiss curriculum for primary and lower secondary schools, and tested as part of a pilot project. The aim of this work is to determine whether VR can create didactic added value for the Swiss primary school system.

Despite the subject's extensive research history, no scientific data appears to be available on the long-term effects of VR learning environments on competence development and student motivation. Research to date has shown that scientific fields in particular are suited to the use of VR.

The research paradigm is based on design science (Hevner, March, Park, & Ram, 2004). Initially, a learning unit on plastics and their effects on the environment, consisting of five learning blocks, was designed. Different ideas for VR applications

---

T. Keller (✉) · E. Brucker-Kley · N. Ebert
ZHAW School of Management and Law, Winterthur, Switzerland

ZHAW, Institute of Business Information Technology, Winterthur, Switzerland
e-mail: kell@zhaw.ch; brck@zhaw.ch; ebet@zhaw.ch; https://www.zhaw.ch/en/sml/institutes-centres/iwi/; https://www.zhaw.ch/en/sml/institutes-centres/iwi/; https://www.zhaw.ch/en/sml/institutes-centres/iwi/

were developed for each of these blocks, resulting in a vision which was discussed with four teachers with regard to didactic compatibility and the evaluation of use cases. The proposal "Environmental Problem Microplastics" selected for implementation not only fits well into Curriculum 21 but is of high social relevance and in-line with the requirements for a VR learning environment as defined in the literature.

2.2 Research Objective

The main objective of this work is to compare the learning success of units utilizing against those not utilizing VR support. A further goal is to determine whether there are differences in gaming experience and gender. In addition, the respondents' opinion of this teaching method is to be questioned and the answers compared with the data collected.

A secondary research objective is to gain experience with the implementation of pedagogical principles in the context of VR learning units. In particular, the focus on establishing whether VR as a technology could lead to new pedagogical approaches.

2.3 Virtual Reality in the Education Domain

Using VR in schools is not a recent idea. The topic has been researched since the 1990s, especially in Anglo-Saxon countries. The field of research has its origin in the area of flight simulation.

Since the 1990s, various authors have analyzed the possibilities of VR and derived potential training benefits. In the following, a selection of relevant publications for education is presented and briefly summarized.

Wickens (1992) justifies the use of VR at school with four factors. Firstly, he mentions the possibility that, thanks to interactive learning environment, higher intrinsic motivation can be achieved. Secondly, the presentation of real learning situations should increase/enhance knowledge transfer. Thirdly, he mentions the aspect of taking on different perspectives and thus discovering certain scenarios in context. Fourthly, he mentions the chance to interact with the world in a natural way.

Winn (1993) argues in his work that the principles of constructivist learning theories and the characteristics of VR are compatible with each other. He sees the key to this compatibility in immersion, in particular in VR's ability to gain experience from a first-person perspective. Dede (2009) and Salzman, Dede, Loftin, and Chen (1999) mention four factors of VR in addition to immersion, all of which are highly compatible with constructivist learning methods. The three-dimensional presentation of content in different reference frameworks promotes in-depth learning and various perspectives on a topic. VR controllers enable interaction that addresses the multisensory stimuli of users and thereby support the safeguarding of knowledge. Furthermore, well-designed immersive worlds increase motivation which leads to more time and concentration being dedicated to the individual tasks in a VR environment. The final factor is the possibility of telepresence, allowing individuals to share experiences regardless of location.

Dede (2009) published a paper on the subject of immersion which garnered much attention. In this paper, he illustrates three ways as to how VR can improve education. The study overlaps to a large extent with the findings of Wickens (1992) and Winn (1993) described above. In the first step, he mentions the ability to adopt both egocentric and exocentric perspectives and thus better depict complex phenomena (multiple perspectives). While he regards the exocentric view as suitable for abstract and symbolic insights, the egocentric perspective should increase the learner's interaction and motivation. The second reason he cites is the possibility of putting the learner in a specific situation (situated learning). According to Dede, situational learning can improve commitment and academic performance. The third aspect is that the transfer of knowledge for learners is simplified by the representation of real situations (transfer).

Table 2.1 summarizes the findings regarding the benefits of VR in education in terms of their functions in a simplified form. The authors' statements overlap at various points. In addition, the analysis reveals that functions and benefits are often mixed and the distinction between immersion and the other possibilities of VR does not follow a clear pattern.

Whether the desired training benefits can be achieved has been investigated since the establishment of this research area. The results of various meta-studies are presented below.

The meta-study by Youngblut (1998) includes the analysis of 20 VR learning units. The evaluation of the results was divided into categories of effectiveness and user-friendliness. Despite positive results, these findings are no longer relevant today for two reasons: Firstly, under the term VR, Youngblut also examined studies that were carried out with virtual desktop environments. Secondly, fully immersive systems were not technologically mature at that time.

Table 2.1 Summarized benefits of VR in education

	Benefits for education					
VR functions		Motivation/ engagement	Knowledge transfer	In-depth learning	Knowledge assurance	Location independent learning
	Immersion	X	X	X	X	
	Interaction	X	X		X	
	Multiple perspectives			X	X	
	3D visualization	X	X	X	X	
	Telepresence					X

Mikropoulos and Natsis (2011) examined 53 scientific papers on VR in education published between 1999 and 2009. Of the 53 studies, 16 used a fully immersive solution with head-mounted displays (HMD). For the rest, a desktop-based solution was used. One finding is that the combination of technological characteristics of VR and individual learning prerequisites and needs must be taken into consideration with regard to learning success. It also found that students and teachers positively received the new technology. It was unclear as to whether VR learners would retain their knowledge for longer. An important conclusion of the study is that every virtual learning environment must be geared toward the didactic goals of the application area.

The meta-study by Merchant, Goetz, Cifuentes, Keeney-Kennicutt, and Davis (2014) examines the effectiveness of desktop-based VR applications in the areas of games, simulations, and virtual worlds for primary and secondary school education. The authors analyzed a total of 67 papers. Since the studies focused on desktop-based VR applications, determining to what degree the results also apply to fully immersive VR applications is only possible to a certain extent. The paper has shown that knowledge transfer encompassing playful elements is far more effective than the other two types of knowledge transfer. The results of testing the students' knowledge shortly after the application of a VR game and at a later date were on a par. According to the authors, this is an indication that knowledge is retained for an extended period using this technology. Whether this knowledge can then be better transferred to other situations by the students was not examined in the study. Another finding is that students learn less well in collaborative learning environments than in non-collaborative ones. The authors were able to prove that the novelty of the technology has a positive effect on performance which subsides with subsequent usage.

Dix (2009) summarizes the challenges that need to be addressed to ensure successful use of VR in the training sector (Table 2.2).

Table 2.2 Challenges of VR for education (Dix, 2009, p. 123)

Category	Challenges
Technology	The costs of VR hardware need to decrease and portability must improve
	The simulation of the environment must improve, thereby increasing the degree of immersion
	The human-machine interaction must become more natural and intuitive
VR learning unit	Adequate learning units, tested by pedagogues, must be created
	Cognitive overload of students needs be avoided
	The monitoring and evaluation of learning effects must be researched in depth
Experience of students	The technology must be user-friendly and easy to operate
	A VR identity (avatar), which can be used in the environments, is to be established
	Privacy protection and security must be ensured
Integration	VR learning environments must be easily integrated into existing learning environments

Despite the interesting characteristics of VR in the context of education, the areas of application should be carefully selected. For a complete list of the conditions under which the use of VR is recommended, please refer to Pantelidis (2010). It can be emphasized that VR can always be used in a situation difficult to represent in the real world and where a simulation facilitates better understanding.

Merchant et al. (2014) examined 25 papers on VR for primary and secondary education (K-12) as part of her meta-study. More than 50% of the surveys are in the field of natural sciences and mathematics. Winn (1993) provides an explanation for this focus, stating that this highlights the possibility that any size comparisons are possible in the virtual world. For example, learners can move within an atom and replace electrons in orbitals or take intergalactic excursions into space. According to Salzman et al. (1999), VR has the potential to complement model-based science teaching.

2.4 VR Enhanced Learning Unit

As previously mentioned, a prototype has been developed for a learning unit within the competence area "Nature and Technology" on the subject of plastics and their effects on the environment. Divided into five learning blocks, the learning unit provides students with knowledge about structure, production, recycling, and environmental consequences with possible approaches to solutions. Ideas for possible VR applications were developed for each of these blocks, but only one block was chosen for implementation. The vision was discussed in four interviews with teachers. The resulting VR application is presented in the following chapters.

2.4.1 Design of Prototype

The lower secondary school in Meilen was selected as a project partner. Based on Curriculum 21 and the features of VR, the potential areas of highest impact have been identified and discussed with experienced teachers. Table 2.3 summarizes the relevant features of the chosen learning unit. In the next step, the prototype was designed the Unity engine with HTC Vive as the HMD was selected as a VR platform.

The VR prototype consists of the following three scenes: "below the water," "micro world," and "enjoy your meal." The prototype is available for download at http://neuelehrkonzepte.ch/.

Scene 1 – Below the Water
In this learning environment, the student starts off underwater. The underwater landscape is decorated with plants, rocks, fish, a car wreck, and a boat. The student receives an instruction to search for illegally disposed waste via an audio instruction.

Table 2.3 Tabular representation of the learning unit

Learning unit	Environmental problems and challenges
Reference to Curriculum 21	NT.3.3 c/BNE/MI
Learning outcomes according to taxonomy levels of Bloom	K1: Students can describe environmental problems caused by the use of plastic K4: Students analyze how microplastics enter the food chain
Learning content	What impact does the use of plastic have on the environment? How and where do environmental problems arise? What impact does plastic have on the environment? What are microplastics? Toxicity of plastics and influence on the hormonal balance of living organisms
Knowledge assurance	Poster – showing the plastic cycle and the impact on the environment and me as an individual Learning documentation – analysis of the products at home and where microplastics could occur.
VR use cases	Students are in a place contaminated with plastic waste Problem of microplastics: What are microplastics? Size comparison based on living organisms in waters

Instructions can be displayed in all scenes at any time at the push of a button. As the student approaches the rubbish heap, the task becomes more specific. The object is to look for the bottle of the sauce the student normally eats with French fries. The ketchup bottle is hidden in the middle of a clump of seaweed and emits microplastics. This is represented by pink dots which radiate from the bottle. A voice explains that the particles are absorbed by the carp eating the seaweed. Next, the student is to pick up the bottle and bring it to the laboratory, walking past the car wreck and the boat to the surface. The scenery on land resembles the shore of a mountain lake. Birds circle in the sky, a hare and a deer are feeding, and in the middle of the clearing is a wooden hut, prominently labeled "Laboratory." The acoustics have changed in the meantime. While the student previously heard underwater diving noises, birds now chirp ashore. With the ketchup bottle in hand, the student enters the laboratory and the "micro world" scene is loaded (Fig. 2.1).

Scene 2 – Micro World

The student is inside the hut and stands facing a blackboard with two types of fish (a pike, a perch) and the ketchup bottle in view. A robotic voice explains that within the laboratory the fish and the ketchup bottle are shown in life size. The sizes are displayed on the blackboard. After looking at the objects, the student leaves through the door out into the micro world and sees a perch enlarged 1,000 times and an equally large ketchup bottle. Four microplastic particles lie on a table. Now the student should compare the particles with the fish and the ketchup bottle to get a feeling of how small microplastics are. Next, the student should dispose of a microplastic particle in the trash can. As soon as the particle touches the bottom of the trash can, a screen and a button appear. The student is asked to press the button. A

Fig. 2.1 Impressions of scene 1

Fig. 2.2 Impressions of scene 2

3-minute film starts about plastics and their consequences for the environment. Once it has finished, the student is asked to look for the exit. As soon as the student walks through the door, the scene "enjoy your meal" starts (Fig. 2.2).

Scene 3 – "Enjoy Your Meal"
The student sits at a camping table, which has been set up in the initial scene in the meantime. The table is set. On the student's plate lie two fish. The student's family is also present. The father sits on a chair, the mother is by the fire, and the brother dances to the music emitting from the loudspeaker. The student is given the task of eating the "right" fish via an audio output. One of the fish is marked with pink dots representing the microplastic particles.

The other fish looks normal. After selecting and lifting up the fish without microplastics, the student is congratulated on successfully completing the unit and is asked to turn around. Instructions to take off the VR glasses now appear on the blackboard (Fig. 2.3).

Fig. 2.3 Impressions of scene 3

2.4.2 Evaluation of Prototype for Usability

The prototype evaluated with students on April 19, 2018, at the Meilen lower secondary school. Of the 16 participants, 10 were female and 6 male. The majority of the students were 14 years old at the time of the study. Around 60% had previous experience with VR, of which 80 % had tried out VR systems at one event. 100% of male and 20% of female participants stated that they play video games. For 120 minutes, the students were able to test the VR learning environment on two systems in succession. Upon completing the learning unit, the students were required to fill out a survey. The survey asked questions pertaining to usability, learning experience, and comprehensibility.

In the following, the results of the survey are presented according to the VR functions in Table 2.1.

Immersion
Nearly 70% of the participants stated that the world depicted looks realistic. The remaining 30% expressed a neutral view. This result is not surprising and can probably be traced back to various reasons. The resolution of the HTC Vive used is 1080 x 1200 pixels per eye. Raja Koduri, the CEO of chip manufacturer AMD until 2017, stated in an interview in 2016 that to ensure a realistic-looking VR experience, a resolution of 15,360 x 8640 (16 k) per eye is required (Koduri, 2016). On the hardware side, VR is therefore still far from possessing optimum properties. The second aspect is the 3D models used. Various compromises had to be made. For example, objects with a low number of polygons were sometimes used due to a lack of alternatives.

Nevertheless, the experience felt realistic for 95% of the participants. The detailed landscape, the audio effects, and the possibility to interact with the world may have been contributing factors. Concrete reasons should be assessed in a further survey.

Furthermore, 95% of the students stated that their level of concentration was higher than in a normal classroom setting. This is most likely due to the fact that this was their first experience with VR in school and the pilot experiment was a special, unusual event for the test persons. In addition, the students were observed by two system supervisors throughout. Reliable data should be collected by means of long-term studies. An interesting approach could be the measurement of body functions, such as heart rate (Keller, Annunzio, & Brucker-Kley, 2018). Such an experiment was carried out by the Universita` della Svizzera italiana in Lugano with a VR application in the tourism sector (Marchiori, Niforatos, & Preto, 2018). It was found that the presentation of content from special perspectives and the interaction with animated objects have the potential to be committed to long-term memory.

Three participants felt uncomfortable navigating the VR environment and one person had to abort early. This result is not surprising as many users complain about a weak stomach during their first experience with a VR environment. Cobb, Nichols, Ramsey, and Wilson (1999) suggest the user's urge to discover everything the first time and thus execute very fast movements as a possible cause. There are also users who are still feel uneasy after experiencing a VR environment multiple times.

Interaction

Nearly 90% of the participants said they would welcome collaborative learning with a classmate in the virtual world. Liu describes this possibility as social learning (Liu, Dede, Huang, & Richards, 2017).

For most of the participants, it was clear how to operate the controllers. This is certainly due to the high technological affinity of this generation. Over 85% of the students understood the instructions; however, only half felt the instructions were sufficient. Nerves may have played a role in this assessment. When experiencing an immersive world for the first time, many users focus on environmental impressions and control. In doing so, they cannot follow audio instructions. Few people used the option of displaying instructions at the touch of a button. Nevertheless, interaction with the objects was considered simple and logical by most of the students.

Learning

The majority of the students stated that the VR learning environment was helpful in understanding the topic of microplastics. In analyzing this question, it is noticeable that eight subjects agreed with this statement but did not select the maximum rating. This may be an indication of to which extent the students have understood the content. The same applies to the result of the question as to whether size comparison in the micro world was helpful for understanding. More than 95% of the students became aware that microplastic enters our food chain.

Having the ability to move around and research freely and audio comments and video were rated by the students as conducive to understanding. The video received the highest number of ratings with the maximum number of points.

Motivation

Around 95% of students stated that VR could increase their interest and motivation to learn. Only one individual marked not applicable which could be due to the fact that the participant felt the VR glasses were too heavy. All students would be interested in learning in a virtual learning environment again.

2.5 Field Experiment for Evaluation of Impact on Learning Success

The field experiment consists of a pre-test, a post-test, a course unit with VR elements, and a course unit based on a conventional teaching method. Both units have the same learning objectives.

Four classes from the same lower secondary school in Meilen partook in this field experiment. All four classes are level A, with two in the first and two in the third year (Table 2.4). The focus was on selecting the classes on the same level. Although the influence of age must be taken into account in the evaluation, the teachers do not consider age difference to have a significant impact. In this case, this has to do with the subject matter, as the VR course unit could also be carried out with sixth grade students.

Two types of group allocation are suggested in the literature: random allocation of students or that of classes. The preferred option would be the allocation of students, taking into consideration that this is difficult to achieve in a school and classroom context. The allocation according to classes is easier but has several disadvantages. For example, an entire class may have been shaped by the teaching style of the teachers. If an experiment is conducted across several schools, other differences, such as city, country, and income, may also have an influence (All, Nuñcz Castellar, & Van Looy, 2016). Since all test persons for this experiment are from the same school and locality, this factor has less of an impact.

For the allocation of the groups, each class was randomly assigned to a group of students. For example, approximately half of each class completed the VR course unit and the other half the conventional course unit. Technically, this was solved by allocating a random number (according to normal distribution) to each student. These numbers were then divided into medians and assigned to each half of a group. In the end, 39 pupils were assigned to the VR course unit and 43 to the conventional course unit. Gender distribution is illustrated in Fig. 2.4 below. Absolute values are shown on the left and relative values on the right.

2.6 Impact on Learning Success

To evaluate the data, the results of the pre- and post-tests as well as the information from the individual results were converted into tables and imported into the statistical software RStudio. The application of a statistical test in itself does not yet give

Table 2.4 List of classes and number of students

Class	Total	Female	Male
1c	18	12	6
1d	20	9	11
3b	22	15	7
3c	22	14	8

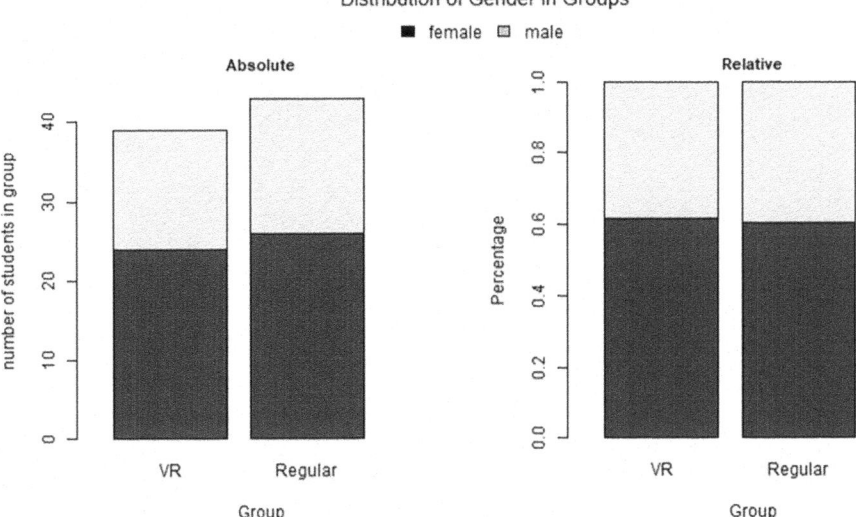

Fig. 2.4 Distribution of gender in groups

any indication as to whether there are significant differences between two samples. For this purpose, a significance level must be determined by the researcher. The significance level can also be described as the probability of error (Kraft & Landes, 1996). Based on the selected significance level, the P-value of the test is considered. If the P-value is below the selected significance level, considerable differences can be assumed. This means that the differences in samples do not appear to be random (Bortz & Schuster, 2010). The 95% significance level is often chosen for statistical analyses. Stigler argues that this is probably due to Fisher because it can reliably show effect sizes even with small samples (Stigler, 2008).

For this reason, the 95% significance level was chosen for each of the following studies outlined in this paper.

2.6.1 Overview

A simple overview of the results of the pre- and post-tests is shown in Fig. 2.5. The graph allows a comparison of the results according to class and covers data for both groups.

When comparing the results of the pre-test and post-test in Fig. 2.5, it becomes apparent that the results of the pre-test are much more widely dispersed than those of the post-test. Furthermore, the medians are visibly lower in the pre-test. It is interesting that both third classes range between 0 % and 100 % in the pre-test. This means that some barely know anything, while others are already very well informed about the topic of microplastics. As nobody reached 100% in the post-test, this also

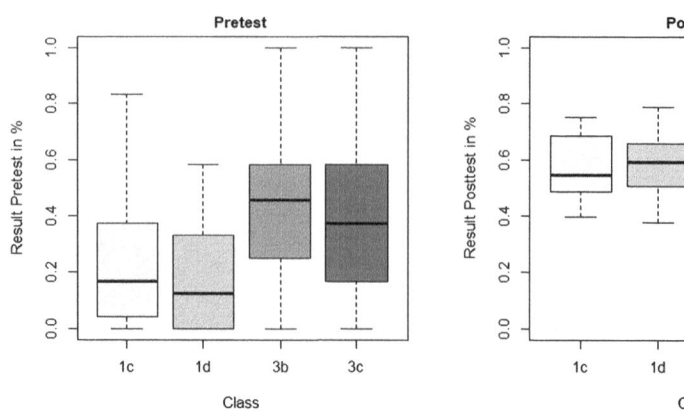

Fig. 2.5 Comparison of test results

led to negative learning successes. This is probably due to the fact that the pre-test and post-test differ in terms of questions.

It is also noticeable that the two first and two third grades each behave similarly. Class 3b seems to have the most knowledge in the post-test. However, this can be put down to the class achieving the highest median in the pre-test. In general, it can probably be assumed that most students achieved learning success. The small variance of the post-test suggests that both learning units were effective.

2.6.2 Hypothesis 1

The first hypothesis claims that the VR learning unit has a positive influence on learning success. This means that the students have more knowledge about the topic and can retrieve that knowledge after completing the VR unit. This hypothesis can be accepted if the results of the pre- and post-tests differ significantly.

The mean value of the results of the post-test is twice as high as that of the pre-test. The median of the post-test is three times higher with half the variance. The results of the pre- and post-tests of the VR learning unit group are visualized for each class in Fig. 2.6 in order to enable comparison.

The result of the Wilcoxon test shows that the results of the pre- and post-tests of the VR unit group differ significantly. This can be deduced from the P-value, which is lower than the defined significance level of 0.05. Hypothesis 1 can thus be accepted, i.e., the application of a VR learning unit leads to positive learning success.

Test Results of Group VR

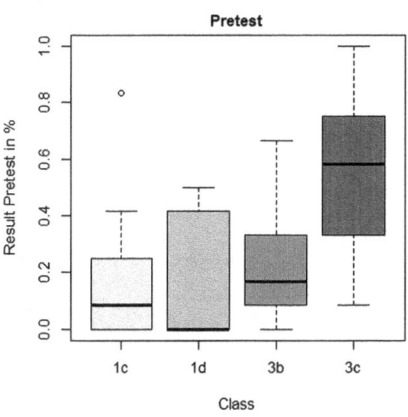 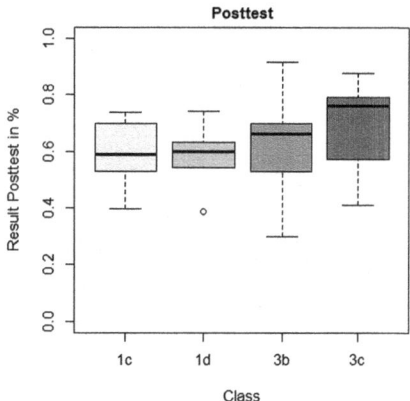

Fig. 2.6 Test results of VR group

2.6.3 Hypothesis 2

The second hypothesis states that a VR learning unit results in greater learning success than a conventional learning unit. For the hypothesis to be accepted, the learning success of the VR group must be significantly greater than that of the conventional learning unit group. Figure 2.7 below shows the learning successes achieved (referred to as "gain") per group and class as box plots.

Looking at Fig. 2.7, it is not clear whether the VR or the conventional learning unit leads to better results. When comparing outcomes between classes and groups, it can be seen that the VR unit indeed leads to slightly higher average results but that dispersion is also somewhat increased. One exception is class 3c. On average, this class performed worse in the VR unit. A possible explanation for this result is that class 3c achieved the highest average in the pre-test and therefore already possessed significant previous knowledge.

The average of the VR unit's learning success across all classes is merely 2% higher than that of the regular unit. Conversely, the median is slightly lower. For a concrete statement, however, a statistical test is required. First, learning success distribution must be determined. For this purpose, learning success data is compared with a theoretical normal distribution. Normal distribution can be assumed if the data points shown in Fig. 2.8 follow the straight line in the middle of the gray confidence interval as closely as possible.

According to Fig. 2.8, a normal distribution can be assumed. However, some data points stray a considerable distance from the straight line. Another approach to examine a data set for normal distribution is the Shapiro test (Bortz & Schuster, 2010).

The calculation of the P-values according to the Shapiro test confirms that normal distribution can be assumed for the learning success of the VR group as well as for the conventional learning unit. This means that the T-test is suitable for testing

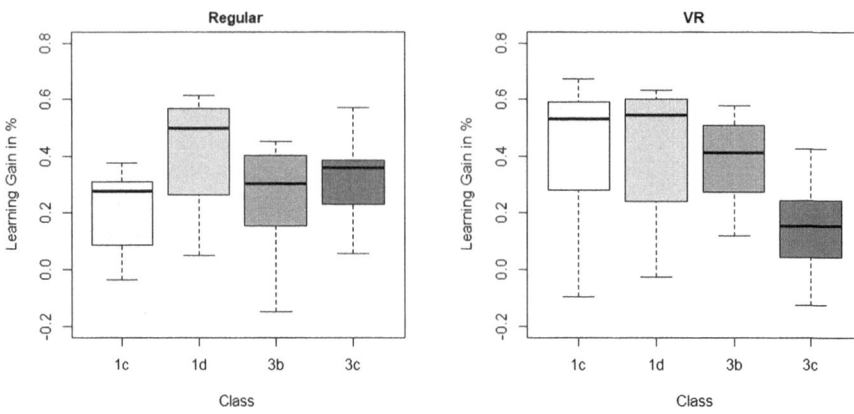

Fig. 2.7 Comparison of learning gain

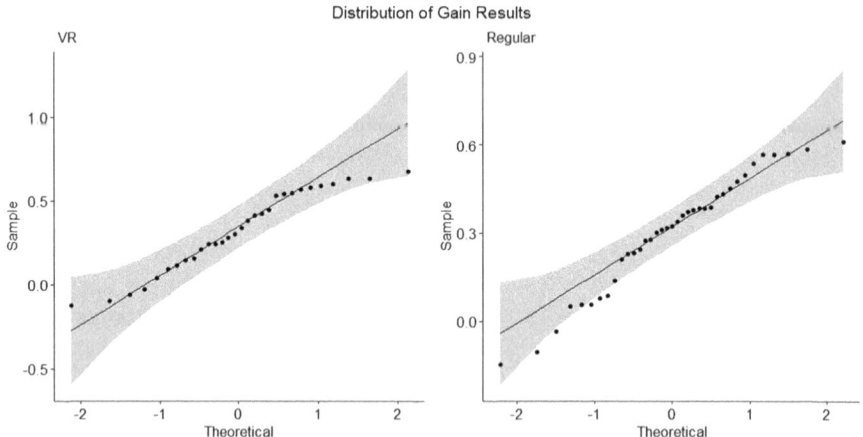

Fig. 2.8 Distribution of gain results

differences between groups. The Levene test can be used to test the equal distribution of variances (Universität Zürich, 2018). The P-value of the Levene test is greater than 0.05, meaning there are no significant differences between the learning success variances of the two groups (Dormann, 2013). Thus, all criteria for the application of the T-test are given.

The calculation of the P-value of the T-test shows a value greater than 0.05, i.e., there are no significant differences between the learning success of the VR group and the conventional learning unit. Based on these outcomes, the second hypothesis, stating that the VR unit is superior to the conventional one, cannot be confirmed.

2.6.4 Further Perceptions

During the implementation of the VR learning unit, it became clear that there are large differences in how intuitively students navigate the VR learning environment. This leads to the question of whether this has an influence on the result, i.e., learning success. The variable "intuitive behavior" does not exist, but it seems obvious that students who frequently play video games can operate more intuitively in a virtual environment. This variable was also collected during execution, and the result of the evaluation is shown in Fig. 2.9.

The middle box plot in Fig. 2.9 shows that although the variance is very similar, the median is approximately 15% higher for groups that play video games at least once a month or more. However, a significant influence of experience with video games cannot be confirmed.

Figure 2.9 also illustrates that all male students indicated that they play video games at least once a week. The opposite is true for female students, with the majority specifying that they never play video games. This leads to the next question as to whether gender has any influence on the result of the VR group. Figure 2.10 below shows the learning success and results of the pre- and post-tests per group.

It is apparent that the male participants have a median of approximately 15% higher gain than the female participants. Based on the overall outcome of the pre- and post-tests, it can be seen that the male students achieved slightly weaker results than the female students. In addition, the variance among male students is somewhat lower, indicating that there are fewer with considerably poor learning outcomes.

The statistical test clearly shows that gender does not lead to significant differences.

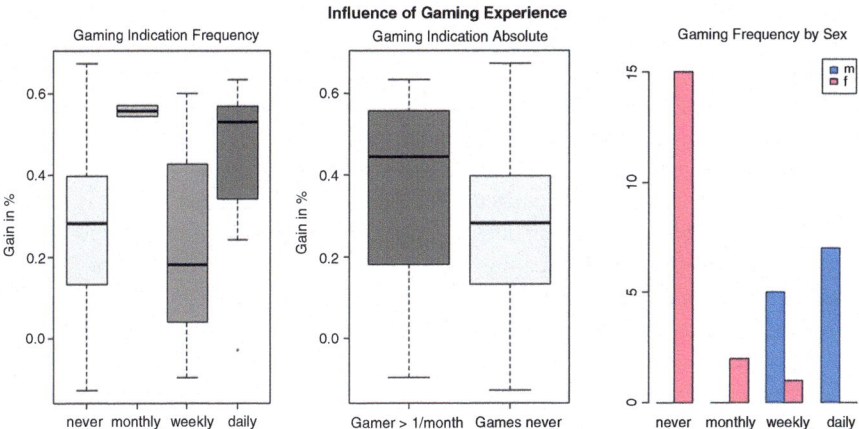

Fig. 2.9 Influence of gaming experience

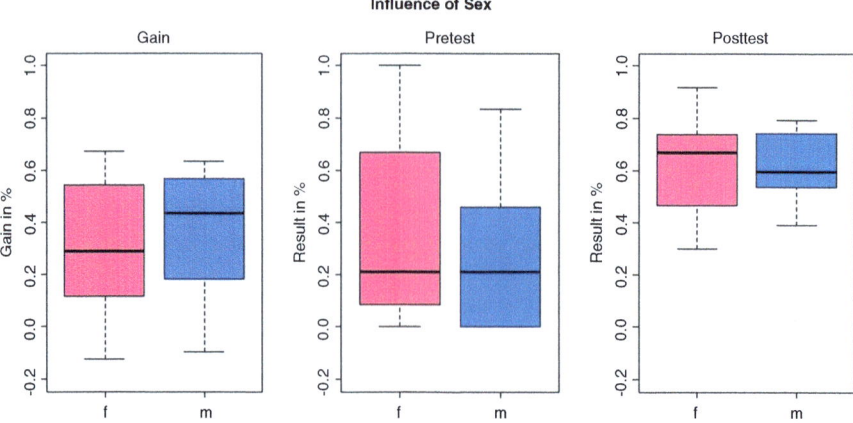

Fig. 2.10 Influence of gender

2.7 Conclusion

Based on the results of this paper, it can be stated that the research question initially formulated can be confirmed. The implementation of the VR course unit microplastics has contributed to positive learning success. However, no evidence could be found for the assumption that the VR learning unit leads to greater learning success than a conventional teaching method in the context of this field experiment. There are various possible reasons for this outcome. Causes could be that the content or design criteria for the VR unit were not adequate. Further investigations are needed.

The VR unit seems to evoke very different emotions in the students. The majority enjoy using the technology and are intrigued by it. However, some either have reservations beforehand or experience fear or discomfort during the simulation. While this confirms that a VR session has the potential to convey very personal content, it also means that these emotions may have a negative impact on the learning success of individual students. This also encompasses the observed factor of intuition, i.e., how easy or difficult it was for individuals to navigate within the VR unit. This field experiment did not focus on determining these factors, hence why further statements in this respect are not possible. An additional confirmation for this influence could be the increased dispersion of the VR learning unit compared to the conventional learning unit, meaning that there are greater differences in learning success within the VR group.

A serious issue in the implementation of the VR course unit are health-related discontinuities. In this field experiment, the learning unit had to be abandoned by four female students. Content could not be conveyed and instead left the students with negative feelings toward the VR learning unit. As previously mentioned, one possible remedy would be to create a learning environment to convey different content. Thus, a VR learning unit would be something familiar and students would be accustomed to navigating and taking in the environment. This would also reduce operational efforts.

One important factor for practical use is the manageability of a fully immersive VR system. The installation takes up a considerable amount of physical space. It is unlikely that this kind of space is available in many schools today. As such, we would like to introduce the idea of making the systems mobile and setting them up in unfrequented rooms. The auditorium was used for this purpose in the pilot experiment. On the hardware side, it is now an affordable investment for end consumers. This significantly lowers the entry hurdle. Since fully immersive systems have only been on the market for a few years, the software range is still modest. The way VR is integrated and the role of the teacher are important factors for the success of the technology in the classroom. Integration should be viewed from an organizational and didactic perspective. During the pilot test, it became clear that system support is time-consuming. In addition, no one complete class can currently study together in the VR environment. These limitations must be taken into account when using the technology in everyday school life. From a didactic perspective, VR should be optimally integrated into the classroom. During the pilot test, the learning unit was not carried out in its entirety. The students were given a reading assignment as preparation. The subsequent learning assignment following the test attempt – which should have ensured the transfer of knowledge according to the model of De Freitas and Neumann (2009) – could not be executed owing to time constraints. Simplicity in operation is important for the success of VR learning units. If the system design is too complex and can only be operated with extensive IT knowledge, it is not likely that the technology will be able to establish itself as a commodity.

In this study, the added value of VR for the Swiss lower secondary school could not be conclusively evaluated. Various signs indicate positive effects. Fully immersive VR systems are still little known to the general public. The prototype created can make an important contribution to presenting VR's practical training possibilities and can function as a starting point for conducting medium- to long-term studies on the assurance of learning.

References

All, A., Nuñez Castellar, E. P., & Van Looy, J. (2016). Assessing the effectiveness of digital game-based learning: Best practices. *Computers & Education, 92–93*, 90–103. https://doi.org/10.1016/j.compedu.2015.10.007

Bortz, J., & Schuster, C. (2010). *Statistik für Human- und Sozialwissenschaftler* (7., vollständig überarbeitete und erweiterte Auflage ed.). Springer, Berlin Heidelberg.

Cobb, S. V. G., Nichols, S., Ramsey, A., & Wilson, J. R. (1999). Virtual Reality-Induced Symptoms and Effects (VRISE). *Presence: Teleoperators and Virtual Environments, 8*(2), 169–186. https://doi.org/10.1162/105474699566152

de Freitas, S., & Neumann, T. (2009). The use of 'exploratory learning' for supporting immersive learning in virtual environments. *Computers & Education, 52*(2), 343–352. https://doi.org/10.1016/j.compedu.2008.09.010

Dede, C. (2009). Immersive interfaces for engagement and learning. *Science (New York, N.Y.), 323*(5910), 66–69. https://doi.org/10.1126/science.1167311

Dix, A. (2009). Human-computer interaction. In L. Liu & M. T. Özsu (Eds.), *Encyclopedia of database systems* (pp. 1327–1331). Springer, Berlin Heidelberg US. https://doi.org/10.1007/978-0-387-39940-9_192

Dormann, C. F. (2013). Das Lineare Modell: T-test und ANOVA in R. In C. F. Dormann (Ed.), *Parametrische Statistik* (pp. 209–223). Berlin Heidelberg: Springer. https://doi.org/10.1007/978-3-642-34786-3_12

Hevner, A., March, S. T., Park, J., & Ram, S. (2004). Design science in information systems research. *MIS Quarterly, 28*(1), 75–105.

Keller, T., Annunzio, G., & Brucker-Kley, E. (2018). *Heart rate variability analysis as a preventive instrument against stress for employees.* 16th International Conference on e-Society, Lissabon, 14–16 April 2018. https://digitalcollection.zhaw.ch/handle/11475/7458

Keller, T., Glauser, P., Ebert, N., & Brucker-Kley, E. (2018). Virtual reality at secondary school– first results. In *Proceedings of the 15th international conference on cognition and exploratory learning in the digital Age (CELDA 2018)* (pp. 53–60).

Keller, T., Hagen, F., & Brucker-Kley, E. (2019). A field study about the impact of a VR learning unit. In *CELDA 2019 16th international conference cognition and exploratory learning in digital age, Cagliari, Italy, 7–9 November 2019* (pp. 307–314).

Koduri, R. (2016, January 15). *AMD's graphics boss says VR needs 16K at 240Hz for "true immersion."* TweakTown. https://www.tweaktown.com/news/49693/amds-graphics-boss-vr-needs-16k-240hz-true-immersion/index.html

Kraft, M., & Landes, T. R. (1996). *Statistische Methoden: Eine Einführung für das Grundstudium in den Wirtschafts- und Sozialwissenschaften* (3., durchges. und aktualisierte Aufl). Physica-Verl. Berlin Heidelberg.

Lehrplan.ch. (2018, November 30). *Lehrplan.ch.* Lehrplan.Ch. https://www.lehrplan.ch/

Liu, D., Dede, C., Huang, R., & Richards, J. (2017). *Virtual, augmented, and mixed realities in education.* Berlin Heidelberg: Springer.

Marchiori, E., Niforatos, E., & Preto, L. (2018). Analysis of users' heart rate data and self-reported perceptions to understand effective virtual reality characteristics. *Information Technology & Tourism, 18*(1), 133–155. https://doi.org/10.1007/s40558-018-0104-0

Merchant, Z., Goetz, E. T., Cifuentes, L., Keeney-Kennicutt, W., & Davis, T. J. (2014). Effectiveness of virtual reality-based instruction on students' learning outcomes in K-12 and higher education: A meta-analysis. *Computers & Education, 70*, 29–40. https://doi.org/10.1016/j.compedu.2013.07.033

Mikropoulos, T. A., & Natsis, A. (2011). Educational virtual environments: A ten-year review of empirical research (1999–2009). *Computers & Education, 56*(3), 769–780. https://doi.org/10.1016/j.compedu.2010.10.020

Pantelidis, V. S. (2010). Reasons to use virtual reality in education and training courses and a model to determine when to use virtual reality. *Themes in Science and Technology Education, 2*(1–2), 59–70.

Salzman, M. C., Dede, C., Loftin, R. B., & Chen, J. (1999). A model for understanding how virtual reality aids complex conceptual learning. *Presence: Teleoperators and Virtual Environments, 8*(3), 293–316. https://doi.org/10.1162/105474699566242

Stigler, S. (2008). Fisher and the 5% level. *Chance, 21*(4), 12–12. https://doi.org/10.1080/09332480.2008.10722926

Wickens, C. D. (1992). Virtual reality and education. *[Proceedings] 1992 IEEE International Conference on Systems, Man, and Cybernetics, 1*, 842–847. https://doi.org/10.1109/ICSMC.1992.271688

Winn, W. (1993). *A conceptual basis for educational applications.* http://www.hitl.washington.edu/research/education/winn/winn-paper.html

Youngblut, C. (1998). *Educational uses of virtual reality technology.* Alexandria, VA: Institute for Defense Analyses.

Chapter 3
Language and Electronic Medium Skills Development Through Autonomous and Ideological Practices

Odette Bourjaili-Radi

3.1 Introduction

The content of this paper will focus on the concepts of autonomous and ideological models, introduced by Brian Street, on both language and computer practices and how school age students in two private schools develop their literacy skills in the two domains of "language" and "computers." The schools, under study, are identified by a code BG (is referred to the co-educational school – boys and girls) which is located in the north suburb of Melbourne and G is referred to girls school which is located in the northwest suburb of Melbourne, Australia. In the courses of the curriculum, the G school students do not carry electronic devices for school use and are still using the printed textbooks and handwrite their school notes, comparing to BG students who are reprimanded for not having their electronic medium devices on hand for using the eBooks which may also be associated with social media.

Some of the concepts raised by the literature apply to both language and computer literacy issues. Hence, this paper is intended to review the literature as this research is still in progress of collecting data. This research is set up to investigate whether the increased use of computers in education is enhancing or hindering students' language literacy development by comparing students' achievement in two private schools and their use of electronic devices. The focus is based on constructing one's own knowledge, as learning is a lifelong endeavor, never fully attained (Bélisle, 2006, p. 56). Botzakis et al., (2019, p. 223) assert that "[t]eaching requires attention to both ideological and autonomous aspects of literacy." However, the focus of this study will be based on five areas to establish any comparison associated with the concepts of autonomous and ideology: first, the definitional and conceptual issues of literacy (McClelland & Cameron, 2019, pp. 144–145); second, language literacy (Chang & Monaghan, 2019, pp. 236–238); third, computer

---

O. Bourjaili-Radi (✉)
La Trobe University, Bundoora, VIC, Australia

literacy, which applies to the acquisition and development of computer skills, particularly those associated with electronic medium (Hatlevik, Throndsen, Loi, & Gudmundsdottir, 2018, pp. 107–119); fourth, the evolution of computer literacy to include new literacies, as new technological components emerge and interlock in computer usage to encompass Information and Communication Technology (ICT) literacy and its applications (Cartelli, 2010, pp. 1–6; Stopar & Bartol, 2019, pp. 280–282); and fifth, parents' opinions are also sought on issues concerning their children's acquisition and development in both computer and language literacy skills.

3.1.1 Definitional and Conceptual Issues of Literacy

Literacy definitions have expanded from an original focus on just reading and writing to include additional changes relating to many aspects of contemporary society. Issues relating to literacy definitions have reflected many dimensions and explanations from different perspectives and disciplinary areas. Collin and Street (2014, p. 356) debate that individuals who learn to read and write are thought to become more logical and literate. Hence, theorists such as Street (1984) have distinguished between an autonomous model and an ideological model of literacy. In the autonomous model, literacy is defined as a set of value-free skills, like decoding the printed words into sounds (decontextualising text) (Street, 1995, pp. 18–19). Viewed from this perspective – the acquisition of reading and writing skills is simply a cognitive process (McClelland and Cameron, 2019, p. 146). There is no mention of how literacy enables people to function socially, culturally, and politically. A corollary of the autonomous model of literacy is the presumption that learning to read and write, in and of itself, will improve the social and economic conditions of people (Street, 1995, pp. 151–152). In critiquing the concept of autonomous literacy by scholars, Street brought into full light the awareness that literacy is not simply a set of context-neutral skills or competencies in mastering graphemes, phonemes, or written and spoken texts. In developing a more inclusive alternative perspective, his focus turned to cultural dimensions of literacy involving attitudes, values, practices, and conventions. He included that

> The autonomous model of literacy works from the assumptions that literacy in itself – autonomously – will have effects on other social and cognitive practices. It assumed that the acquisition of literacy will in itself lead [to] higher cognitive skills, improved economic performance, greater quality, …. This model … disguises the cultural and ideological assumptions and presents literacy's values as neutral and universal. … The alternative ideological model of literacy offers a more culturally sensitive view of literacy practices as they vary from one context to another. (Street, 2005, pp. 417–418)

Street (1993) identified many issues relating to the models and notions of literacy. In relation to the ideological model of literacy, he argued that it

> recognises a multiplicity of literacies; that the meaning and uses of literacy practices are related to specific cultural contexts; and these practices are always associated with relations

of power and ideology. They are not simply neutral technologies. … Literacy practices are constitutive of identity and of personhood – whichever forms of reading and writing we learn and use have associated with them certain social identities, expectations about behavior and role models. …, 'what it is to be a person', to be moral and to be human in specific cultural contexts is frequently signified by the kind of literacy practices within which a person is engaged. (1993, pp.139–140)

Both models of literacy have been interpreted in different ways by different scholars. For example, Blake and Blake's (2005, p. 172) interpretation of the autonomous model is "the prevailing Western view of literacy, a single thought." In extending a modified view of literacy into the social domain, Bélisle (2006) included three complementary approaches to literacy that stand out in educational analysis:

an autonomous model of literacy is based on the assumption that reading and writing are simply technical skills; a socio-cultural model, based on the recognition of all literacies as socially and ideologically embedded; and a strong claim model based on anthropological statements of the revolutionary power of instrumented thinking processes. (2006, p. 52)

After the 1990 International Literacy Year, Bélisle (2006) added that literacy had come to be seen in a broader way as knowledge acquisition: "to be literate is not only to identify and satisfy information needs through mastery of print," but involves the capacity and the inclination constantly to "continue constructing one's own knowledge, as learning is a lifelong learning endeavour, never fully attained" (p. 54). In line with Bélisle (2006), Kimber and Wyatt-Smith (2008, p. 330) reported that the strategy adopted an inspirational tone, "urging teachers to embrace and capture the potential of new technologies in classroom practice." They stated that pedagogies integrating ICT can enhance learning. "ICT provide tools and environments that support interactive conceptual learning, focused on constructing and creating knowledge. It exhorts teachers to empower students to purposefully select activities, applications and modes of communication and to engage students in simulations, modelling and creative activities." Kimber and Wyatt-Smith's (2008) work echoed Bélisle (2006, p. 64) who also reported that pedagogy is influential communication, providing children with the information and the tools to successfully integrate into society.

Consequently, the autonomous model has been criticized many times over the years as a result of questioning its strategies, applications, and goal directions particularly in response to the rapid development of technology and its wide use, by all ages, in contemporary society. According to Barton (2007, pp. 118–119), the autonomous view suggests that "there is a great divide between literate and non-literate, both at the individual level and at the cultural level, and that there are cognitive consequences associated with literacy itself". Subsequently, Reder and Davila (2005) in agreement with Barton (2007) elaborated on the "great divide" views of the consequences of literacy, which have posited fundamental and far-reaching cognitive differences as a consequence of being (or not being) literate, not only between societies and individuals but also between local and global contexts. In his later writing, Street (2003) pursued the distinction between literacy events and literacy practices to further clarify the notions of literacy. He applied these notions to what was challenged in the "New Literacy Studies" (NLS) (Mandinach & Cline, 2000).

Heath (2007, pp. 204–206), however, was not satisfied with Street's explanations of the concepts of "literacy and social practices" and looked at it from a contemporary perspective of how young people convey and receive information in the NLS/multimodality of "literacy practices." Heath stated that multimodal literacies involve all media forms that combine visual literacy, information literacy, digital literacy, and conventions. The initial formulation of Street's theory of literacy was broadly applied without taking into account the extensive use of the electronic medium, its rapid changes moving away from traditional literacy, and its impact on contemporary society and the young. It was only in his later writings that Street engaged more extensively with issues associated with language and digital/computer literacies.

3.1.2 Defining Language and Computer Literacies

Hence, Street's (1984) autonomous and ideological models of literacy that were subsequently replaced by the notions of literacy events and practices partially apply to computer literacy. Many technological dimensions have been considered in moving to the current term of ICT and digital literacy (Markauskaite, 2006). Markauskaite utilized Street's (1984) models by relating the different purposes of ICT literacy to different teaching and learning practices. She pointed out that

> [i]n this model, ICT is an integral part of all literacy practices. ... [She includes the notion of ICT literacy in a specific context with dimensions which are intended to provide benefits in the first instance]; *in an autonomous model 'benefits to individual'* [and in the second instance of the] *ideological model 'benefits to society.'* (Markauskaite, 2006, pp. 10–16)

Understandings of computer literacy include literacy events with many dimensions underpinning literacy practices at the global level such as information literacy, visual literacy, technology literacy, and digital literacy (Cohen & Cowen, 2008; Barton, 2007). The term digital literacy developed to include media literacy and the ability to interpret information. Digital literacy encompasses computer hardware, software (particularly those used most frequently by businesses), the Internet, cell phones, PDAs, iPods, iPads, and other digital devices. McLean (2010, p. 14) stated that "..., social networking sites such as MySpace, Instagram, Twitter, Facebook and others offer their members opportunities to engage in multimodal consumption and production of a range of texts, including photos, videos, text comments, symbols and images." Young people using these skills to interact with society are called digital citizens (Lankshear and Knobel, 2006, pp. 12–24). Digital literacy has also different meanings, according to Leahy and Dolan (2010, pp. 210 –221) which includes terms such as "computer literacy" (the technical knowledge of computer professionals); "information literacy" includes the ability to verify, interpret and validate the information; "cyber literacy" includes competence with using the Internet, digital communication and the Web. Digital literacy is used to refer to the use of electronic equipment by all members of society, for personal and social interactions and for educational and business needs. It is underpinned by basic skills in

ICT: the use of computers to retrieve, access, store, produce, present, and exchange information and to communicate and participate in collaborative networks via the Internet (McLean, 2010, pp. 13–22). Despite the need to become computer literate, Blake and Blake (2005, p. 172) reported that the use of ICT also requires language literacy skills, "[r]eading and writing are [also] used [in order] to transmit information, to interpret, to respond to the expression of human thought." Language literacy acquisitions are fundamentally essential for the exchange of information required in our society.

3.2 Language Literacy

More generally, in current usage, the term language literacy implies an interaction "between social demands/practices and autonomous individual competence, ranging from individual skills, abilities and knowledge, to social practices and functional competencies to ideological values and political goals" (Winch et al., 2006, pp. xxxii–xxxvi). Malatesha and Aaron (2010, p. 310) stated that "letter knowledge requires the ability not only to be aware of the phonemes of the language but also to relate these sounds to the letters of the alphabet." They added that increasing awareness of phonemes can also increase children's knowledge about reading and writing in a particular language. From an ideological perspective, language literacy is a broad term used to indicate not only the importance and the ability of individuals to read and write in a designated language but also their ability to interpret the world as presented to them in the texts (Blake & Blake, 2002, p. 10). Hence, writing is clearly a form of communication, which also connotes the activity of forming letters and words and sentences which can signify meaning to a prospective reader. The National Assessment Program – Literacy and Numeracy (NAPLAN) is an annual formal assessment for students in Years 3, 5, 7, and 9 in Australian schools which raised a controversial issue by the results of 2019 annual assessment (Carey, 2019, pp. 1 & 6). The Education Minister, Mr. Merlino stated that "Year 9 students were stubbornly disengaged from the national test, as preliminary results for 2019 revealed a lack of improvement in literacy and numeracy …" The NAPLAN is organized by the Australian Curriculum, Assessment, and Reporting Authority (ACARA) which is hosted by all public, private, and Christian schools across Australia. "NAPLAN tests are designed to oversee the sorts of skills that are essential for every child to progress through school and life, such as reading, writing, spelling, grammar and numeracy." According to ACARA (2019b), NAPLAN is not about passing or failing, but about assessing learning progress. The learning progress considered by the Australian Curriculum (n.d.) includes general capabilities of literacy, numeracy, information, and communication technology alongside other concepts. Hence, the writing is briefly mentioned in the discussion papers, but there is a need to elaborate on its importance in any literacy discussion.

3.2.1 Students' Writing

Handwriting has been largely forgotten in the literacy and ICT debates. But Ljungdahl (2010, p. 357) stressed that handwriting develops skills needed for good readers and writers. Increasingly, writing is done on the keyboard, enhancing legibility, but only in contexts where keyboards or alternative digital technologies are available. In other contexts, which are still frequent in both classrooms and high stakes environments such as examinations, the acquisition of handwriting skills free the student to focus on the quality of ideas and clarity of expression, including accurate spelling. In addition, good (consistent) handwriting visually reinforces the memory of word patterns and can help in speaking, spelling, and writing more effectively. This applies to the students at G school and was confirmed by their teachers. They read widely and saw a relationship between reading and their effective writing skills. Carroll et al. (1995, p. 5) asserted that the value is in the handwritten language when practiced independently; the handwriting reinforces the acquisition of literacy skills. In line with Carroll et al. (1995), De Craene and Cuthell's (2006, pp. 1–5) study revealed that children, who handwrote their work and engaged more in reading printed texts, showed development in their motor and cognitive skills at a young age. In line with the literature, the G students who practiced their handwriting skills were able to express their ideas and wrote lengthy essays. This strategy was consistent with strategies adopted by their teachers who expect their students to handwrite their drafts as many times as they needed until they reached the curriculum expectations. Their reasons were that students were provided with the opportunity to reflect on issues (such as spelling and grammatical errors, expressions and the like) that they might improve on by redrafting their pieces of writing. In support to the teachers consisting practices, Feder and Majnemer (2007, p. 312) asserted that "[f]ailure to attain handwriting competency during the school age years, has far-reaching negative effects on both academic success and self-esteem." Despite the widespread use of computers, they added, that "legible handwriting remains an important life skill that deserves greater attention from parents and educators" (Ljungdahl, 2010, pp. 363–367). Children typically handwrite in a classroom environment and for examinations. Although some work involves computers, children engage in handwriting throughout their school life (Williams et al. 2019, pp. 2–3). The data in Table 3.1 compares in percentage the settings of the two schools and their policies for using/not using electronic devices.

Table 3.1 demonstrates 80% of students in G school do not own any electronic devices for school use, while 20% use their domestic personal computer (pc) to produce their school work. The question was asked to Year 12 students if how do they feel about being unable to use any electronic devices at school. Their responses were: "This helps us to improve our handwriting to be faster at composing the required writing which will earn us a high mark at the end of year exams. Handwriting the essays in the exam are easily readable and clear to the examiners." This makes a substantial difference in the passing rate of 70% of G students compared to 30% of BG students at the end of year exams. The G students' responses echoed in De

Table 3.1 BG students compulsory use of electronic devices and G students do not use any electronic devices at school

Students	No electronic devices at school %	Electronic devices %	Research projects using electronic devices at school %	Passing rate at year 12 %
G school	80		20	70
Electronic devices used at home	20			
BG school				30
Laptop		45	80	
iPads		44		
Mobile phones		11		
Total	100	100	100	100

Souza and Towndrow (2010, p. 26), who stressed the importance of handwriting for students who "still use pen and paper format in their exams." While 89% of students at BG school were directed to solely use their electronic devices to perform all their school works, they stressed that at times, "we could not read our own handwriting." It is a hindrance to us at the end of year exams. Nevertheless, Ljungdahl (2010, p. 357) stressed that handwriting develops skills needed for good readers and writers by stating that "[g]ood handwriting visually reinforces the memory of word patterns and can help in speaking, spelling, and writing more effectively."

The definitions of literacy are of increasing breadth and reflect a growing emphasis on context. The relevance of this study particularly relates to the text composition. This applies to G school where the students are contented to handwrite their school work as required. The social situations have changed and brought with them changes to the definition of language literacy with the additional emergence of new technologies in educational, domestic, and workplace environments. For the purpose of this study, the main focus will be to compare the relationship between language literacy and computer literacy, which involves the use of computer peripherals and software applications and their tools.

3.3 Computer Literacy

Computer literacy definitions vary depending not only on the different levels of regular and power users (software developers, programmers and network infrastructure experts) but also on how literacy is perceived and applied by educational and industrial/workplace theorists. Computer literacy involves not only the understanding of what is possible with (and what influences the use of) computers but also the physical use of combined equipment (peripherals) and software applications (Williams, 2002, p. 8). At a less specialized level and from the autonomous view, this applies to BG students; computer literacy involves the knowledge of how to turn on a computer, start and stop software applications, as well as save, retrieve, and print documents. In relation to software, Cohen and Cowen (2008, p. 546) defined computer literacy as "the ability to effectively use [autonomously] computer tools, such as word processors, spreadsheets, databases, presentation and [integration of] graphic software." From a possibly wider perspective, Moursund's (2003, p. 9) definition of computer literacy, which also reflects an autonomous model, is "a functional level of knowledge and skills in using computers and computer-based multimedia as an aid to communication with oneself and others for the purposes of learning, knowing and for using one's knowledge." Ideologically, the term computer literacy is commonly used to characterize a degree of knowledge and awareness about computers and their role in society. Computer literacy, according to Cartelli (2010, pp. 1-6), applies to an understanding of computer characteristics, capabilities, and applications, as well as an ability to implement this knowledge in the skillful, productive use of computer applications suitable to individual roles in society. From an ideological view, computer literacy has evolved into a broad term that incorporates the use of the Internet and other digital devices.

3.3.1 The Internet

The Internet is an integral part of computer literacy. It is a "powerful tool and endless source of information, which is easy to find and easy to produce" (Knierzinger & Turcsanyi-Szabo, 2001, p. 926). Computer literacy has evolved into a broad term that encompasses a range of related literacies, including digital, network, ICT, and electronic devices in different fields of communication, including the Internet (Cesarini, 2004, pp. 1–4). More recently, computer literacy has expanded to multidimensional-related literacies known as ICT. The ideological dimensions of computer literacy or ICT revolve around online communication (globally), the Internet, and wireless electronic devices to facilitate access to digital resources.

The Internet has become more and more important in young people's lives at school and at home. Ma et al. (2008, p. 197) stated that "the Internet is affecting all subjects in K-12." Ma et al.'s study included those described by Tapscott's (1998) term the "Net-generations" who are fluent with digital technology, including all sorts of digital and electronic devices. Not only students are making more use of the Internet, but the service providers are reaching further with the development of ICT literacy into the lives of the young users. The nature and scope of ICT capability are not fixed but are responsive to ongoing technological developments. "This is evident in the emergence of advanced internet technology over the past few years and the resulting changes in the ways that students construct knowledge and interact with others" (Australian Curriculum, n.d.).

3.3.2 ICT Literacy

ICT literacy is a broad term that includes multiple communication devices, various services, and applications associated with it. ICT literacy is increasingly regarded as a broad set of generalizable and transferable knowledge, skills, and understandings that relate to communication tools used to access, manage, integrate, evaluate, and create information in order to function in a knowledgeable society (Martin, 2006, pp. 8–9; Ainley, 2010, p. 2). ICT literacy covers the new and emergent technological devices combined, introducing new literacies (internet, iPads and others) as they become available. Harris (2005, p. 34) stated that ICTs are "social information spaces." They are designed as much for the reciprocal "sharing of information" as they are for "seeking and disseminating information." He elaborates that "sharing" involves exchanging information among users, and "seeking" implies going to sources outside one's immediate social system. Out-of-school and in-school digital literacies are used by youth interactively and purposefully, in ways that are increasingly "hypertextual," connected and communicated (Bussert-Webb & Diaz, 2012, p. 5). These changes have made computer literacy skills more available to include interactions and communications through social events and practices. The changes become more apparent in Street's notions. Literacy events and practices apply to the acquisition of computer literacy skills. The literacy events happen when the Net Generation (Rohatgi et al., 2016, pp. 103–116) acquired the new literacy and put it into practice. On the other hand, autonomously, the digital natives apply their own language which they have invented by engaging in the use of the electronic devices as they emerge. The digital culture that the young people identify with has shifted emphasis from the traditional written language to re-form a language that the Net-Generation created (Mountifield, 2006, pp. 172–173). They are digitally embodied in multimodal forms of literacy and are associated in the constructions of identity and community (Nævdal, 2007, p. 1113). They will continue to apply their experience to further practice with more emergent technology.

3.4 Research Methodology

This study has adopted an ethnographic methodological approach which relates to educational research. The methods encompass the collection and analysis of quantitative and qualitative data (Shah, 2019, pp. 46–47). This method involves participant observation. The focus in ethnography is on description of current circumstances and of particular groups of people rather than individual or historical events in these contexts (p. 48). The total numbers of students observed are 180 students: 90 students at the BG school and 90 students at G school. All students are at secondary level, years 6–12, and age ranges from 13 to 18 years old. The nature of the present study has three methods associated with an ethnographic quantitative approach: (1) the implications of the increase use of ICT; (2) qualitative, the students' perceptions of and identified use of ICT both at home and at school (Burns, 1997, pp. 9–10); and (3) parents report on their children's acquisition of computers and language literacy skills between the two private schools. Given the importance of ethnography method in obtaining first-hand and in-depth results, it is recommended to provide more awareness about the effectiveness of the method and more attention to its implementation among the research projects both in educational and health research areas (Shah, 2019, pp. 48–49).

This methodology will be used to analyze the shift from reading the printed text and handwriting to engaging with electronic medium devices. Seeking students' and their parents' opinions will be a source of descriptive data that will assist in arriving at a judgment of how computers are enhancing or hindering the development of language literacy skills comparing the two private schools to those who are using the electronic devices and those who are not. This is a continuous progress of observation and pre-surveying and interviewing students and their parents. The main variables are the electronic devices usage at home and at school.

3.4.1 Results

At the BG school, students use their devices between 7 to 9 hours a day between school and homework, while the G students only carry their textbooks and do not have any electronic devices to use at school. Figure 3.1 displays the percentage of middle school students at BG (Years 6–9) who use more than one device, while G school students do not use any electronic devices at school, but both BG and G students use them at their domestic environment.

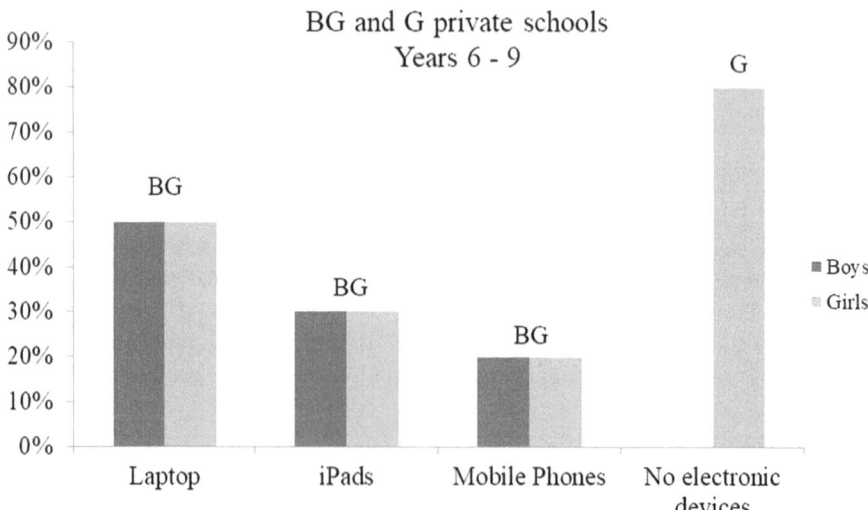

Fig. 3.1 Middle school (years 6–9) students' use/not use of electronic devices

Figure 3.1 shows that 50% of boys and 50% of their counterpart, at BG school, are using their laptops to access information from their ebooks, the Internet and for writing purposes, while 30% of boys and 30% of girls use their iPads and 20% use their mobiles phones. Their activities include homework and leisure time. Hence, 80% of students at G school do not use any electronic devices at all at school, but they still experience self-efficacy in operating their PC away from school. They are as familiar with the electronic devices as much as the BG students are. Regardless, they are also the Net Generation (Rohatgi et al., 2016, pp. 103–116); every day, students come into contact with computer or any form of technologies and learn about them in less formal ways outside the school. "ICT skills are acquired through family, through friends, self-tuition, and through many other sources" (Milić & Škorić, 2010, p. 63). Hence, Hatlevik et al. (2018, pp. 107-119) stated that "... ICT self-efficacy is positively related to computer and information literacy when controlled for other student characteristics and background contextual variables." Furthermore, students' ICT self-efficacy at both schools plays important roles in understanding students' computer use and accessing information literacy. However, the senior students at BG school are compelled to use more specific devices, depending on the demand of their subjects.

Figure 3.2 illustrates 70% of boys and 70% of girls are using laptops, while 25% of boys and 20% of girls are using iPads at the BG school. The mobile phones are less used, and 5% of boys and 10% of girls may use their mobile phones to access and manipulate the required data. The experienced Year 12 students who practiced the use of the electronic devices such as iPads with the inclusion of Bluetooth keyboard are able to save their work on Google drive. More questions were asked; how do they access their documents and why using the Google drive rather the iCloud

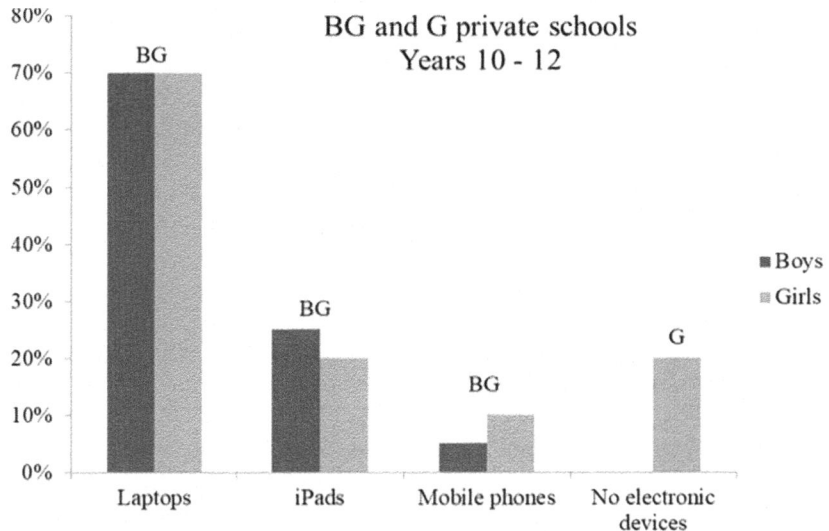

Fig. 3.2 Senior (Years 10–12) students' use/not use of electronic devices

drive? Their responses were that "the iCloud provides only five gigabytes of free capacity to save their data and when the capacity exceeds the required amount, they have to pay a fee, where Google drive is not restricted to any data capacity and also free." The G students do not use electronic devices; 20% of them "commented that the storage they used for their data is only in their exercise books." Further comments, it is safer, "we do not worry about computer viruses and the deletion of our work."

The use of ICT in different settings such as the home or school environment for different purposes such as recreation or working on school-related tasks may provide opportunities for students to gain mastery experience. As such, mastery experiences are considered "to be crucial antecedents of students' self-efficacy, which in turn determine their achievement" ideologically (Rohatgi et al., 2016, pp. 103–116). Therefore, seeking the parents' opinions is vital to obtain their assessment on their children's acquisition of literacy skills.

3.5 Parents Report on Students' Acquisition of Computers and Language Literacy Skills

The questionnaire reached the parents after they were formerly informed and signed the approval forms to allow their children to participate in the study. The survey sought parents' opinions on issues concerning their children's acquisition and development in both computer and language literacy skills. The parents' questionnaire included questions about their initial reason for buying a personal computer; estimate time used by the individual members of the household, and to list other amusement equipment possessed by the household and its frequent use. The questionnaire also covered other issues relating to the types and frequency of use of personal computers at home.

The majority of parents, whose children attend the BG school, felt that their children were spending more time on the computer than reading any type of printed text. They generally felt that the high use of computers at school and home are not allowing their children to develop their language literacy skills as expected at their age. They also felt that spending time exploring the electronic medium is good for developing computer literacy but not the language literacy. Nevertheless, the majority of parents were convinced of the necessity of technology in their domestic environment for their children's educational needs.

Figure 3.3 illustrates 43% of parents purchased the PC for their children's education (to do schoolwork) and 26% for their children to keep up with technology (learn how to use the computers). Adding the two together, 69% of parents purchased the computers partly for their children to use. The majority of parents in the survey felt that "their children need to keep up with the current development of technology." "For technology is taking part in all aspects of our society and our lives." Parents' responses were "there is not much of a choice, everything is

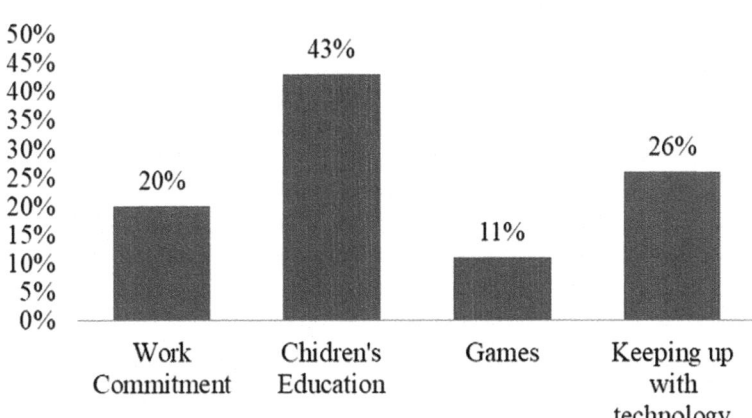

Fig. 3.3 Parents initial reasons for buying a personal computer

computers. … Children need to have good knowledge of computers, …, that is the way the world is going." Eleven percent of parents who bought their PC just for games is also reported; "playing games is keeping up with technology that is going to benefit the children in the future, keep the children amused and expand their knowledge and share ideas with friends." They stated that the computer games make their children become "… computer literate [which] is an advantage when entering the workforce." "Games and other tools give them [the children] confidence to use computers for other uses, increase awareness and familiarization".

The majority of the households in this study own amusement equipment other than computers such as PlayStation and Nintendo. Seventy-two percent of the BG parents' responses were: "besides using the school electronic devices at school, also their children have access to electronic equipment alongside their domestic computers". The BG parents were not expected that the school where their children attend were going to make school electronic devices compulsory". Sixty-five percent of parents made the comments that "our children are using the electronic devices more than seven to nine hours a day between school and home work."

The G parents agree with the school policy not to allow their children to use electronic devices at school. Eighty percent of parents responded that "we are pleased that our children are not exposed to the electronic devices during school time." "Our children are autonomously ready to improve on their cognitive practices and skills, due to their wide reading away from the destruction of the electronic devices." "The acquisition of language literacy will lead them to improve into a high quality performance in their exams due to their handwriting eligibility." Their reasons are in line with Street's (1984) autonomous model of literacy benefits to "individual" and in the second instance of the ideological model of literacy benefits to "society."

It should be remembered here that the PC is not the only type of computer chip-based electronic technology in these households. The other electronic devices such as video games and mobile phones are used by the children beside their household pc. The increased use of mobiles, both at home and school, initially was for emergency reasons, in case the students need to contact their parents or vice versa. Hence, every student at GB school carries a mobile phone, their reasons were that "they are not destructed by others and are much focused on their work by listening to music". This is in well-established electronic schools like the BG school, whereas the G school students leave their mobiles in their lockers. They check it for messages at recess and lunchtime. However, Albion and Tondeur (2018, pp. 1–3) found that "a large-scale of studies that Australian children aged 8–9 years were using ICT at school in conventional ways with little evidence of use to support creative and project-based activities." This suggests that children may be acquiring basic skills with ICT as envisaged in the ICT general capability in the Australian Curriculum but are less likely to be developing as creators of digital solutions. Far from improving over time, skills measured by that assessment have decreased. One plausible explanation for such a decrease is that the skills measured in the assessment relate mostly to the use of applications on personal computers, but the focus of schools and students has shifted to emerging forms of ICT such as tablets and handheld devices like smartphones. "New technologies require different skillsets and the rate of change in ICT is sufficiently rapid that attempts to compare very specific skills over time may be futile if they have been made less relevant by changes in ICT" (Albion & Tondeur, 2018, p. 2).

3.6 Conclusion

Today, young people face a challenging situation. While they have the opportunity to benefit from powerful digital technologies which open up new learning opportunities, they also need to deal with handling and making sense of such devices in a complex and non-stable world. Consequently, the BG school students are constantly using their digital devices for seven to nine hours a day, increasing their accessibility and perception through the development of learners' understanding and creativity, computational thinking, media literacy and digital citizenship. The obvious limitations for the BG students are the lack of practicing their handwriting skills. Hence, the implications on young people's engagement in digital culture, from an autonomous and ideological view, have a focus on digital texts as social and textual entities.

The implications and the acquisition of handwriting skills free the student to focus on the quality of ideas and clarity of expression (Ljungdahl, 2010, p. 358). However, the literature suggests that being competent in literacy implies that one knows which practices, attitudes, and values are appropriate in a given situation. This applies to the G school students who are autonomously mastering the language literacy without the destruction of the digital devices, and the ideological dimensions can present much more compelling and in depth challenges. The prominent messages stemming from the literature and the comparison of the two private schools are that young children should be developing an enriched vocabulary as an indicator of oral language proficiency which is essential for comprehension of both oral and written language. Technological changes have happened so rapidly that changes to literacy are shaped not only by technology but by our ability to adapt and acquire the new literacies that emerge with its applications (Leu, Kinzer, Coiro, & Cammack, 2004; Florian, 2004).

Computer literacy and its relationship to language literacy development among school age children need further and continuous study. Technology is still advancing rapidly, and further changes to the education system infrastructure and domestic environments are likely. It is, therefore, necessary to have a closer look at the ways in which individual student made use of the computers and their associated literacy tools. In future studies, a collaborative work between teachers and researchers will be necessary to progress the formulation of multimodal "new literacies" and "digital literacies," and intermodal pedagogic "spellings" and "grammars" will be needed to accommodate the New Literacies Studies in classroom contexts. Further studies will assist in facilitating productive participation along these lines among the researchers and teachers in ICT, English, and literacy education.

References

Ainley, J. (2010). What can Australian students do with computers. *Research Developments. ACER: Camberwell, 23*(23), 1–4.

Albion, P. R., & Tondeur, J. (2018). Information and communication technology and education: Meaningful change through teacher agency. In *Second handbook of information technology in primary and secondary education* (Springer international handbooks of education) (2nd ed., pp. 1–16). Netherlands: Springer. Retrieved from https://eprints.usq.edu.au/33783/.

Australian Curriculum. (n.d.). Information and communication technology (ICT) capability. Retrieved from https://www.australiancurriculum.edu.au/f-10-curriculum/general-capabilities/information-and-communication-technology-ict-capability/.

Australian Curriculum, Assessment and Reporting Authority. (2019). General capabilities. Retrieved from https://acara.edu.au/curriculum/foundation-year-10/general-capabilities.

Barton, D. (2007). *Literacy: An introduction to the ecology of written language* (2nd ed.). Oxford: Blackwell Publishing.

Bélisle, C. (2006). Literacy and the digital knowledge revolution. In A. Martin & D. Madigan (Eds.), *Digital literacies for learning* (pp. 51–67). Facet Publishing.

Blake, B. E., & Blake, R. W. (2002). Literacy and Learning: A Reference Book. ABC-CLIO. Santa Barbara.

Blake, B. E., & Blake, R. W. (2005). *Literacy primer*. New York: Peter Lang.

Burns, R. B. (1997). *Introduction to research methods* (3rd ed.). South Melbourne: Longman.

Bussert-Webb, K. M., & Diaz, M. E. (2012). New literacy opportunities and practices of Latino/a children of poverty in and out of school. *Language and Literacy Journal, 14*(1), 1–25.

Carey, A. (2019). Schools Victoria pushes reform: Jobs link proposal for year 9 NAPLAN. *The Age Newspaper*, pp. 1 and 6.

Carroll, A., Psihoyos, L., & Swerdlow, J. L. (1995). Information revolution. *National Geographic, 188*(4), 5.

Cartelli, A. (2010). Theory and practice in digital competence assessment international. *Journal of Digital Literacy and Digital Competence, 1*(3), 1–17.

Cesarini, P. (2004). Computers, technology, and literacies. *The Journal of Literacy and Technology, 4*(1), 1–16.

Chang, Y., & Monaghan, P. (2019). Quantity and diversity of preliteracy language exposure both affect literacy development: Evidence from a computational model of reading. *Scientific Studies of Reading., 23*(3), 235–253. Retrieved from https://www.tandfonline.com/doi/full/10.1080/10888438.2018.1529177.

Chen, X., & Lee, V. G. (2010). Promoting comprehension in middle school and high school: Tapping into out-of-school literacies of our adolescents. In K. Ganske & D. Fisher (Eds.), *Comprehension across the curriculum perspectives and practices K – 12* (pp. 119–145). New York: The Guilford Press.

Cohen, V. L., & Cowen, J. E. (2008). *Literacy for children in an information age: Teaching, reading, writing and thinking*. Belmont: Thomson Wadsworth.

Collin, R., & Street, B. V. (2014). Ideology and interaction: Debating determinism in literacy studies. *Reading Research Quarterly., 49*(3), 351–359. Retrieved from https://ila.onlinelibrary.wiley.com/doi/abs/10.1002/rrq.75.

De Craene, M., & Cuthell, J. (2006). Clickerati generation update: The digital divide starts early. *The Educational Technology: ICT in Education,* 1–5.

De Souza, D. E., & Towndrow, P. A. (2010). The generative use of ICT in the language arts: Strategies in learning task design and implementation. In C. M. L. Ho, K. T. Anderson, & A. P. Leong (Eds.), *Transforming literacies and language: Multimodality and literacy in the new media age* (pp. 23–48). London: Continuum.

Feder, K. P., & Majnemer, A. (2007). Handwriting development, competency, and intervention. *Devlopmental Medicine and Child Neurology Journal, 49*(4), 312–317.

Florian, L. (2004). Uses of technology that support pupils with special educational needs. In L. Florian & J. Hegarty (Eds.), *ICT and special educational needs: A tool for inclusion* (pp. 7–20). Buckingham: Open University Press.

Harris, F. J. (2005). *I found it on the internet: Coming of age online*. Chicago: American Library Association.

Hatlevik, O. E., Throndsen, I., Loi, M., & Gudmundsdottir, G. B. (2018). Students' ICT self-efficacy and computer and information literacy: Determinants and relationship. *Computers & Education, 118*, 107–119.

Heath, S. B. (2007). Afterword. In V. Ellis, C. Fox, & B. Street (Eds.), *Rethinking english in schools: Towards a new and constructive stage* (pp. 199–206). London: Continuum International Publishing Group.

Kimber, K., & Wyatt-Smith, C. (2008). Assessing digital literacies: Can assessment ever be the same? In L. Unsworth (Ed.), *New literacies and the english curriculum: Multimodal perspectives* (pp. 328–352). London: Continuum.

Knierzinger, A., & Turcsanyi-Szabo, M. (2001). Internet, education and culture: Should we care? In D. Watson & J. Andersen (Eds.), *Networking the learner. Seventh IFIP World Conference on Computers in Education (WCCE)* (pp. 925–932). Norwell: Kluwer Academic Publishers.

Lankshear, C., & Knobel, M. (2006). Digital literacy and digital literacies: Policy, pedagogy, and research considerations for education. *Digital Kompetanse Journal, 1*(1), 12–24.

Leahy, D., & Dolan, D. (2010). Digital literacy: A vital competence for 2010?. In N. Reynolds and M. Turcsányi-Szabó (Eds.). *Key Competencies in the Knowledge Society. International Federation for Information Processing (IFIP) TC 3 International Conference*, KCKS 2010, Held as Part of WCC 2010, Brisbane, Australia, September 20–23, 2010. Proceedings, Vol. 324, 210–221.

Leu, D. J., Kinzer, C. K., Coiro, J. L., & Cammack, D. W. (2004). Toward a theory of new literacies emerging from the internet and other communication technologies. In R. B. Ruddell & N. J. Unrau (Eds.), *Theoretical models and processes of reading* (5th ed., pp. 1570–1613). Newark: International Reading Association.

Ljungdahl, L. (2010). Handwriting. In G. Winch, R. Ross Johnston, P. March, L. Ljungdahl, & M. Holliday (Eds.), *Literacy: Reading, writing and children's literature* (4th ed., pp. 357–369). South Melbourne: Oxford University Press.

Ma, H. J., Hongyan, J., Wan, G., & Lu, E. Y. (2008). Digital cheating and plagiarism in schools. *Theory Into Practice, 47*(3), 197–203.

Malatesha, J. R., & Aaron, P. G. (2010). Assessment of reading problems among English language learners based on the component model. In A. Yücesan Durgunoglu (Ed.), *Language and literacy development in bilingual settings* (pp. 304–331). New York: Guilford Press.

Mandinach, E. B., & Cline, H. F. (2000). It won't happen soon: Practical curricular, and methodological problems in implementing technology-based constructivist approaches in classrooms. In S. P. Lajoie (Ed.), *Computers as cognitive tools: No more walls* (pp. 377–389). Mahwah, NJ: Lawrence Erlbaum Associates.

Markauskaite, L. (2006). Towards an integrated analytical framework of information and communications technology literacy: From intended to implemented and achieved dimensions. *Information Research, 11*(3), 1–23.

Martin, A. (2006). Literacies for the digital age: Preview of part 1. In A. Martin & D. Madigan (Eds.), *Digital literacies for learning* (pp. 3–25). London: Facet Publishing.

McClelland, M. M., & Cameron, C. E. (2019). Developing together: The role of executive function and motor skills in children's early academic lives. *Early Childhood Research Quarterly, 46*, 142–151. Retrieved from https://www.sciencedirect.com/science/article/pii/S0885200617301369.

McLean, C. A. (2010). A space called home: An immigrant adolescent's digital literacy practices. *Journal of Adolescent &Adult Literacy, 54*(1), 13–22.

Milić, M., & Škorić, I. (2010). The impact of formal education on computer literacy. *iJET, 5*(2), 60–63.

Mountifield, H. (2006). The information commons: A student-centred environment for IT and information literacy development. In A. Martin & D. Madigan (Eds.), *Digital literacies for learning* (pp. 172–181). London: Facet Publishing.

Moursund, D., Bielefeldt, T., Ricketts, D., & Underwood, S. (1995). *Effective practice: Computer technology in education. International Society for Technology in Education*. Oregon: Eugene.

Moursund, D. G. (2003). Project-based learning using information technology. Retrieved from https://www.researchgate.net/publication/247276594_Projectbased_learning_using_information_technology

Nævdal, F. (2007). Home-pc usage and achievement in English. *Computers and Education, 49*(4), 1112–1121.

Reder, S., & Davila, E. (2005). Context and literacy pratices. *Annual Review of Applied Linguistics, 25*, 170–187.

Rohatgi, A., et al. (2016). The role of ICT self-efficacy for students' ICT use and their achievement in a computer and information literacy test. Computers & Education. Vol 102, pp 103–116.

Shah, A. (2017). Debate: Ethnography? Participant observation, a potentially revolutionary praxis. *HAU: Journal of Ethnographic Theory, 7*(1), 45–49.

Stopar, K., & Bartol, T. (2019). Digital competences, computer skills and information literacy in secondary education: Mapping and visualization of trends and concepts. *Scientometrics, 118*(2), 479–498. Retrieved from https://link.springer.com/article/10.1007/s11192-018-2990-5.

Street, B. (1984). Literacy in theory and practice. Cambridge University Press. Cambridge.

Street, B. (1993). Introduction: The new literacy studies: In Street, B. (Ed.) Cross-Cultural approaches to literacy. Cambridge University. Cambridge, pp 1–22.

Street, B. (1995). Social literacies: Critical approaches to literacy in development, ethnography, and education. Longman, London.

Street, B. (2003). What's "New" in New literacy studies? Critical approaches to literacy and practice. *Current Issues in Comparative Education, 5*(2), pp 77–91.

Street, B. (2005). Recent applications of new literacy studies in educational contexts. *Research in the Teaching of English, 39*(4), pp 417–423.

Tapscott, D. (1998). Growing up with digital: The rise of the net generation. McGraw-Hill. New York.
Williams, G. J., Larkin, R. F., Coyne-Umfreville, E., & Herbert, T. C. (2019). The effects of planning and handwriting style on quantity measures in secondary school children's writing. *Frontiers in Psychology, 10*(1143), 1–11. Retrieved from http://irep.ntu.ac.uk/id/eprint/36890/1/14132_Williams.pdf.
Williams, K. (2002). Literacy and computer literacy: Analyzing the NRC's "being fluent with information technology". *Journal of Literacy and Technology, 2*(2), 1–20. Retrieved from http://www.literacyandtechnology.org/uploads/1/3/6/8/136889/literacy.pdf.
Winch, G., et al. (2006). Introduction: To literacy in the modern world. In G. Winch, R. R. Johnston, P. March, L. Ljungdahl & M. Holliday (Eds.), Literacy: Reading, writing and children's literature, Third Edition. Oxford University Press, South Melbourne. Pages. xxxi– xl.

Chapter 4
Technology-Enhanced Learning of Motions Based on a Clustering Approach

Quentin Couland, Ludovic Hamon, and Sébastien George

4.1 Introduction

Motion capture is increasingly used in multiple domains such as video-game, animation movies, virtual reality (VR), sport, medicine, industry, and education. Thanks to breakthroughs made in electronics, human-computer interface (HCI), and data processing, it is reasonable to assume that capturing, editing, and sharing human gestures will be soon generalized. This assumption has a strong impact on education and on every domain implying human movements. Indeed, different kinds of information can be extracted from human motion analysis. One can easily generate low-level descriptors such as kinematic and dynamic data (Nunes & Moreira, 2016; Larboulette & Gibet, 2015). Gestures may have a meaning for verbal (Huang, Zhou, Li, & Li, 2015) or non-verbal communication (Chang, Chang, Zheng, & Chung, 2013). In addition, high-level data linked to human emotion (Kobayashi, 2007), intention (Yu & Lee, 2015), and action (Kapsouras & Nikolaidis, 2014) can be reified and built. Monitoring learner activities can imply the generation of a large amount of motion data that cannot be manually analyzed (Gu & Sosnovsky, 2014). Automatic methods, such as machine learning techniques, can ease such a task. This set of techniques can process high-dimensional data for classification purposes, feature extraction, regression problems, etc. (Ng, 2016). In an educational context, these algorithms are used to study and classify learner actions (Lokaiczyk, Faatz, Beckhaus, & Goertz, 2007) and/or behavior (Markowska-Kaczmar, Kwasnicka, & Paradowski, 2010), from motions thanks to supervised learning. However, this kind of algorithms implies: (i) the existence of a large

---

Q. Couland (✉) · L. Hamon · S. George
LIUM - EA 4023, Le Mans Université, Le Mans, France
e-mail: quentin.couland@univ-lemans.fr; ludovic.hamon@univ-lemans.fr; sebastien.george@univ-lemans.fr; https://lium.univ-lemans.fr/en/team/quentin-couland/; https://lium.univ-lemans.fr/en/team/ludovic-hamon/; https://lium.univ-lemans.fr/en/team/sebastien-george/

database of specific annotated motions for each task to learn (ii) and the knowledge of the different class names in advance. There is a lack of work regarding the automatic extraction of relevant information in pedagogical situations from learner motions. This can be explained by several technical and scientific issues: the heterogeneity, the complexity, the high-dimensional nature of such data, and the need to correlate this information with the observation needs of the teacher. Some of these issues could be overcome by the use of clustering algorithms, in order to avoid the requirements related to supervised ones (database size and labeling), and by using morphology-invariant descriptors relevant in the given context. The goal of this work is to use kinematic descriptors along with clustering techniques in order to (i) make and visualize well-separated clusters representing user profiles, (ii) use clusters features and inter-clusters distance to lead him to the cluster of acceptable motions, and (iii) create a TEL environment using clustering techniques usable by an expert in order to assist them in their motion evaluation task.

The goal of this work is to create a new TEL environment dedicated to motion learning, using clustering techniques, in order to assist the expert in their evaluation task. The creation of such a system requires the solving of some scientific and technic challenges: (i) the separation of motions in well-defined cluster, based on their properties, (ii) obtaining a separation corresponding to the degree of success of the task; and (iii) the validation of this approach and the use of this system in a real learning case. These challenges were addressed through three experimentations, all related to throwing motions. Results show that while it was possible to achieve a good separation of the motions in different clusters corresponding to different strategies of throwing, it was not possible to obtain a separation corresponding to the degree of success of the motions. Furthermore, the experimentation conducted in order to validate the usability and the usefulness of this system showed an improvement in the quality of the learners' motion.

The remainder of the chapter is structured as follows: Sect. 2 presents a review of motion-based analysis methods with a focus on educational-based work, showing the lack of unsupervised and generic approach for motion analysis. Our new approach using clustering techniques is shown in Sect. 3. The unsupervised approach allows using few unlabeled data in order to assist the expert. The experimentation on the separation of user profiles and its related protocol, results, and discussion are detailed in Sect. 4. Section 5 presents the TEL developed in order to validate the use of such a system in a real learning situation, showing an improvement in the learner motions. Finally, perspectives and future work end this study.

4.2 Related Work

Human learning motion can use captured motions, in order to assist the student in their learning task. In this context, the motion is mainly represented as a sequential evolution of human postures through time. Usually, a fixed time-step separates each posture (called "frame"). One way to represent a posture is to build a set of joints, hierarchically structured thanks to a graph, each node describing a joint. This set of joints is organized according to a skeleton model, i.e., a tree data structure, in which the root represents the low body part of the torso (i.e., the hip bone) and the nodes represent the body joints. Each node contains the position and the orientation, related to its parent node. It is possible to extract kinematic and dynamic descriptors from this structure such as the speed of the joint, its acceleration, its displacement through time, etc. (Nunes & Moreira, 2016) (Larboulette & Gibet, 2015). Zhu and Hu worked on the learning of specific motions for re-education (Zhou & Hu, 2008). The skeleton model was not systematically considered, because different kinds of sensors were used to gather motion data, depending on the observed movement. The data were used in order to analyze the patient's gait. No automatic analyses of the recorded movements were made; the observations and deductions of information were always made by a human expert. For Japanese archery learning, Yoshinaga and Soga developed a system based on a Kinect sensor to capture learner skeletons and its variations through time (Yoshinaga & Soga, 2015). Expert movements were also recorded and learners could compare their motions with the expert ones. The analysis was empirically made by humans. Le Naour et al. proposed a superimposition of the expert model and the student one in order to learn the throwing motion in American football (Le Naour et al., 2019). The quality of the motion was assessed with the help of the dynamic time warping algorithm computed between the expert and the learner motion and the regularity of the learner motion between different sessions. The superimposition is allowed for a better motion reproduction. Chan et al. used a TEL environment in order to learn dance motions (Chan, Leung, Tang, & Komura, 2011). Expert motions were recorded and showed to the learner. The learner motions were then compared to the expert ones, highlighting the parts of the student's body that were not synchronized with the expert, by using a distance threshold. A score was given to the student, to evaluate their performance. Maes et al. also worked on the visualization of the expert movements, the learning of the motion step-by-step, and the evaluation of the learner motion through a score in the same context (Maes, Amelynck, & Leman, 2012). In the last case, the score gives no hints about which part of the motion must be corrected, and thus the system gave no pedagogical feedbacks. Xu et al. developed a TEL environment in order to help children learning specific motions (Mingliang et al., 2019). These motions were related to the Chinese culture: operating looms, shooting arrow, riding horses, etc. The system makes use of a database of sub-motions and two hidden Markov models to achieve this goal. The first one allowed the segmentation of the motions, and the second one adapted the learning process to the student if the motions were not correct. While using automatic methods, a database containing motions related to the considered study case must be captured beforehand, in order to cover the widest range of possibilities. Furthermore, no pedagogic feedback was inferred from the performed motions.

There are a lot of TEL environments dedicated to motion learning. These systems can be used in various contexts such as rehabilitation (Zhou & Hu, 2008), surgical procedure learning (Pepley et al., 2017), and sports motion learning (Yoshinaga & Soga, 2015; Le Naour et al., 2019). An evaluation of the learner's motion was sometimes proposed, whether as a score, motion data visualization (expert and learner 3D avatar in VR, sometimes superimposed), or as a visualization of the learning path (in case the motion was segmented). A lot of these systems were not based on generic models allowing to consider different tasks as well as observation and analysis needs. Indeed, the expert's knowledge is often hard-coded during the design phase. Consequently, a heavy re-engineering is required in order to adapt them to other contexts. The generic aspect of such a system must be considered during the design phase, in order to be reusable in other contexts.

Studies using supervised and unsupervised algorithms to analyze facial expressions, gestures, and actions exist, and some of them were based on 3D captured data. Patrona et al. presented a framework for action recognition and evaluation based on extreme machine learning (Patrona, Chatzitofis, Zarpalas, & Daras, 2018). Using fuzzy logic, a feedback (depending on the activity context) is given to the learner, such as the velocity at specific frames, in order to improve the realized motion. This feedback requires a reference motion and a large corpus of existing motions, as the goal is to classify the motion into predefined categories from different datasets (CVD exercise, MSRC-12 and MSR-Action3D). Hachaj and Marek used a set of expert rules relating to the learner displacements (e.g. the distance covered by the learner in a time step), in order to classify motions (Hachaj & Ogiela, 2015). Although these approaches were efficient, the motions were related to simple and everyday activities (e.g., walking, jogging, running) that did not require a cognitive effort or strong motor skills to learn. Furthermore, the goal was not to evaluate the success degree of the motion and the descriptors could not be used to give a pedagogical feedback. Lui et al. worked on video databases from which two sets of descriptors were extracted (Lui, O'Hara, & Draper, 2011). These descriptors were, on the one hand, spatial and temporal localized features that were used with a Bag of Features approach and a manifold product on the other hand. The results showed an acceptable data partitioning, especially with the set of descriptors dedicated to the manifold product. The performed motions were also trivial in terms of cognitive effort, and the descriptors could not be used to give feedbacks to the learner. Due to the nature of the motions, the degree of success of the task was not evaluated. Pirsiavash et al. assessed the quality of motions without any a priori on the considered methods (Pirsiavash et al., 2014). The data are extracted from videos and consist of pixel gradients, joint trajectory, and successive postures of the performer. The considered motions were related to Olympic diving and figure skating. The motion was associated with the expert judge scores and fed to an SVM algorithm, allowing to extract the most relevant motion features linked to the scores. The system then gives a score, assessing the quality of the new motions. The results of this work show that while the scores are still far from the expert ones, they are better than the scores given by nonexpert humans.

With a sufficient amount of data for the training phase, supervised machine learning algorithms are efficient when the searched and estimated hypothesis is well designed for the problem complexity. However, these kinds of algorithms need a large amount of labeled data related to the given context. The data labeling is usually a costly task in terms of time and resources. Furthermore, some pre-processing steps can change the nature of the data (e.g. PCA), and some decision/separation frontier cannot be easily interpreted by humans (i.e., such as those built by SVN or neural networks). Consequently, analyzing and giving feedbacks to the learner can be a hard or impossible task. Unsupervised learning approaches do not need labeling data to group them into different clusters. However, there is a lack of studies using unsupervised machine learning algorithms to automatically extract useful pedagogical information from 3D motion data in a pedagogical context. This approach could allow the automatic detection of the most distinguishing features of a set of motions, to group them as learner profiles according to the observation needs of the teachers. In addition, a more efficient help could be provided to the expert in advising the learner by the observation of (i) the features of the acceptable motion groups and (ii) the current distance separating the current performed motion from these groups. The development of this kind of system must take into account the motion variation, in order to achieve the same desired goal or task (whether it is a set of postures in space and time or the position of an object).

The presented work is based on the three following hypothesis: (i) for one identified task to learn, it is possible to group motions in separable clusters, with each cluster made of motions with common features; (ii) it is possible to automatically group gestures according to the degree of success of the motion-based task; and (iii) it is possible to use clustering methods in order to create an interactive TEL system assisting the expert in its evaluation and advising task. This approach, as well as three experiments conducted to validate these hypotheses, is detailed in the next sections.

4.3 A Clustering Approach for Motion Analysis

For a manual task to learn, there is usually not a unique and perfect motion to achieve it. In most of the cases, the features of a targeted gesture are defined by one or several experts. Establishing which of those features are relevant, allowing to tell if the motion is successful or not, depends on the context and the expectations of the professionals, which can vary from one expert to another. This means that, for a given a learning situation, the set of discriminant features is not the same for every expert. Using supervised learning algorithms implies that a database containing labeled motions exists. The degree of success of the task must be stored within the labels of each sample. In practice, most of the databases focus on trivial motions, such as sitting, running, walking, etc. The chosen approach relies on the automatic analysis of motions through clustering techniques to avoid most of the drawbacks of the supervised approach. The overall and implemented method can be seen in Fig. 4.1. From a captured motion-based corpus, a first pre-processing step applies several filters to clean the data if needed (e.g., frames loss or corrupted, framerate variation, etc.). The next step allows the extraction of well-chosen kinematic, dynamic, and geometric descriptors (Larboulette & Gibet, 2015). One should be careful about them, as some descriptors are morphology-dependent (e.g., those

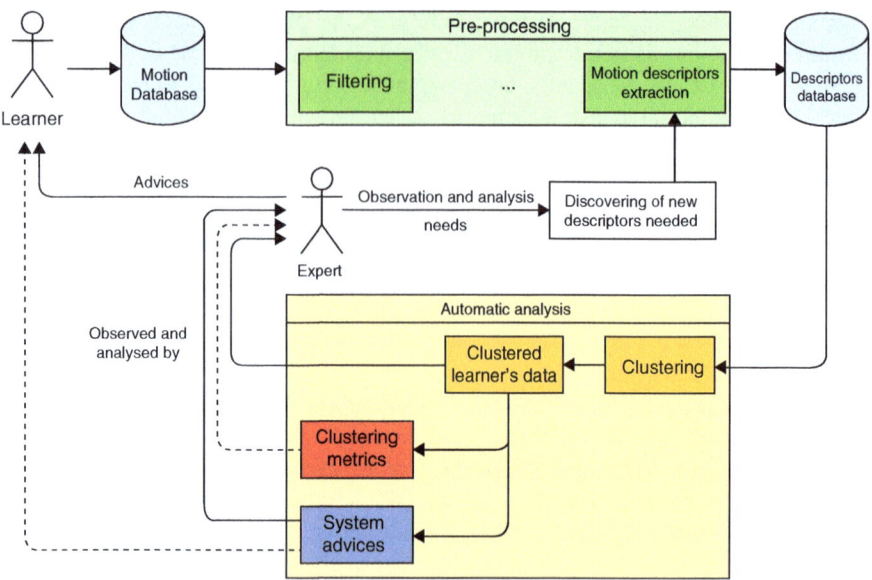

Fig. 4.1 The Motion Learning Analytics (MLA) system, dedicated to human motion learning

related to the distance between two joints), and some are not (e.g., the joint rotation). The data are then analyzed through the descriptors linked to the observation needs of the teacher. These descriptors are then used in a clustering process, using the k-means algorithm, from which several metrics are computed to assess its quality. The use of an IT environment allows observing the state of the current motion in terms of (i) features compared to those of the acceptable motion groups and (ii) distance between this motion and these groups. From the observation of this state, the expert can give feedback to the learner while refining their observation needs.

This chapter focuses on two parts of Fig. 4.1 automatic analysis block, namely, the clustering process and the feedback system (system advices), implying that clean data are available. An example of such data can be seen in Fig. 4.2c. The goal is to find a set of descriptors, algorithms, and metrics to (i) separate the motion corpus in different groups, (ii) give an indication of the degree of success for each group, and (iii) automatically give advices to the learner from the group features and the current motion state through a visualization of the data. Such separation-based system would allow analyzing the unperceived or hard-perceived properties of the motion clusters, giving information related to the characteristics of different and acceptable motion profiles, and thus giving a more accurate advice for the improvement of the learner motion. The next section presents the experimentation conducted, in order to validate the presented hypotheses.

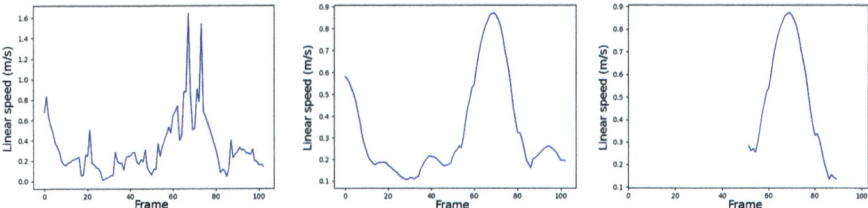

Fig. 4.2 (**a**) Speed of the captured motion through time of the right-hand of a user, (**b**) initial speed filtered, and (**c**) extracted throwing part (Couland, Hamon, & George, 2018)

4.4 Experimentation on Clustering with Kinematic Descriptors

This section is dedicated to an experimentation for the validation of the first two previous hypotheses. As a reminder, these assumptions are the following: (i) it is possible to separate the data into well-defined clusters, and (ii) it is possible to obtain a separation corresponding to the degree of success of the motion. The validation of the first hypothesis would prove that it is possible to obtain different learner profiles regarding the considered task, allowing the expert to adapt their advices for each group. The validation of the second hypothesis would prove that it is possible to obtain various degrees of success of the motion regarding their characteristics, allowing to determine a threshold of what is considered an acceptable motion and a better understanding of how to improve a motion, going from one profile to another.

4.4.1 Protocol

For this experimentation, a database made of motions requiring some dexterity was created. The bottle flip challenge was the chosen task. The goal is to throw a bottle, such as it completely rotates once on the horizontal axis and lands correctly on a table. The distance from the person performing the gesture to the table was empirically set to 70 cm (27.5 inches), indicated by a mark on the floor. The MOCAP Perception Neuron suit made of Inertial Measurement Units (IMU) was used for the capture (https://neuronmocap.com/). It allows capturing 72 joints (some of which are interpolated) at the rate of 60 frames per second. The skeleton of the subject was measured according to the official measuring guide provided with the suit, in order to have data skeletons made in accordance with the user morphology. Due to the nature of the sensors, the experimental protocol ensures that (i) no device generating electromagnetic perturbations was close to the user and (ii) all metallic accessories were removed (including rings, bracelets, watches, belt with metallic buckle, etc.). During the experiment, the MOCAP suit had to be regularly recalibrated, due to the inherent drift of the sensors. Each subject had to perform the motion a hundred times and for every throw, the success (or not) of the task was recorded.

Figure 4.2a shows the artifacts of the suit sensors, on the hand's speed data. Such data are not usable, as the original signal is distorted by the noise. In order to compensate these errors, a Savitsky-Golay filter was applied on each motion (Fig. 4.2b). Then, the throwing part of the motion was automatically segmented to extract the motion part of interest (Fig. 4.2c). This method is based on the detection of one or more local minimums to the left and the right of the global maximum value of the speed values for the dominant hand. It is particularly suited for throwing motions, as the characteristic of such a motion implies having the highest speed value at the moment the object is released. From those cleaned data, some descriptors were computed. Since the subjects have different morphologies, morphology-invariant descriptors were chosen: speed and acceleration (vector norm and direction, components along each axis in both cases). The descriptors were computed from three moments of each cleaned motion: the beginning of the throw, the maximum value of the speed norm for the dominant hand (corresponding to the release of the bottle), and the end of the throw. The chosen clustering method is the k-means algorithm to give a first insight of the possible separation. In addition, this algorithm is faster than other clustering methods (i.e., execution time scales linearly with data size) and has easily explainable results. The k values ranged from 2 to 10 for this experimentation.

In order to analyze the clustering results, the following metrics suited to our approaches were chosen.

To evaluate the separation quality of the obtained clusters, the Average Silhouette Score (*ASS*) was computed (Rousseeuw, 1987). The Silhouette Score (SS) is a metric indicating if a sample belongs well to its assigned cluster (compared to other clusters). The Average Silhouette Score (ASS) is the mean of every sample SS. It gives an indication about the cluster homogeneity: the highest this value has, the better the clusters are separated. This value ranges from -1 to 1, with 1 meaning that every sample is close to the others in the same clusters (the clusters are well separated) and 0 indicating that the clusters are overlapping. In this last case, a possible explanation is that the number of clusters is either too low or too high. An ASS between 0 and 0.25 means that no structure is found in the data, a value between 0.25 and 0.5 indicates that a weak structure is found (potentially artificial), and an ASS above 0.5 suggests that an acceptable structure is found, while an ASS value above 0.7 means that a strong structure is found (Struyf, Hubert, & Rousseeuw, 1997). In this context, the metric allows verifying the separation quality of the clusters, thus giving an indication about the relevancy of the computed descriptors and clustering algorithm in terms of separation.

To assess the separation quality in terms of motion groups representing the same degree of success of the task (in our case a successful or failed throw), a metric such as the accuracy of the clustering seems to not be a relevant indicator. For example, if the k-means algorithm is considered, this metric, based on the computation of a Euclidian distance, is relative to the measured data, the required accuracy of the measuring system and the learning situation. This accuracy is often ascertained by an advanced expert both in the application domain and in computer sciences. In order to verify the difference between the ground truth and the obtained labeling (i.e., failed/success motion), the precision, the recall, the F1-score and the Adjusted Rand Index (ARI) were chosen. These metrics were only computed for $k = 2$, as the ground truth is defined for $k = 2$ (successful/failed). As a reminder, the F1-score is a combination of two metrics (recall and precision) representing the labeling accuracy. This value ranges from 0 to 1, with 1 indicating a perfect matching. The ARI is a measure of the similarity between two data partitioning. This index maximum value is 1, corresponding to a perfect matching between the two labeled clusters and their labeled data. 0 corresponds to a random cluster assignment, and negative values are obtained if the clustering is orthogonal to an extent.

4.4.2 Results

The recorded data consisted of 1300 motions, performed by 13 different subjects. Elevem subjects were right-handed, and 2 were left-handed. For the clustering, different sets of joints have been considered: hand (H), forearm (FA), and arm (A), these body parts being the most solicited during the movement. The computed descriptors were speed norm (SN); speed value in x, y, and z (Sxyz); speed directions in x, y, and z (SDxyz); and speed norm and directions in x, y, and z (SNDxyz). The precision *(P)*, recall *(R)*, F1-score *(F1)*, and Adjusted Rand Index *(ARI)* are given for $k = 2$, as it corresponds to the ground truth. The Average Silhouette Score *(ASS)* is also given for $k = 2$, as it is the k value that gives the best value in most of the cases (the *ASS* values show non-significant variations for other k values when k = 2 does not give the best *ASS* values). The clustering was performed on (i) the mixed data (left and right-handed together), (ii) left-handed data only, and (iii) right-handed data only. Table 4.1 shows the obtained results. F1-score, *ASS* and *ARI* values slightly decreased when joints were added to the dominant hand, meaning that the dominant hand was the most important joint for this case. The highest *ASS* scores were obtained for speed values along the three axes, in the right-handed (0.73) and mixed (left and right-handed) data (0.54). Left-handed best *ASS* values are for the speed norm values (0.41), yet they are lower than the right-handed and mixed data *ASS* values for the same data (0.42 and 0.48). The *ARI* stayed close to 0, regardless of the joints and descriptor combination (ranging between 0.05 and 0).

4.4.3 Discussion

The combination of the speed vectors in each axis is a good separation criterion, as suggested by results shown in Sect. 4.2. The best ASS values were obtained for the descriptors extracted from the dominant hand, suggesting that other body parts only add noise. This can be partially explained by the fact that every joint motion is

Table 4.1 clustering metrics for various joint combinations for the bottle flip challenge experiment

Joints	H					H, FA					H, FA, A				
Metric	ASS	P	R	F1	ARI	ASS	P	R	F1	ARI	ASS	P	R	F1	ARI
Left and right-handed															
SN	0.48	0.25	0.33	0.29	0.04	0.44	0.25	0.33	0.29	0.04	0.43	0.25	0.33	0.29	0.04
Sxyz	*0.54*	0.18	0.67	0.3	0.05	0.52	0.27	0.32	0.29	0.05	*0.51*	0.18	0.68	0.29	0.05
Sdxyz	0.24	0.21	0.53	0.3	0	0.27	0.25	0.25	0.25	0.04	0.22	0.18	0.72	0.27	0.04
SNDxyz	0.21	0.18	0.47	0.3	0	0.27	0.25	0.26	0.26	0.04	0.22	0.26	0.28	0.27	0.04
Left handed															
SN	*0.41*	0.39	0.39	0.39	0.02	*0.42*	0.38	0.39	0.39	0.01	*0.41*	0.31	0.61	0.39	0.01
Sxyz	0.35	0.32	0.57	0.39	0	0.34	0.32	0.57	0.39	0	0.33	0.35	0.43	0.39	0
Sdxyz	0.31	0.34	0.48	0.4	0	0.27	0.34	0.54	0.39	0	0.23	0.34	0.48	0.4	0
SNDxyz	0.27	0.34	0.49	0.4	0	0.25	0.33	0.48	0.39	0	0.22	0.34	0.52	0.41	0
Right handed															
SN	0.42	0.18	0.29	0.22	0	0.36	0.17	0.28	0.21	0	0.34	0.17	0.28	0.21	0
Sxyz	*0.73*	0.19	0.12	0.15	0.01	*0.71*	0.19	0.12	0.15	0.01	*0.71*	0.19	0.12	0.15	0.01
Sdxyz	0.28	0.15	0.45	0.28	0	0.2	0.16	0.49	0.27	0	0.26	0.19	0.13	0.15	0.01
SNDxyz	0.26	0.16	0.45	0.28	0	0.19	0.19	0.52	0.27	0	0.26	0.17	0.87	0.15	0.01

4 Technology-Enhanced Learning of Motions Based on a Clustering Approach

Table 4.2 Relative distance of the clusters centroids, for the right hand, with the speed directions in x, y, and z, for $k = 2$

	Beginning	Maximum	End
X (side)	0.0398	0.5071	0.0110
Y (upward)	0.0415	1.7497	0.0998
Z (forward)	0.0847	2.0477	0.0536

related to the other and that the hand movement is the one with the widest range of values (in terms of speed).

While the *ASS* had an acceptable value (*ASS* ≈ 0.5) for the mixed data, better results were obtained when right-handed and left-handed people are separated (*ASS* ≈ 0.75). The acquisition problems of the suite can explain this phenomenon (and are discussed below in this section). In terms of relative distance, the most discriminant features were the maximum speed value, in both Z (forward) and Y (upward) directions (regarding to the subject), as seen in Table 4.2.

The clusters were indeed separable; however, the ARI stayed close to 0 for every case (*max(ARI)* ≈ *0.05*), indicating a random cluster assignment. That means that the obtained clusters cannot be related to the outcome of the throw. Consequently, the current descriptors (speed, acceleration, and direction) with the proposed separation model are uncorrelated from the degree of success of the task. One can argue that the considered task itself does not present a significant variation from one throw to another, in terms of speed and acceleration. Furthermore, the computed descriptors all rely on speed or acceleration, and that can possibly limit the variability of the results. Other high-level descriptors exist (Larboulette & Gibet, 2015) and could be used to analyze the motions. For example, the jerk (rate of change of the acceleration during the motion) can give an indication on how smooth the motion is, and the curvature, which is a measure of how fast a curve is changing through time, can give a more accurate information about the wrist rotation. The geometric descriptors, such as the rotation of joints through time, and the displacement of the center of mass are also interesting values to consider.

In this experimentation, several problems arose. First, the distance between the subject and the table was not constant, as some people took a small step back before throwing. The table was also slippery, and the bottle slid on the table. Thus the distance between the subject and the impact point of the bottle cannot be measured with consistency regarding the throws of all subjects.

The MOCAP suit limits the experiment to its sensors accuracy, and their constraints for a good use, opposed to, for example, an infrared camera system. Having accurate rotation data of the wrist would be interesting, as it represents a crucial part of the motion. Furthermore, a frame-by-frame analysis showed that the data flow was not constant. The mandatory software, for getting the data, used some undocumented method to counterbalance the data loss, which creates the artifacts seen in Fig. 4.1a. While the pre-processing steps took care of these problems, nothing can ensure that the used method did not alter the initial data. Furthermore, the left side of the suit (from the shoulder to the hand) outputted noisy data. When the clustering

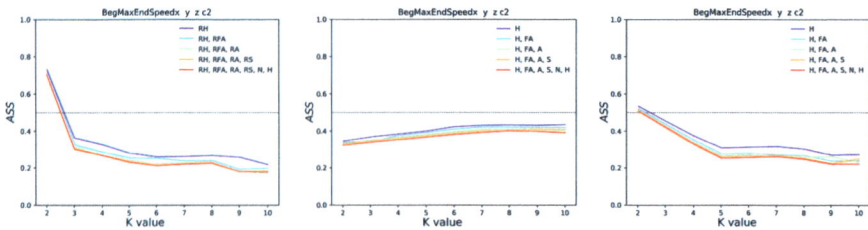

Fig. 4.3 ASS score for various joint combinations and k ranging from 2 to 10 of (**a**) the right-handed subjects (**b**) the left-handed subjects (**c**) left and right-handed subjects together

was performed, mixing left-handed and right-handed data gave worse results than keeping only the right-handed subjects, due to the noisy nature of the left-handed data (Fig. 4.3). This noise was visible on the captured data, and it seems that the suit has difficulties to handle a capture of the full body.

4.4.4 Ball Throwing

As the motion variability of the previous task can be discussed, another experiment was conducted to verify if the computed descriptors, combined with the k-means algorithm, can separate the motions according to the ground truth. In this experiment, a subject must throw a ball in one of the two bins, placed in a line front on him (one placed 2 m (6.56 ft) from them, another one placed 3.5 m (11.48 ft) from them). The subject has to perform 100 throws, without any constraints about the throwing motion. For each throw, the degree of success of the throw, the bin aimed at, and the type of throw (i.e., basket type launch or bowling type launch) were recorded. In this experiment, only right-handed data and a subset of the suit sensors were used, to limit the artifacts. Having multiple labeling for each motion allows working on the degree of success, as well as the descriptor ability to discriminate different throw strategies. The same joint combinations, as well as the same metrics, were used to evaluate the results. For each metric, the results are given for $k = 2$, as it is the number of clusters that gives the best results. The results have shown that the *ASS* and *ARS* values stay the same as the first experimentation for the successful/failed labeling, indicating that the separation of the motions was still not feasible with the proposed method. However, the clustering gives good *ASS* and *ARI* scores (0.59 and 0.83 respectively) for the throwing type, with the norm and "norm + directions" descriptors (Table 4.3), suggesting that the data were separable regarding this criterion. Adding joints other than the dominant hand does not (or marginally) improve the results.

Table 4.3 clustering metrics for various joint combinations for the ball throwing experiment

Joints	H					H, FA					H, FA, A				
Metric	ASS	P	R	F1	ARI	ASS	P	R	F1	ARI	ASS	P	R	F1	ARI
All data (ground truth = success/fail)															
SN	0.59	0.51	0.89	0.64	0.01	0.6	0.5	0.86	0.63	0	0.6	0.5	0.86	0.63	0
Sxyz	0.56	0.48	0.89	0.62	−0.01	0.54	0.48	0.89	0.62	−0.01	0.54	0.48	0.89	0.62	−0.01
Sdxyz	0.23	0.41	0.25	0.31	−0.01	0.23	0.54	0.77	0.64	0.04	0.24	0.55	0.77	0.64	0.05
SNDxyz	0.26	0.53	0.89	0.67	0.04	0.27	0.55	0.77	0.64	0.05	0.26	0.53	0.77	0.63	0.03
All data (ground truth = closest/farthest bin)															
SN	0.59	0.65	1	0.79	0.21	0.6	0.64	0.98	0.78	0.19	0.6	0.64	0.98	0.78	0.19
Sxyz	0.56	0.54	0.88	0.67	0.01	0.54	0.54	0.88	0.67	0.01	0.54	0.54	0.88	0.67	0.01
Sdxyz	0.23	0.65	0.34	0.45	0.02	0.23	0.68	0.86	0.76	0.2	0.24	0.69	0.86	0.77	0.22
SNDxyz	0.26	0.68	0.98	0.8	0.26	0.27	0.71	0.88	0.79	0.26	0.26	0.69	0.88	0.77	0.22
All data (ground truth = throwing type)															
SN	0.59	0.87	0.95	0.91	0.83	0.6	0.83	0.95	0.89	0.79	0.6	0.83	0.95	0.89	0.79
Sxyz	0.56	0.06	0.05	0.05	−0.09	0.54	0.06	0.05	0.05	−0.09	0.54	0.06	0.05	0.05	−0.09
Sdxyz	0.23	0.08	0.1	0.09	−0.07	0.23	0.54	0.95	0.69	0.39	0.24	0.53	0.95	0.68	0.37
SNDxyz	0.26	0.74	0.95	0.83	0.68	0.27	0.55	1	0.71	0.42	0.26	0.56	0.95	0.7	0.42

4.4.5 Discussion

These two experiments allowed us to evaluate a clustering approach for the automatic analysis of motions with the MLA platform. With the considered set of joints, kinematic descriptors, and k-means algorithm, it was possible to obtain a good separation of motions regarding some observable properties of these motions. In our case, the throwing type could be detected thanks to the kinematic properties. It means that, for the considered task, it is possible to obtain multiple clusters corresponding to different throwing strategies. Analyzing which descriptors are the most discriminant for each cluster can give a hint about the different strategies used by the learner, thus leading to the determination of multiple learner profiles. However, it was not possible to achieve an acceptable separation corresponding to the degree of success of the task. Having such a separation would have allowed to automatically determine if a motion was within the acceptable range or not. The lack of experts in the bottle flip challenge field, and thus the lack of evaluation criterion of the gesture itself, was also a hindrance for the choice of descriptors and the analysis of the motion.

In both of these experiments, the analysis is binary: the motion is either in one group or the other (successful/failed, throwing from above/from below, etc.). In a real motion learning context, it is not always possible to separate the results with only two categories. Moreover, the expert does not take part in the analysis process: their knowledge is only used in the selection of the relevant descriptors. While an autonomous system can be useful, the goal is to provide a set of tools to help the experts in their motion analysis task. The feedback system developed to answer these requirements is presented in the next section.

4.5 Feedback System

The next step of this work consisted in developing a TEL environment able to assist the expert in their motion analysis and advise task. Since multiple experts can have different viewpoints about the properties of the targeted motion to learn, the term " targeted motion " will be used in this section to designate the learning objective.

The system must give (i) advices to the learner about specific modalities of their gestures and (ii) a visualization of the main flaws or lacks of the learner motion. This system requires the expert to record (i) some targeted motions (at least a dozen) and (ii) some non-acceptable motions for each identified flaw. The more data for each group, the better the identification of acceptable motion groups and their features in the next step will be. The expert is then asked to designate one or more motion descriptors for each mistake, in order to be able to extract these motion descriptors from the expert data. The descriptor specification is made as follows:

- The name of the motion's flaw
- The used descriptor(s) for this flaw

4 Technology-Enhanced Learning of Motions Based on a Clustering Approach   65

- The joint(s) on which this/these descriptors(s) will be computed, along with the dominant hand of the learner if relevant (e.g., if "right" must be replaced with "left" in the joints name if the person is left-handed)

An example of such a specification can look as follows:

- Flaw: leaning forward when throwing
  - Descriptor: mean speed
    - Joint: left shoulder, dominant hand side: no
    - Joint: right shoulder, dominant hand side: no
- Flaw: elbow moving during the throw
  - Descriptor: mean speed
    - Joint: left arm, dominant hand side: yes
    - Joint: left shoulder, dominant hand side: yes

Descriptor values can be normalized, in order to have a consistent scale when evaluating the importance of the fault compared to another one. These data are then used in a clustering process, in order to obtain two groups for each identified flaw, one corresponding to the targeted motions, the other to the non-acceptable motions. A naïve approach would assign each data to the corresponding label, i.e., acceptable or not. However, this makes the assumption that the expert data are separable regarding this labeling. In practice, when the expert is recording multiple motions with mistakes made deliberately, a self-correction can appear. Indeed, the expert tends to unconsciously correct their motion. This can lead to outliers, i.e., flawed motions being more similar to acceptable ones. The clustering phase allows putting these motions into the group they truly belong to, without manually deleting those outliers. Consequently, this method can produce overlapping groups. In this case, the acceptable motions are not sufficiently different from the non-acceptable ones or the used descriptors are not significant to represent the motion flaw.

The learner data are then compared to the expert ones. In order to give relevant feedback regarding the most important flaws of the learner motion, this comparison is made by computing the Euclidean distance of the projection of the mean of the learner data point on the line that goes through each cluster center. Let c_g be the centroid of the targeted motion cluster, c_b the centroid of the non-acceptable motion cluster, and c_a the centroid of the learner motions. We define

$$A = y_{c_b} - y_{c_g}$$

$$B = x_{c_b} - x_{c_g}$$

$$C = \left(x_{c_g} * y_{c_b}\right) - \left(x_{c_b} * y_{c_g}\right)$$

The distance D is then defined as:

$$D = \frac{A * x_{c_a} + B * y_{c_a} + C}{\sqrt{A^2 + B^2}}$$

The use of this distance is based on the hypothesis that if the projection of the learner means data on the aforementioned line is located inside the trapezoid linking the two expert motions groups (Fig. 4.4), this flaw is more easily correctable than if it is outside of this trapezoid. The system then takes the two most prominent flaws (in terms of the distance D) and highlights the two mistakes that the learner must correct before anything else. This requires that the expert write down, for each flaw, at least one relevant advice to correct the gesture.

An experiment has been conducted in order to validate the proposed evaluation process. The goal was to throw darts, aiming at the center of a target, with respects to the sport official rules, including the target size, the darts length and mass, and the throwing distance (2.37 meters). An interview conducted with an expert of the darts game allowed us to find four majors flaws usually found in the beginner motions:

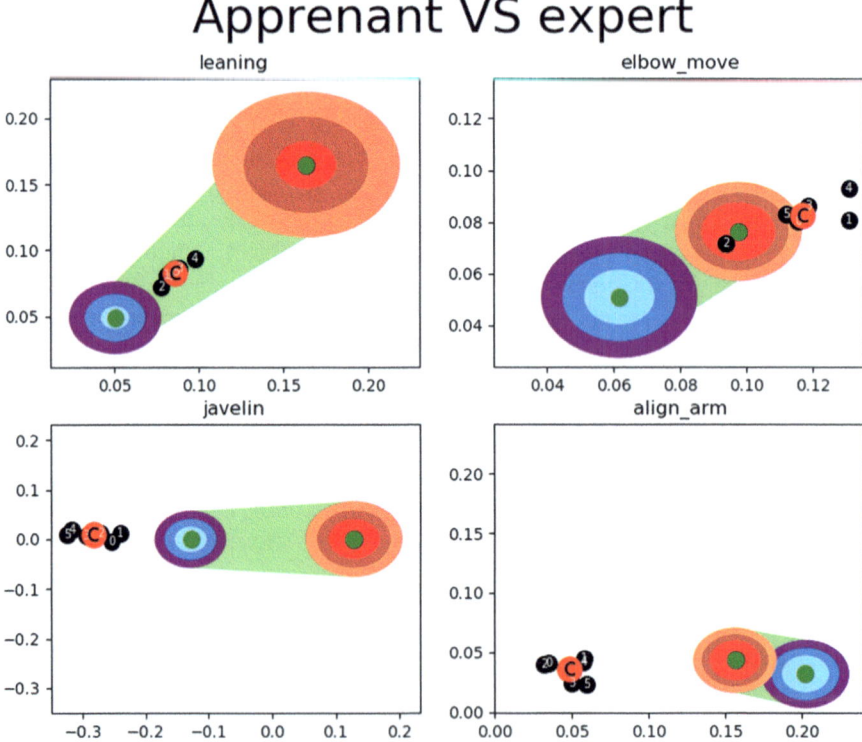

Fig. 4.4 An example of the visual feedback proposed by the system. There is one visualization for each flaw. The blue group consists of the acceptable motions, while the red one consists of the flawed motions. The red point labeled "C" is the centroid of the learner motion

- *Leaning*: the learner leans towards the target when throwing a dart, resulting in the dart landing lower than expected.
- *Elbow move*: when throwing a dart, the elbow moves instead of only rotating, which leads to a less controlled motion.
- *Javelin*: the learner's arm goes next to (or even behind) their head, instead of staying in front of the head during the throw.
- *Align arm*: the arm tends to go toward the center of the body (to the left for a right-handed person, and vice versa).

These four flaws can be detected in the motion data. Each of these flaws is not exclusive, i.e., a beginner can perform a motion with several flaws. In addition, other flaws exist. Nevertheless, they would require other capture devices and data to detect them. For example, the moment the dart was released by the learner can be detected with an appropriate infrared capture system following the dart motion, thanks to some reflectors on it. Since we aim to study an evaluation process only based on body-motion data, we only considered flaws that can be detected with the analysis of human movement with the above-mentioned capture suit in this study.

Forty-five subjects were separated into 3 different groups, according to the use of the advice system: (group 1) the advices were given by the expert based only on their observation, (group 2) the advices were given only by the system, and (group 3) the advices were given by the expert using their observation and the evaluation of the system to refine their analysis. The distance to the center of the target and the distance between each motion to the centroid of the cluster for each flaw were noted. Each subject had to throw 36 darts, divided into 4 series of 9 throws each. Between each series, the system can give two feedbacks (groups 2 and 3) and can be used to visualize the learner data (group 3). The preliminary results show that there is an improvement in the motion shape of the learner (i.e., correction of the four flaws) for each group, without getting a significant difference from one group to another. However, no significant improvement was obtained for the distance of the darts to the center of the target. This can be explained by the fact that the user will focus on the imitation of the targeted motion shape to the detriment of the throw accuracy. In addition, this shape can strongly differ from the initial motion of the user. Consequently, it seems that not enough throws are made by the learners to both improve the accuracy of the throw and the motion shape. Furthermore, a real learning situation would last longer.

4.6 Conclusion and Perspectives

A new approach regarding the analysis of 3D motions was presented in this chapter. The goal is to give a method to analyze the motion, through explainable descriptors extracted from it, leading to personalized feedback given to the learner in order to improve their motion. After acquiring and processing the motion data, some descriptors based on speed, acceleration, and direction were extracted. These descriptors were then used in a clustering process, in order to find different explainable types of motions. This approach relied on three hypotheses: (i) it is possible to separate the motions into explainable clusters, (ii) it is possible to obtain partitions corresponding to the degree of success of the task, and (iii) it is possible to use clustering methods in order to create an interactive TEL system assisting the expert in its evaluation and advising task. While the second objective did not reach the expectations, the results of the first objective showed that the separation of the clusters is indeed possible, validating this hypothesis and the used descriptors (with the proposed method for the first two tasks presented in this study) in terms of discriminant features.

The computation of more descriptors is planned, as the current ones may be limited, regardless of the application context. Most of the high-level descriptors used in various studies about human motions are a combination of multiple low-level ones based on kinematic, dynamic, and geometric properties (Larboulette & Gibet, 2015). It would be possible to propose a template language in order to allow the user to specify their own descriptors. This would allow computing a predefined set of descriptors for every motion from a combination of low-level descriptors. As the data are made of time series, the use of the dynamic time warping (DTW) algorithm, computing a similarity distance between the trajectory of two motions (Morel, 2017), would provide another measure, giving inter and intra-cluster information about the motions. Future work will also focus on performing recursive clustering on obtained clusters, in order to find if the motions, in each cluster, are separable according to the degree of success of the task or other features.

The feedback system can be improved in multiple ways. As an engineering perspective, a graphical user interface (GUI) will be developed to tweak the parameters of the different phases and algorithms (e.g. motion segmentation, clustering parameters, etc.). Regarding the clustering phase on the expert data, it would be possible to automatically detect which data points are the furthest from the cluster center its assigned to, in order to delete them to reduce the overlapping effect between motion groups. The system selects the advice to give (i.e., the most important mistakes to correct). However, this choice does not consider (i) the severity of the flaw and (ii) the specificity of each flaw (e.g.. if the arm is not aligned towards the target, there is no indication about the side causing the problem). A comparison of the differences of each descriptor between the expert and the learner data could provide a hint and lead to a more precise feedback.

References

Chan, J. C. P., Leung, H., Tang, J. K. T., & Komura, T. (2011). A virtual reality dance training system using motion capture technology. *IEEE Transactions on Learning Technologies, 4*, 187–195.

Chang, C.-Y., Chang, C.-W., Zheng, J.-Y., & Chung, P.-C. (2013). Physiological emotion analysis using support vector regression. *Neurocomputing, Issue, 122*, 79–87.

Couland, Q., Hamon, L., & George, S. (2018). Enhancing Human Learning of Motions: An Approach Through Clustering. *European Conference on Technology Enhanced Learning.*

Gu, Y., & Sosnovsky, S. (2014). Recognition of student intentions in a virtual reality training environment. *Proceedings of the Companion Publication of the 19th International Conference on Intelligent User Interfaces*, pp. 69–72.

Hachaj, T., & Ogiela, M. R. (2015). Full body movements recognition - unsupervised learning approach with heuristic R-GDL method. *Digital Signal Processing, 46*, 239–252.

Huang, J., Zhou, W., Li, H., & Li, W. (2015). Sign Language Recognition using 3D convolutional neural networks. *IEEE International Conference on Multimedia and Expo (ICME) 2015*, pp. 1–6.

Kapsouras, I., & Nikolaidis, N. (2014). Action recognition on motion capture data using a dynemes and forward differences representation. *Journal of Visual Communication and Image Representation, 25*(6), 1432–1445.

Kobayashi, Y. (2007). The EMOSIGN - analyzing the emotion signature in human motion. *IEEE International Conference on Systems, Man and Cybernetics, 2007. ISIC*, pp. 1171–1176.

Larboulette, C., & Gibet, S. (2015). A review of computable expressive descriptors of human motion. *Proceedings of the 2Nd international workshop on movement and computing*, pp. 21–28.

Lokaiczyk, R., Faatz, A., Beckhaus, A., & Goertz, M. (2007). Enhancing just-in-time e-learning through machine learning on desktop context sensors. *Modeling and using context: 6th international and interdisciplinary conference, CONTEXT 2007, Roskilde, Denmark, August 20–24, 2007. Proceedings*, pp. 330–341.

Lui, Y. M., O'Hara, S., & Draper, B. A. (2011). Unsupervised learning of humain expressions, gestures, and actions. *Face and Gesture, 2011*, 1–8.

Le Naour, T., Hamon, L., & Bresciani, J. P. (2019). Superimposing 3D Virtual Self + Expert Modeling for Motor Learning: Application to the Throw in American Football. *Frontiers in ICT 6.*

Maes, P.-J., Amelynck, D., & Leman, M. (2012). Dance-the-music: An educational platform for the modeling, recognition and audiovisual monitoring of dance steps using spatiotemporal motion templates. *EURASIP Journal on Advances in Signal Processing, 1*, 35.

Markowska-Kaczmar, U., Kwasnicka, H., & Paradowski, M. (2010). Computational intelligence for technology enhanced learning. *Intelligent techniques in personalization of learning in e-learning systems*, pp. 1–23.

Mingliang, X., et al. (2019). Personalized training through Kinect-based games for physical education. *Journal of Visual Communication and Image Representation, 62*, 394–401.

Morel, M. (2017). *Multidimensional time-series averaging: application to automatic and generic evaluation of sport gestures*, s.l.: s.n.

Ng, A. (2016). *CS229 - machine learning course, lecture N 19: Stanford engineering everywhere, Stanford University.* [Online] Available at: https://see.stanford.edu/Course/CS229 [Last access: 2016].

Nunes, J. F., & Moreira, P. M. (2016). *Handbook of research on computational simulation and modeling in engineering.* s.l.:s.n.

Patrona, F., Chatzitofis, A., Zarpalas, D., & Daras, P. (2018). Motion analysis: Action detection, recognition and evaluation based on motion capture data. *Pattern Recognition, 76*, 612–622.

Pepley, D., Gordon, A., Yovanoff, M., Mirkin, K., Miller, S., Han, D., & Moore, J. (2017). Training Surgical Residents With a Haptic Robotic Central Venous Catheterization Simulator. *Journal of Surgical Education 74*(6), 1066–1073.

Rousseeuw, P. J. (1987). Silhouettes: A graphical aid to the interpretation and validation of cluster analysis. *Journal of Computational and Applied Mathematics, 20*, 53–65.

Struyf, A., Hubert, M., & Rousseeuw, P. (1997). Clustering in an object-oriented environment. *Journal of Statistical Software, Articles, 1*(4), 1–30.

Yoshinaga, T., & Soga, M. (2015). Development of a motion learning support system arranging and showing several Coaches' motion data. *Procedia Computer Science, 60,* 1497–1505.

Yu, Z., & Lee, M. (2015). Human motion based intent recognition using a deep dynamic neural model. *Emerging spatial competences: From machine perception to sensorimotor intelligence,* Septembre, pp. 134–149.

Zhou, H., & Hu, H. (2008). Human motion tracking for rehabilitation - A survey. *Biomedical signal processing and control,* pp. 1–18.

Chapter 5
Comparing Face-to-Face to Online Instruction in Secondary Education: Findings of a Repetitive Factoral Experiment

Stephan Poelmans, Katie Goeman, and Yves Wautelet

5.1 Introduction

In the past decade, a lot of research in the information system (IS) literature has focused on explaining e-learning (EL) success in terms of acceptance and deployment of integrated systems and distinct tools by teachers and learners. The information systems success model (ISSM) developed by DeLone and McLean offers a robust approach, suitable for studying both mandatory and voluntary use of a multitude of ISs in various types of contexts (DeLone & McLean, 2003). It focuses on actionable system and information characteristics that can be the target of IS design and configuration efforts (Wixom & Todd, 2005). This represents a key element in design research studies regarding OL systems, i.e., IT platforms and tools that scaffold learning activities (Wang, Wang, & Shee, 2007).

Delone and McLean's ISSM proposes that the quality of an information system (its hardware, software, and infrastructure), the quality of the information it provides, and the quality of the provided IT service (or support) will directly affect subsequent use or intention to use and users' satisfaction. Both system and information quality can be measured as multifaceted constructs, comprising several subdimensions or facets such as reliability, relevance, accuracy, information presentation, etc. Satisfaction and use of the system will finally lead to certain individual and organizational net benefits. Net benefits are defined as "the most important success measures as they capture the balance of positive and negative impacts" of an IS (DeLone & McLean, 2003, p. 25). The ISSM also contains feedback loops, since an increase in benefits will increase the level of satisfaction and stimulate further usage

---

S. Poelmans (✉) · K. Goeman · Y. Wautelet
Research Centre for Information Systems Engineering (LIRIS Brussels),
University of Leuven (KU Leuven), Brussels, Belgium
e-mail: stephan.poelmans@kuleuven.be; katie.goeman@kuleuven.be; Yves.wautelet@kuleuven.be

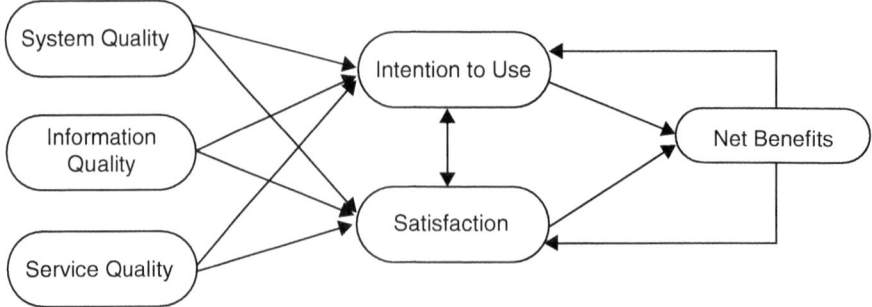

Fig. 5.1 The information systems success model (DeLone & McLean, 2003)

of the system (Fig. 5.1). The multidimensional approach, and the potential to refine and extend each dimension contingent on the objectives and context of the empirical investigation, ensures that personal, organizational, and technical drivers of success can be considered in one parsimonious model (Poelmans & Wessa, 2013; Seddon, 1997).

To date, a multitude of studies have tested the DeLone and McLean's ISSM to investigate several categories of information systems (see the meta-analysis by Petter & McLean, 2009). Prevalent ISs to which the ISSM has been applied include enterprise systems (e.g., Wei, Loong, & Leong, 2009), knowledge management systems (KMS) (e.g., Kulkarni, Ravindran, & Freeze, 2007; Wu & Wang, 2006), and e-government applications (e.g., Wang & Liao, 2008).

A number of studies also used the DeLone and McLean IS success model in an e-learning context (e.g. Kurt, 2019; Cidral, Oliveira, Di Felice & Aparicio, 2018; Pham & Tran, 2018; Dağhan & Akkoyunlu, 2016; Mohammadi, 2015; Hassanzadeh, Kanaani, & Elahi, 2012; Eom & Stapleton, 2011; Lee, 2010; Wang et al., 2007). Almost all of these reports analyze learners' perceptions by means of a cross-sectional survey-based research design and point to the importance of system and information quality as drivers of learners' satisfaction and other measures of e-learning success (such as OL system usage, usage intention, perceived usability, perceived benefits, and perceived goal achievement). Whereas Wang et al. (2007) investigated e-learning from the point of view of employees, other studies targeted higher education students and/or focused on the success of a specific OL environment or system.

Despite the availability of such empirical research endeavors, there is a shortage of experiments in real-life school settings, probably due to organizational complexity (Grubišić, Stankov, Rosić, & Žitko, 2009) or ethical issues. We further notice there is limited understanding of the objective and subjective nature of the net benefits related to OL system usage. To our knowledge, previous contributions did not scrutinize antecedents of both learners' performance (objective indicator) and learners' perceived benefits (subjective indicator), and their interrelationships. We suggest this is an important asset to the current knowledge building regarding OL system acceptance and usage, and therefore we propose to extend the ISSM and to study this issue by means of an experiment in a comparative manner.

5.2 Focus and Context of the Study

In this chapter we describe an experimental study focused both on evaluating the outcomes of a particular OL approach in a secondary school, as compared to a face-to-face (F2F) mode of teaching, and on assessing potential influencing variables. The study was initiated by the coordinator of a group of secondary schools. In order to keep up with the fast pace of technological change and to better adapt to the learning needs of the "millennium learners" (Ananiadou & Claro, 2009), the school group was urged to understand how to infuse OL tools in order to create a more attractive and effective learning environment. More particularly, the aim was to assess whether the learner outcomes in terms of satisfaction and performance remain the same or improve by using the existing e-learning system Smartschool (www.Smartschool.be) more in depth, with a focus on online instruction. As a response to this initiative, we address in this study two main research questions:

1. Do secondary school pupils benefit from online instruction when compared to face-to-face instruction?
2. Which factors contribute to individual differences between pupils in terms of benefits?

5.3 Research Method

This methodology section is organized as follows. The first part describes the general onset of the study (design, participants, procedure). In particular, we focus on the deployment of a factoral experiment as a means to compare both instruction modes in terms of outcomes and their prominent influencing factors. The second part addresses the proposed research model and its related hypotheses, which is based on ISSM theory and related empirical studies. A following part is dedicated to the analyses of the collected data, the interpretations and the discussion of the findings. The last part presents the conclusions, including the strengths, limitations, and future research.

5.3.1 Research Design

We conducted an experiment in a mid-sized secondary school in the Dutch-speaking region of Belgium as a first iteration in design-based research, "a methodology (…) that seeks to increase the impact, transfer and translation of education research into improved practice" (Anderson & Shattuck, 2012: 16). Following Grubišić et al. (2009), we opted for a factoral experimental design, in which two or more parallel groups and two or more cycles are created (see Fig. 5.2). In each case, the same lesson was taught by the same instructor using the two delivery methods, both online

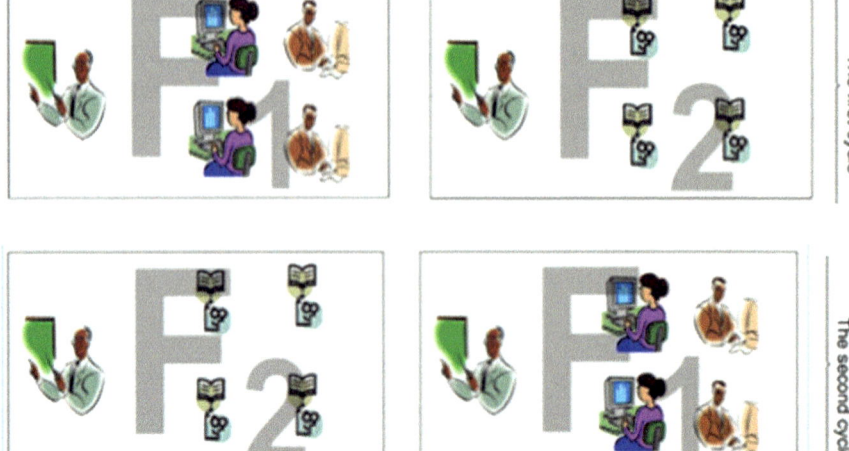

Fig. 5.2 A factoral design (see Grubišic et al., 2009)

(OL) and face-to-face (F2F). Pupils taking the course were tested twice, each time after being instructed. The groups rotated in each cycle.

We strongly advocate the use of the factoral experiment with two parallel groups and two cycles in order to overcome typical biases due to undesired group or topic effects. As Grubišic' et al. (p. 595) pointed out: "If we find that in each cycle one and the same factor is more efficient than the other, then we can conclude that a certain factor is better regardless of a difference between taught domain knowledge. In the same way, if the same factor is more efficient in each cycle, in spite of the groups that it has been introduced in, then we can conclude that a certain factor is better regardless of a difference between the groups." A repetition of such a factoral approach (in several classes and grades in the underlying study) strengthens the findings.

Due to the fact that the factoral design was reiterated six times with different teachers and learners, the potential biases due to subject effects are minimized, and a more appropriate empirical design for effectiveness evaluation was applied.

5.3.2 Participants

The full sample consisted of 151 pupils between 12 and 18 years old, from the 7th until the 12th grade of secondary education. 70% were male. 39.7% of the participants were enrolled in a general secondary education program, 32.5% in technical secondary education, 19% in a vocational program, and 9% in a secondary arts program.

5.3.3 Procedure

Within a class, 10 to 15 pupils were randomly assigned to one of the test conditions (OL or F2F). In the course of 1 week, one group received a F2F lesson, and the other group received the digital equivalent. The next week, the order was reversed. For example, a pupil belonging to group 1 received a history lesson in OL mode. In that same week, group 2 received the F2F version of that lesson, by the same teacher. In the following week, group 1 received F2F a subsequent history lesson, whereas group 2 received the OL equivalent. As a result, each pupil followed one F2F and one OL lesson. After each lesson, all pupils took the same closed book tests which were constructed in accordance with the regular school procedures and regulations. Test scores ranged from 0 to 10. In total, 24 lessons were organized, covering 5 subjects and 12 different groups. The subjects were Mathematics, History, Geography, French, and Economics (see Fig. 5.3).

Each of the six teachers who were involved prepared two lessons for their subject. The learning contents were part of the regular curriculum. Each lesson in the OL condition was developed as an OL path, with a number of pre-ordered learning activities and contents, which offer "a road map to learners" (De Smet, Schellens, De Wever, Brandt-Pomares, & Valcke, 2014). Each developed digital path contained multiple learning objects including online text materials, pictures, (OL) exercises and hyperlinks to external websites, and video clips. Each pupil worked individually on a desktop computer, using a headphone. Teachers were present in the classroom, but they only assisted pupils in the event of technical problems, not with content-related questions.

5.3.4 Research Model and Hypotheses

The proposed research model follows the rationale set forward in the ISSM of DeLone and McLean (2003) (see Fig. 5.4), yet it is updated and adapted in order to fit better with a user-centered approach to explain OL system usage. It incorporates three original constructs of the ISSM: system, information, and service quality. It also subdivides the outcome construct of the ISSM, net benefits, into perceived and observed benefits. Furthermore, it replaces the original construct "intention to use" by "preference" and extends the model by integrating "perceived enjoyment." In the following section, we elaborate on each of the model's components and their corresponding hypotheses.

The observed benefits are conceived as differences in learning performance between the OL and F2F conditions. The latent construct of perceived benefits is defined as the "perceived usefulness of the OL system for learning, as compared to the classroom-based way of teaching." We assume that perceived benefits are important; learners evaluate previous experiences with ICT and make a total judgment as to whether the benefits outweigh the practical problems (Kirkman, 2000). Learners

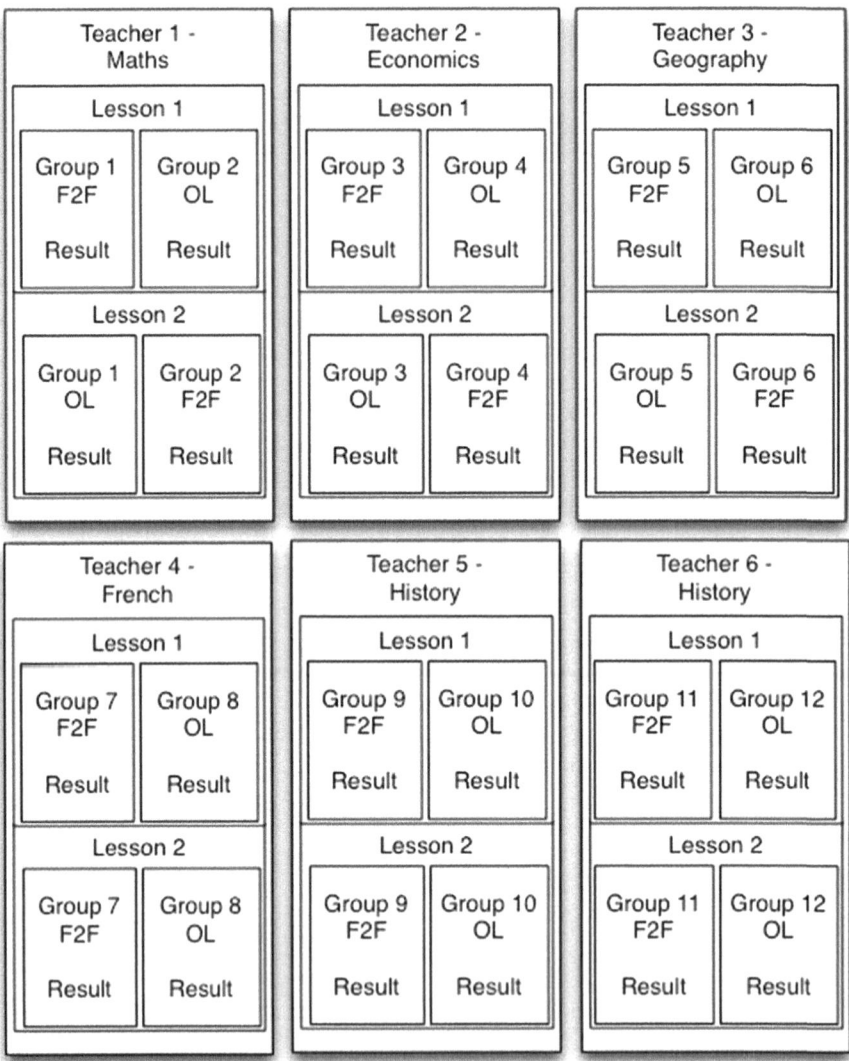

Fig. 5.3 The repeated factoral design

must believe the technology can be a useful tool for improving or enhancing learning (Butler & Sellborn, 2002). In line with this stance, we ascertain the value of perceived benefits and consider it to be a real proxy and predictor of the tested benefits. Thus, we state:

H1: Perceived benefits have a positive impact on observed benefits.

The model further posited that net benefits are dependent on three primary beliefs: preference, satisfaction, and enjoyment. Within a secondary school or a class context, "voluntary (intention to) use" is restricted; educational institutions or

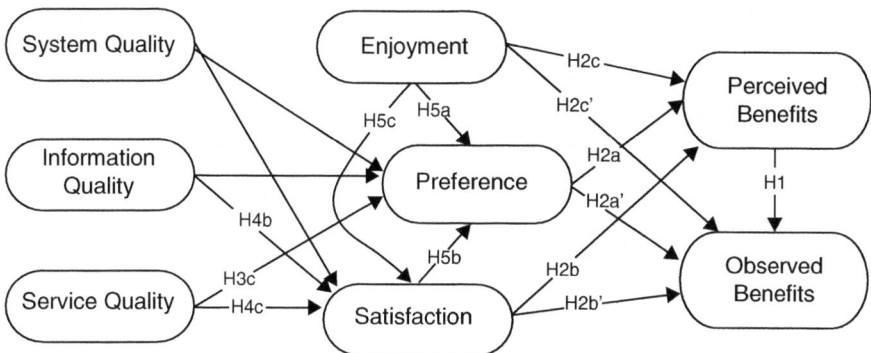

Fig. 5.4 The proposed structural model

teachers usually decide on when and how to use OL tools. As a consequence, we included the concept of use preference as a replacement for the ISSM's "intention to use", as proposed by Hsu and Lu (2007) and Bourgonjon, Valcke, Soetaert, and Schellens (2009). Preference is defined as "the positive and preferred choice for the continued use of e-learning systems in the classroom." We contend that preference for a system will affect pupils' learning experiences positively and thus lead to better results, i.e., improved net benefits.

Satisfaction is another principal success determinant, expressed as "the feelings and attitudes that stem from aggregating a user's efforts and benefits from using an information system" (Wixom & Todd, 2005). As such, satisfaction is conceived as reflecting an aggregated attitude that positively influences the system's net benefits (as proposed by DeLone & McLean, 2003).

Perceived enjoyment is defined as "the extent to which using technology is perceived to be enjoyable in its own right, independent of any performance consequences" (Cheng, 2011). Evidence sufficiently validated perceived enjoyment as a significant driver of intention to use, usage, and ease of use of OL systems (e.g., Cheng, 2011; Teo & Noyes, 2011). We argue that an increase in perceived enjoyment stimulates pupils to make use of the OL course materials. In other words, perceived enjoyment is a driver of both net benefits. Following the above rationale, we posit:

H2a and H2a': Observed and perceived benefits are both positively affected by use preference.

H2b and H2b': Observed and perceived benefits are both positively affected by satisfaction.

H2c and H2c': Observed and perceived benefits are both positively affected by perceived enjoyment.

The ISSM further distinguishes between the quality of the hard- and software (system quality), the quality of the information that is provided by the system, and the quality of the service that is provided to use the system. In our instructional context, we defined information quality as "the level of difficulty of the OL system, the multimedia components and the related learning activities." System quality is, in line with the ISSM literature, conceived as "the degree to which the system is easy to manipulate and interact with."

As pupils were not trained beforehand, the only service they received was technical teacher support during the lesson. Thus, in this study service quality is conceived as the degree to which technical teacher support was available and sufficient. Congruent with the ISSM, we propose system, information, and service quality as determinants of use preference and satisfaction.

H3a, H3b, and H3c: Use preference is positively influenced by system quality, information quality, and service quality.

H4a, H4b, and H4c: Satisfaction is positively influenced by system quality, information quality, and service quality.

In the literature, enjoyment has been established as a direct determinant of (intention to) use learning systems (cf. Saade, Tan, & Nebebe, 2008). In our model, preference is used instead. Likewise, it is plausible to contend that as a pupil enjoys the sheer use of the OL environment, she/he will likely prefer its further use and be more satisfied with it. Consequently, we propose perceived enjoyment as a determinant of both use preference and satisfaction. In the ISSM, intention and satisfaction could influence each other. As such, a feedback loop can only be tested in a longitudinal study, and not in the cross-sectional factorial experiment we applied. Alongside the arguments above, we posit:

H5a and H5b: Preference is positively influenced by perceived enjoyment and satisfaction.

H5c: Satisfaction is positively influenced by perceived enjoyment.

5.3.5 Measures

Several previously validated instruments were employed (Wang et al., 2007). Both self-reported (perceived) and objectively measured (observed) gauges were used to evaluate the pupils' learning performance. The observed benefits were calculated as differences in test performance between pupils in the OL and F2F condition, i.e., a differential score between −10 and 10.

Table 5.1 shows the factor loadings and internal consistency measures for all retained items. All constructs show sufficient internal consistency with Cronbach's alphas of higher than 0.7 (Nunnally & Nunnally & Bernstein, 1994). Table 5.1 also displays the composite reliability and average variance extracted (AVE) for each construct, both of which are above the expected thresholds of 0.7 and 0.5 for all latent constructs, suggesting adequate convergent validity (Hair, Blake, Babin, & Tatham, 2006). Discriminant validity is achieved (i) when the items load much higher on their own latent variable than on other variables and (ii) when the square root of each construct's AVE is larger than its correlations with other constructs

Table 5.1 Internal consistency of the measures

Construct	Items and their factor loadings	Composite reliability	Cronbach's alpha	AVE
Perceived benefits	PB1: 0.79; PB2: 0.86; PB3: 0.76	0.85	0.73	0.65
Preference	Pref1: 0.90; Pref2: 0.94; Pref3: 0.90; Pref4: 0.92	0.95	0.93	0.83
Satisfaction	Sat1: 0.88; Sat2: 0.72; Sat3: 0.88	0.87	0.78	0.69
Perceived enjoyment	PE1: 0.90; PE2: 0.94; PE3: 0.92	0.95	0.91	0.85
Information quality	IQ1: 0.68; IQ2: 0.81; IQ3: 0.80; IQ4: 0.83; IQ5: 0.83	0.89	0.85	0.63
Construct	*Items and their factor loadings*	*Composite reliability*	*Cronbach's alpha*	*AVE*
System quality	SQ1: 0.77; SQ2: 0.67; SQ3: 0.88; SQ4: 0.73	0.83	0.72	0.55
Service quality	SeQ1: 0.91; SeQ2: 0.96	0.93	0.86	0.87

(Chin, 1998). While omitting the display of all item cross-loadings in the interest of brevity, we confirm that all items loaded on their constructs as expected. In the case of multiple determinants, the variance inflation factor was below the 2.0 level, excluding collinearity issues.

5.3.6 Applied Data Analyses

We tested the measurement and research model by applying a partial least squares (PLS) modeling approach, using the SmartPLS application (Ringle, Wende, & Will, 2005). PLS combines a structural model (i.e., paths between constructs) with a measurement model (i.e., relationships between a construct and its indicators (or items)). It uses an ordinary least squares approach and bootstrapping to obtain estimates of model parameters and their significance.

5.4 Results

This section provides an overview of the descriptive and explanatory data analyses. It incorporates findings about the different constructs of the research model, followed by the assessment of the different hypotheses.

5.4.1 General Descriptives

Table 5.2 presents the descriptives for the different constructs. Remarkably, pupils' performance in the OL condition was significantly poorer than when instructed in a traditional way (with test scores of 75.7% for the F2F versus 56.8% in the OL condition). On average, the OL instruction was modestly accepted: the information, system, and service quality received rather positive scores of between 3.30 and 3.55 (on a scale of 1 to 5), with a mean score for satisfaction of 3.09. Perceived benefits, perceived enjoyment, and in particular preference, however, received scores below the neutral point (3). It seems pupils appreciated the quality of the system and the OL materials but would not opt for them if they were allowed to choose independently. Given the particular onset of the study, there were limited or no interactions with peers or the teachers. We deem it is plausible that the pupils have missed the integration of interactive practice, which can be regarded as a premise for "students to become proficient in any area of study" (Kuyatt & Baker, 2014, p. 15).

The most salient outcomes of the comparative analyses (Table 5.3) can be summarized as follows:

1. Significant differences were detected between observed and perceived benefits.
2. The observed benefits' score, i.e., the differences in test results among respondents from the 7th grade, is −4.96, which is significantly lower than the scores of the pupils in other grades.
3. The observed benefits' score of the pupils enrolled in general secondary education (−3.43) is significantly lower than that of vocational, technical, and arts pupils. The perceived benefits' score of the general education pupils (2.29) is significantly lower than the scores of the technical and arts pupils.
4. The observed benefits' score for mathematics is significantly lower than that for other course subjects. The "perceived benefits'" scores are the highest for French.

Table 5.2 Global descriptives

	Mean	Std. D.	Min	Max
Test results F2F	7.57	2.25	0	10
Test results OL	5.68	2.75	0	10
Test results difference	−1.89	3.34	−10.0	10.00
Perceived benefits	2.63	0.82	1.00	5.00
Preference	2.24	1.05	1.00	5.00
Satisfaction	3.09	0.86	1.00	5.00
Perceived enjoyment	2.61	1.02	1.00	5.00
Information quality	3.30	0.68	1.00	5.00
System quality	3.55	0.66	1.00	5.00
Service quality	3.49	0.98	1.00	5.00

Table 5.3 Mean scores according to grade, subject, and program type

School grade[a]	7th	9th	10th	11th	12th
N	24	49	28	21	29
Observed benefits	−4.96[b]	−1.86	−0.25	−0.71	−1.83
Perceived benefits	2.31	2.65	2.90	2.43	2.74
Subjects	*Geography*	*Economics*	*French*	*History*	*Mathematics*
N	30	28	30	39	24
Observed benefits	−1.97	−2	−0.03	−1.44	−4.71[b]
Perceived benefits	2.79	2.79	2.96[b]	2.39	2.22
Education type	*General*	*Vocational*	*Arts*	*Technical*	
N	49	28	14	60	
Observed benefits	−3.43[b]	−1.68	−0.64	−0.25	
Perceived benefits	2.29[b]	2.79	2.55	2.90	

[a]There were no students of the 8th grade
[b]Significance is based on Kruskal-Wallis or one-way ANOVA

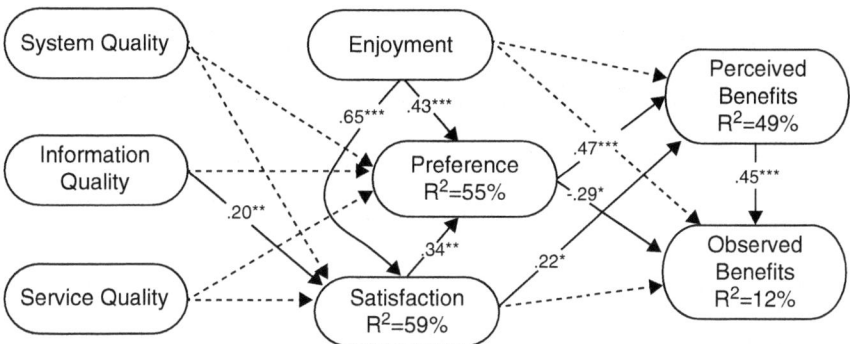

Fig. 5.5 The tested structural model

5.4.2 Hypotheses Tested

The tested model is depicted in Fig. 5.5. Enjoyment plays a key role in explaining satisfaction and use preference, compared to the limited importance of system, service, and information quality. Information quality and satisfaction are significantly related ($\beta = 0.20$; $p < 0.05$). The impact of enjoyment on the net benefits is fully mediated via satisfaction and preference. Preference has a strong impact on perceived benefits ($\beta = 0.47$, $p < 0.001$) but a negative impact on observed benefits ($\beta = -0.29$, $p < 0.05$). Thus, the data suggests that pupils who are in favor of OL system usage are not the pupils with the best test results. Satisfaction is only weakly related to perceived benefits. It has no impact on the observed benefits, but a considerable effect on preference. A strong relationship is found between perceived and observed benefits ($\beta = 0.45$; $p < 0.001$).

5.5 Discussion and Interpretation

In what follows, we discuss and assess the results of this study in different ways. We describe the findings and their implications for practice and theory building. Moreover, we discuss at length the study's strengths and limitations and propose opportunities for future studies. Next to this, the benefits of the adapted ISSM in order to study and understand pupils' usage of OL systems are put forward.

5.5.1 Findings

Our experiment reveals that secondary school pupils have better test results in a face-to-face instructional situation. The overall test difference which shows worse results for the OL model, 1.89 on a 10-point scale, is confirmed across subjects, teachers, school years, and educational types. This finding is also strengthened by a rather low overall scores on the perceived benefits (M = 2.63) and pupils' preference for using the system (M = 2.24). Given the radical nature of the OL approach, where pupils had to deal with the new IS, the online nature of the contents without any assistance or pre-course training, and the novelty of it in their educational context, these findings are comprehensible. The explanatory model built upon the ISSM that we tested helps to explain why the OL instruction mode resulted in lower scores on perceived and observed benefits.

The model includes both instrumental and emotional determinants of preference and satisfaction. It is clear that the emotional variable, perceived enjoyment, is the most important determinant of satisfaction and preference, the latter being a dominant predictor of net benefits. Perceived enjoyment has a modest mean of 2.61, and its impact on user preference and satisfaction is strong and significant ($\beta = 0.43$ and 0.65, respectively, (with $p < 0.05$)). In other words, if pupils think they (will) enjoy working with an OL system, they really prefer its use and are satisfied with it.

The instrumental determinants that focus on observable qualities of the deployed system, i.e., service, system, and information quality, are not the reason for the lack of preference for the OL instruction mode. Only information quality impacts satisfaction significantly (but not strongly) ($\beta = 0.20$; $p < 0.05$), indicating that a higher level of appreciation of the OL contents slightly increases satisfaction. Yet, the lesser importance of these three factors should be interpreted cautiously. As Table 5.1 indicates, pupils did give a rather positive score on the three constructs (M between 3.30 and 3.55). This implies that the OL material, the learning activities and supporting software (Smartschool with external hyperlinks), and hardware have been configured adequately. Under the assumption that an OL system is badly designed or not supported, a significant negative impact of these factors on satisfaction and preference might be expected. Nevertheless, it is also plausible that the limited interactivity of the OL system was a particular influence on the findings. As mentioned before, pupils worked on their own and only had contact with the teacher in the event of technical problems. Previous studies indicated that increased teacher-to-pupil and pupil-to-pupil interactions via online facilities impacted learner grades positively (Palloff & Pratt, 1999; Poon, Low, & Yong, 2004).

Another upshot is the considerable difference in observed benefits for pupils of the 7th grade (12 to 13 years old). For this cohort, the negative test result differences were more pronounced than for the rest of the respondents. We found an average test result difference of −4.96 as compared to averages between −1.86 and −0.25 for the other grades (Table 5.3). Apparently, younger pupils possess less self-regulation skills and are less able to work autonomously, which is a requirement of the particular OL approach.

5.5.2 Contributions

Despite its merits and suitability, the number of OL studies inspired by the ISSM model is not overwhelming. The great majority of extant ISSM studies were conducted in higher education and focused on the success of specific OL environments using a cross-sectional survey-based research design.

Our approach not only targets the less-studied group of secondary education learners but also integrates a theory-driven research model with an experimental design in an ecological setting. Moreover, it includes both perceived and objectively measured learning outcomes and the construct of "preference" as a substitute for "intention to use." The latter is particularly pertinent in a context of non-voluntary usage, which is common in secondary education, where pupils cannot but deploy a given system. The resulting validated model is re-usable for future research endeavors in- and outside the context of secondary education research, and it can be applied within an experimental design or in a survey-based investigation.

From a methodological point of view, the factoral approach enabled us to minimize potential biases due to group or topic effects. The repetition of the design (in several classes and grades in the underlying study) strengthens the findings. To our knowledge, this set-up has not yet been applied in a previous educational study, and it deserves to be applied more widely. The study's findings add further evidence for the appropriateness of using the ISSM to scrutinize OL in secondary education. More particularly, it adequately frames pupils' perceptions and usage behavior, as well as the predictors and the outcomes of these two crucial factors in OL acceptance research.

5.5.3 Implications

At first glance, our findings are somewhat contradictory to the current body of research findings which stresses the importance and beneficial contributions of e-learning. However, our results should not be regarded as being opposed to such a stance or as a call to conventional in-class education. We have explored the limits of OL in secondary education, and our results primarily point to aspects and considerations that need to be addressed when introducing OL systems in schools. In particular, two main concerns for both practitioners and researchers are raised by this study.

First, when following new trends in education, such as "flipping the classroom" (FtC) (e.g., Stone, 2012; Wong & Chu, 2014), one should take into account the nature of the materials and learner characteristics. In a context where pupils are used to conventional classroom teaching, the transition to more technology-enhanced instruction is not evident, not even for millennials (the subjects of the underlying study). We contend that pupils today may be technology-oriented, but when it comes to learning, they have limited capabilities in supporting their learning process effectively. Reading and comprehending learning materials independently and on-screen, without focused guidance, seems less fruitful than F2F lessons. In the light of FtC, where pupils are provided with OL artifacts they need to process themselves as homework, outside of the classroom, our findings mark a warning. Teaching should not be confined to providing learning materials and follow-up class-based activities, as pupils need to be scaffolded in their knowledge acquisition process as well. A consequence of this stance implies the consideration of a framework regarding "self-regulated learning" (e.g., Lee & Lee, 2008), explaining learners' cognitive strategies, management, and control of their effort on classroom tasks, and/or the self-determination theory, a theory of motivation that taps into our natural tendencies during a task-achievement process such as learning (e.g., Jang, Reeve, & Halusic, 2016).

5.6 Conclusions

This study contributes to the OL research field by assessing the antecedents of perceived and observed benefits of OL instruction as compared to F2F teaching, in secondary education. 151 pupils and 6 teachers from a secondary school participated in a repetitive factorial experimental design, which facilitated the comparison of instructional formats in an empirical sound way, while yielding interesting information for practitioners. The DeLone and McLean ISSM underpins the experimental approach. The model was extended through an emotional factor, perceived enjoyment, as well as both perceived and observed measures of net benefits.

In general, both the observed test results and the perceived benefits are an indication of the lower effectiveness of OL relative to F2F lessons. This finding is confirmed across subjects, school years, and different educational types.

Our results point to the importance of perceived enjoyment as a determinant of the success dimensions which function as predictors of net benefits. However, the pupils preferring the system and attributing a degree of enjoyment to it are not necessarily the best performing ones.

These findings are important for educational policy makers and professionals. They indicate that a shift toward OL should not be taken for granted. Given the self-discipline and self-regulated learning that is required by a more autonomous OL approach, efforts should be made to find the optimal equilibrium between F2F and OL instruction, while focusing on both enjoyment and performance orientation.

A considerable number of IS acceptance studies include perceived benefits in their models. In this study, we found that the use of perceived and observed measures in the same study is a merit; the perceived benefits are strongly related to observed measures. Given the participants' age, their ability to reliably estimate the real benefits is remarkable. It strengthens the validity of the other findings as well. The involvement of 6 teachers and a substantial number (151) of pupils, the carefully established repetitive factorial experiment, and the theoretically underpinned assessment model are the strengths of the research presented above.

A first plausible limitation of the study is the fact that teachers were only allowed to intervene in the event of technical problems. In other words, a quite radical OL approach was introduced. A second limitation is related to the limited number of cycles employed within the larger framework of a design-based research approach. The quest for sound, validated sets of guidelines for educational design, adapted to one's organization, preferably involves multiple iterations in a longitudinal set-up (Anderson & Shattuck, 2012; Strobel, Jonassen, & Ionan, 2008) and multiple methods (Wang, Vogel, & Ran, 2011).

Follow-up studies could refine the measurement instruments and further extend the proposed model with context and individual characteristics related to teaching and cognitive presence (Joo, Lim, & Kim, 2011), playfulness, and motivation (Atkinson & Kydd, 1997), alongside self-regulated learning (Lee & Lee, 2008). Subsequent research will focus on a new iteration of an intervention targeting active learning and the engagement of pupils, based on design principles for blended learning.

Acknowledgments We thank Mr. Y. Weyts, the former head of the school group at the time of the study. He actively participated in the design of the experiment and suggested useful improvements. He granted us access to the facilities of the school. Finally, we are equally grateful to the teachers and pupils who participated and spent time and effort in designing and completing the learning paths and activities.

Appendix: Questionnaire Items

Constructs	Items
Perceived Benefits	PB1 To what extent is learning in Smartschool better than a conventional class (given by a teacher)?
	PB2 By using Smartschool, I can understand the course material.
	PB3 By using Smartschool, I could study my lesson.

Constructs	Items
Satisfaction	Sat1 To what extent are you satisfied with the lesson in Smartschool? Sat2 Are you satisfied with this way of teaching? Sat3 Are you satisfied with the use of Smartschool within the school?
Preference	Pref1 If I had to choose between a learning path in Smartschool and a conventional class, I would choose a learning path in Smartschool. Pref2 I prefer to use Smartschool. Pref3 If it was up to me, Smartschool would be used more frequently. Pref4 In the future, I would like work more with Smartschool in the classroom.
Perceived Enjoyment	PJ1 I find the use of Smartschool enjoyable. PJ2 Learning via Smartschool is pleasant. PJ3 I find it pleasurable to learn via Smartschool.
System Quality	SQ1 Smartschool is easy to use. SQ2 To what extent did you experience technical problems during the class? SQ3 Did you find it easy to work with Smartschool? SQ4 How responsive was the system (the pages shown on the screen)?
Information Quality	IQ1 Was the learning path (with its components) clear and understandable? IQ2 How much do you appreciate the contents presented (text, videos, pictures)? IQ3 Were the presented assignments in the system clear? IQ4 Could you understand the topic with the available information? IQ5 The topic was well presented in the learning environment.
Service Quality	SeQ1 If I needed help from the teacher, I received valuable help. SeQ2 The support I got was sufficient.

References

Ananiadou, K., & Claro, M. (2009). *21st century skills and competences for new millennium learners in OECD countries. OECD education working papers.* Paris: OECD Publishing.

Anderson, T., & Shattuck, J. (2012). Design-based research: A decade of progress in education research? *Educational Researcher, 41,* 16–25. https://doi.org/10.3102/0013189X11428813

Atkinson, M., & Kydd, C. (1997). Individual characteristics associated with World Wide Web use: An empirical study of playfulness and motivation. *The Database for Advances in Information Systems, 28,* 53–62. https://doi.org/10.1145/264701.264705

Bourgonjon, J., Valcke, M., Soetaert, R., & Schellens, T. (2009). Students' perceptions about the use of video games in the classroom. *Computers & Education, 54,* 1145–1156. https://doi.org/10.1016/j.compedu.2009.10.022

Butler, D. L., & Sellborn, M. (2002). Barriers to adopting technology for teaching and learning. *Educause Quarterly, 9*(4), 105–127. https://www.learntechlib.org/p/92849/

Cheng, Y.-M. (2011). Antecedents and consequences of e-learning acceptance. *Information Systems Journal, 21*(3), 269–299. https://doi.org/10.1111/j.1365-2575.2010.00356.x

Chin, W. W. (1998). The partial least squares approach to structural equation modeling. In G. A. Marcoulides (Ed.), *Modern business research methods* (pp. 295–336). Mahwah, NJ: Lawrence Erlbaum Associates.

Cidral, W. A., Oliveira, T., Di Felice, M., & Aparicio, M. (2018). E-learning success determinants: Brazilian empirical study. *Computers & Education, 122,* 273–290.

Dağhan, G., & Akkoyunlu, B. (2016). Modeling the continuance usage intention of online learning environments. *Computers in Human Behavior, 60*, 198–211. https://doi.org/10.1016/j.chb.2016.02.066

De Smet, C., Schellens, T., De Wever, B., Brandt-Pomares, P., & Valcke, M. (2014). The design and implementation of learning paths in a learning management system. *Interactive Learning Environments, 24*, 1076–1096. https://doi.org/10.1080/10494820.2014.951059

DeLone, W., & McLean, E. (2003). The DeLone and McLean model of information systems success: A ten-year update. *Journal of Management Information Systems, 19*, 9–30. https://doi.org/10.1080/07421222.2003.11045748

Eom, S. B., & Stapleton, J. (2011). Testing the DeLone-Mclean model of information system success in an e-learning context. In S. Eom & J. Arbaugh (Eds.), *Student satisfaction and learning out- comes in e-learning: An introduction to empirical research* (pp. 82–109). Hershey, PA: Igi Global.

Grubišić, A., Stankov, S., Rosić, M., & Žitko, B. (2009). Controlled experiment replication in evaluation of e-learning system's educational influence. *Computers & Education., 53*, 591–602. https://doi.org/10.1016/j.compedu.2009.03.014

Hair, J., Blake, W., Babin, B., & Tatham, R. (2006). *Multivariate data analysis*. Upper Saddle River, NJ: Prentice Hall.

Hassanzadeh, A., Kanaani, F., & Elahi, S. (2012). A model for measuring e-learning systems success in universities. *Expert Systems with Applications, 39*, 10959–10966. https://doi.org/10.1016/j.eswa.2012.03.028

Hsu, C. L., & Lu, H. P. (2007). Consumer behavior in online game communities: A motivational factor perspective. *Computers in Human Behavior, 23*, 1642–1659. https://doi.org/10.1016/j.chb.2005.09.001

Jang, H., Reeve, J., & Halusic, M. (2016). A new autonomy-supportive way of teaching that increases conceptual learning: Teaching in students' preferred ways. *The Journal of Experimental Education*. Advance online publication. https://doi.org/10.1080/00220973.2015.1083522

Joo, Y. J., Lim, K. Y., & Kim, E. K. (2011). Online university students' satisfaction and persistence: Examining perceived level of presence, usefulness and ease of use as predictors in a structural model. *Computers & Education, 57*, 1654–1664. https://doi.org/10.1016/j.compedu.2011.02.008

Kirkman, C. (2000). A model for the effective management of information and communications technology development in schools derived from six contrasting case studies. *Journal of Information Technology for Teacher Education, 9*, 37–52. https://doi.org/10.1080/14759390000200077

Kulkarni, U. R., Ravindran, S., & Freeze, R. (2007). A knowledge management success model: Theoretical development and empirical validation. *Journal of Management Information Systems, 23*, 309–347. http://www.jstor.org/stable/40398863.

Kurt, O. E. (2019). Examining an e-learning system through the lens of the information success model: Empirical evidence from Italy. *Education and Information Technologies, 24*, 1173–1184. https://doi.org/10.1007/s10639-018-9821-4

Kuyatt, B. L., & Baker, J. D. (2014). Human anatomy software use in traditional and online anatomy laboratory classes: Student-perceived learning benefits. *Journal of College Science Teaching, 43*(5), 14–19.

Lee, J.-K., & Lee, W.-K. (2008). The relationship of e-Learner's self-regulatory efficacy and perception of e-Learning environmental quality. *Computers in Human Behavior, 24*, 32–47. https://doi.org/10.1016/j.chb.2006.12.001

Lee, M.-C. (2010). Explaining and predicting users' continuance intention toward e-learning: An extension of the expectation–confirmation model. *Computers & Education, 54*, 506–516. https://doi.org/10.1016/j.compedu.2009.09.002

Mohammadi, H. (2015). Investigating users' perspectives on e-learning: An integration of TAM and IS success model. *Computers in Human Behavior, 45*, 359–374. https://doi.org/10.1016/j.chb.2014.07.044

Nunnally, J. C., & Bernstein, I. H. (1994). *Psychometric theory* (3rd ed.). New York: McGraw-Hill.

Palloff, R.M. & Pratt, K. (1999). Building Learning Communities in Cyberspace: Effective Strategies for the Online Classroom. Jossey-Bass Publishers, San Francisco, CA, USA.

Petter, S., & McLean, E. (2009). A meta-analytic assessment of the DeLone and McLean IS success model: An examination of IS success at the individual level. *Information & Management, 46*(3), 159–166. https://doi.org/10.1016/j.im.2008.12.006

Pham, Q. T., & Tran, T. P. (2018). Impact factors on using of e-learning system and learning achievement of students at several universities in Vietnam. In *Computational science and its applications – ICCSA 2018* (Lecture notes in computer science) (Vol. 10963, pp. 394–409). https://doi.org/10.1007/978-3-319-95171-3_31

Poelmans, S., & Wessa, P. (2013). A constructivist approach in a blended e-learning environment for statistics. *Interactive Learning Environments, 23*, 385–401. https://doi.org/10.1080/10494820.2013.766890

Poon, W., Lock-Teng Low, K. & Gun-Fie Yong, D. (2004). A study of Web-based learning (WBL) environment in Malaysia. *International Journal of Educational Management, 18*(6), 374–385. https://doi.org/10.1108/09513540410554031

Ringle, C. M., Wende, S., & Will, A. (2005). SmartPLS 2.0 (beta). Germany, University of Hamburg. http://www.smartpls.de.

Saade, R., Tan, W., & Nebebe, F. (2008). Impact of motivation on intentions in online learning: Canada vs China. *Issues in Informing Science and Information Technology, 5*, 137–147.

Seddon, P. B. (1997). A respecification and extension of the DeLone and McLean model of IS success. *Information Systems Research, 8*(3), 240–253. https://doi.org/10.1287/isre.8.3.240

Stone, B. S. (2012). *Flip your classroom to increase active learning and student engagement.* Columbia, MO: University of Missouri.

Strobel, J., Jonassen, D. H., & Ionan, I. G. (2008). The evolution of a collaborative authoring system for non-linear hypertext: A design-based research study. *Computers & Education, 51*(1), 67–85. https://doi.org/10.1016/j.compedu.2007.04.008

Teo, T., & Noyes, J. (2011). An assessment of the influence of perceived enjoyment and attitude on the intention to use technology among pre-service teachers: A structural equation modeling approach. *Computers & Education, 57*(2), 1645–1653. https://doi.org/10.1016/j.compedu.2011.03.002

Wang, M., Vogel, D., & Ran, W. (2011). Creating a performance-oriented e-learning environment: A design science approach. *Information & Management, 48*, 260–269. https://doi.org/10.1016/j.im.2011.06.003

Wang, Y., Wang, H., & Shee, D. (2007). Measuring e-learning system success in an organizational context: Scale development and validation. *Computers in Human Behavior, 23*(4), 1792–1808. https://doi.org/10.1016/j.chb.2005.10.006

Wang, Y.-S., & Liao, Y.-W. (2008). Assessing eGovernment systems success: A validation of the DeLone and McLean model of information systems success. *Government Information Quarterly, 25*(4), 717–733. https://doi.org/10.1016/j.giq.2007.06.002

Wei, K., Loong, A., & Leong, Y. (2009). Measuring ERP system success: A respecification of the DeLone and McLean's IS success model. In *Symposium on progress in information & communication technology* (pp. 7–12). http://citeseerx.ist.psu.edu/viewdoc/download?doi=10.1.1.160.5014&rep=rep1&type=pdf.

Wixom, B. H., & Todd, P. A. (2005). A theoretical integration of user satisfaction and technology acceptance. *Information Systems Research, 16*(1), 85–102. https://doi.org/10.1287/isre.1050.0042

Wong, K., & Chu, D. W. (2014). Is the flipped classroom model effective in the perspectives of students' perceptions and benefits? In R. K. Zhang & L. F. Kwok (Eds.), *Hybrid learning. Theory and practice: 7th international conference, ICHL 2014, Shanghai, China, August 8–10, 2014* (pp. 93–104). https://doi.org/10.1007/978-3-319-08961-4_10

Wu, J., & Wang, Y. (2006). Measuring KMS success: A respecification of the DeLone and McLean's model. *Information & Management, 43*(6), 728–739. https://doi.org/10.1016/j.im.2006.05.002

Part II
Technology Supported STEM School Education

Chapter 6
Coding and Computational Thinking: Using Arduino to Acquire Problem-Solving Skills

Veronica Rossano, Teresa Roselli, and Gaetano Quercia

6.1 Introduction

Computational thinking (CT) is a way of thinking that allows a human to define solutions that a non-human agent can use to solve a set of problems. One of the major misconceptions about CT is that it is a typical skill for computer scientists. CT and coding are often used as synonyms, but they are not (Wing, 2008; Israel, Pearson, Tapia, Wherfel, & Reese, 2015; Resnick et al., 2009).

CT refers to four basic skills: decomposition of problems, to break a complex problem down into a number of simple problems; pattern recognition, to recognize sequences and similarities; abstraction, to remove characteristics in order to define the essential characteristics necessary to solve a problem; and algorithm design, to define a step-by-step solution for a class of problems (Wing, 2006). Coding, on the other hand, is the ability to write a program that a machine can understand and apply to solve a problem. Thus, CT is the art of solving a problem, whereas coding is the art of translating that solution into a language that a computer can understand and run.

The importance of CT has been underlined since the 1980s by Seymour Papert. Developing procedural thinking for children is important to develop basic skills for problem-solving and deep learning. The first children's programming language, LOGO (Papert, 1980, 1991), was defined to allow children to experience CT and enable them to build simple programs. For years, it was used occasionally by teachers who were particularly interested in Papert's studies. Only in the recent years coding and CT studies have spread around the world.

The current challenges in the educational technology field are, on the one hand, to make children aware that computers, and technologies in general, can be smart

---

V. Rossano (✉) · T. Roselli · G. Quercia
Department of Computer Science, University of Bari, Bari, Italy
e-mail: veronica.rossano@uniba.it; teresa.roselli@uniba.it

only if they are programmed by humans and, on the other, to prepare future citizens to be able to use smart objects and tools (Merino-Armero, González-Calero, Cózar-Gutiérrez, & Villena-Taranilla, 2018). One of the most dangerous and widespread misconceptions among young people is "technology is smart since the circuits are smart." As Jeannette Wing (2006 - p. 33) stated, computational thinking is "a universally applicable attitude and skill set that everyone, not just computer scientists, would be eager to learn and use." As much empirical evidence confirms that CT and coding are effective in improving problem-solving skills, divergent ways of thinking, creativity, communication, and group work (Marques, Guimarães, & Salgado, 2019; Lye & Koh, 2014; Siegle, 2017; Silva, da Silva, Toda, & Isotani, 2018). In Burke (2012) and Wolz et al. (2011), for example, CT is integrated in existing activity to acquire English writing skills, and Choi et al. (2013) use CT and programming to enhance learners' positive attitude toward mathematics. Israel et al. (2015) state that the inclusion of computing skills has positive effects also with struggling learners, including students with disabilities and those living in poverty. In addition, CT skills allow students to develop interdisciplinary skills, and it helps to create connection between disciplines which is a basic for interdisciplinary thinking in the workplace (Cabo & Lansiquot, 2016). In this context also, the use of robots to acquire coding skills is growing. In Merino-Armero et al. (2018), an educational robot was effective to increase motivation in acquiring solving map-reading tasks. But also unplugged approaches have been proved as effective to develop CT skills; this confirms that problem-solving ability can be developed regardless of the use of programming and/or coding (Brackmann et al., 2017).

Google offers the Exploring Computational Thinking (ECT) program[1], a collection of lesson plans, videos, and other resources on computational thinking (CT) to allow users to acquire CT skills. Moreover, to underline that CT is not only referred to STEM but it is effective in any school subjects, the website offers didactic resources that can be used in different subjects, for example, algebra, music, and US history.

Another interest aspect in CT and coding education is the approach used during the learning process. To engage the student in the educative activities, it is basic to design a learning path that allows them to interact, participate, and build artifacts. This educational approach is named constructionism (Harel & Papert, 1991), which is a constructivist learning theory that states that learner can acquire knowledge effectively if they can interact with real objects.

In this context, the aim of the research is to verify if the use of physical technology, such as Arduino board, can be effective in teaching coding and developing CT skills. To this aim, a learning path has been designed and developed. The activities have been organized in order to introduce junior high school students, with no experience in coding, to the process of building the algorithm from simple exercises to more complex tasks. In addition, to make the activities more engaging, some wooden models have been built to allow students to see the effects of programming

---

[1] https://edu.google.com/resources/programs/exploring-computational-thinking/#!home

on physical objects. A brief description of the structured pathway and some results of the experiment were presented in Rossano et al. (2018). Here a more in-depth presentation of the learning activities and experimental results are illustrated. The activities have been described from an operative point of view to allow the reader to apply the same learning path in other contexts.

The chapter is organized as follows: Sect. 6.2 describes the state of the art of technological solutions for coding and CT; Sect. 6.3 describes the design and implementation of the learning path; and Sect. 6.4 describes the pilot study to measure both the students' appreciation of the technological approach and the students' knowledge gain. Finally, the results of the user study are discussed, and conclusions are drawn.

6.2 Tools and Resources for CT

All children are attracted by technology. They use different kinds of electronic devices to play, study, and communicate. Until a few years ago, these tools were used exclusively by adults, but today, with the generation of "digital natives," it is common to see smartphones in children's hands.

Different ways of interaction have been observed, also different ways of thinking and learning. Starting from Papert's work, many technological solutions have been implemented in order to let the pupils acquire technological and computational skills. Some of them are toys sold by toy stores, and others have been designed and implemented in order to be used in educational contexts and are more complex and expensive. Bee Bot®, for example, is a floor robot that pupils, from 3 years old, can program using directional commands (e.g., forwards, backwards, left and right turns) to follow a path. Bee Bot® is one of the most used to teach CT and coding since childhood (Di Lieto et al., 2017; Cho, Lee, Cherniak, & Jung, 2017; González & Muñoz-Repiso, 2018).

For the same learning purpose, there are also unplugged solutions. The Montessori play set, named Cubetto (https://www.primotoys.com/fr/), for example, is based on a tangible approach; children will be able to learn programming without the support of screens. Other solutions combine technology with physical objects, such as coding blocks from Osmo (https://www.playosmo.com/en/) that is a tangible play platform to learn coding with physical blocks that interact with iPad and iPhone. There are also solutions based on a software approach; the best known is the Hour of Code (https://code.org/), where different games based on Scratch are supplied. Scratch (Maloney, Resnick, Rusk, Silverman, & Eastmond, 2010) is a visual programming language that can be easily used by children to build media-rich projects, such as stories, games, and animation. It is based on Papert's Logo project and is currently one of the most widely used languages to introduce the programming at different ages (Vaca-Cárdenas et al., 2015).

To improve motivation and engagement in programming skill acquisition, in the recent years, also robotic education has spread (Díaz-Lauzurica & Moreno-Salinas,

2019). The idea is to create artifacts that can be programmed to do some tasks. This allows students to work with real hardware that will be able to do real physical work when programmed. The LEGO® Mindstorms are an example: they allow the development of programmable robots based on Lego building blocks. This approach has been successfully applied in different contexts (Haak, Abke, & Borgeest, 2018; Wu, de Vries, & Dunsworth, 2018; Umbleja, 2017). Another device commonly used in teaching and learning contexts is Arduino (Plaza et al., 2018), which is an open-source hardware and software for building digital devices and interactive objects that can sense and control objects in the physical and digital world. The Arduino board uses a variety of microprocessors and microcontrollers that can be programmed using a language similar to C. The microcontrollers, unlike the microprocessors, which integrate only the processing unit (CPU), include permanent and volatile memories and I/O ports. This makes Arduino an autonomous system: the program, saved in the permanent memory, instructs the microprocessor which uses volatile memory to store data that are useful during the execution of the program. Moreover, there are different sensors which allow Arduino to measure light, temperature, degree of flex, pressure, proximity, acceleration, carbon monoxide, radioactivity, humidity, and barometric pressure. Thus, the Arduino board can be used to solve real complex problems with physical objects, allowing students to program artifacts that can be touched. The learning process is more engaging and motivating.

6.3 Learning Activities: Design and Implementation

Until now, there have been many teaching experiences using coding to introduce the concept of problem-solving and computational thinking from the early years of school (Lye & Koh, 2014). In this context, the research aims at defining a learning path for the acquisition of the basic concepts of programming with the use of Arduino and Scratch4Arduino (Rossano et al., 2018). The learning path addresses middle school students and aims at improving motivation and engagement in technological subjects. The learning path was designed to introduce some basic skills related to problem-solving and coding, such as algorithm design, logical connectives, and if-then-else and iterative statements. As previously mentioned, to improve motivation and engagement, the Arduino Uno logic board, the IDE[2] Scratch for Arduino, and some wooden models built for this specific purpose were used during the learning activities.

The activities were defined using the *learning by doing* and *tinkering* approaches, in order to involve students during the teaching process. The proactive dimension allows students to participate actively during learning activities, thus stimulating both motivation and engagement (Pesare, Roselli, & Rossano, 2017). In addition, to

---

[2] Integrated Development Environment is a software application that offers facilities useful to code in a defined language.

let the students acquire knowledge and skills by interacting with real objects, the challenge proposed was to build a circuit and a program to handle a train level crossing and two traffic lights. For these reasons, some wooden models were built to show the results of the coding activities.

The eight activities (Table 6.1) have increasing difficulty levels, and usually the output of one activity is the input for the next one.

Table 6.1 List of the designed and implemented learning activities

Activity name and No.	Learning objective	Level of difficulty	Instruments
Activity #1 LED controlled by switch	Introducing the electronic components of Arduino	Easy	1 LED 1 220 ohm resistor 1 switch Wires
Activity #2 Blinking LED	Introducing the algorithm	Easy	1 LED 1 220 ohm resistor Wires
Activity #3 Blinking LED more than once	Introducing the repeat statement	Medium	1 LED 1 220 ohm resistor Wires
Activity #4 Turn on and turn off the LED	Introducing the if-then-else statement	Medium	1 LED 3 220 ohm resistors 2 switches Wires
Activity #5 AND operator	Introducing the AND logical operator	Medium	1 LED 3 220 ohm resistors 2 switches Wires
Activity #6 OR operator	Introducing the OR logical operator	Medium	1 LED 3 220 ohm resistors 2 switches Wires
Activity #7 The traffic light	Applying the knowledge and skills acquired to a real case study	Difficult	6 LED 6 220 ohm resistors Wires
Activity #8 Rail crossing	Applying the knowledge and skills acquired to a real case study	Very difficult	2 LED 2 220 ohm resistors 1 servo motor 2 switches Wires

6.3.1 Activity #1: LED Controlled by a Switch

This was the first and easiest activity, for the students to have the first contact with electronic components. The main aim of the activity was to introduce Arduino board and each single component of the circuit. For this reason, in this activity no coding actions were required to handle the task.

The Arduino board was used as a power source. When connected to a USB port or to an external battery, Arduino provides 5-volt power between its 5 V pin and the Ground (GND) pin. The circuit lights up the LED when the switch is pressed.

The circuit to be produced as output is shown in Fig. 6.1.

What Students Learn
In this activity the student learns the components of Arduino and how to assemble them. The task is to build a circuit able to turn on a LED when a button is pressed.

How to Build the Circuit
1. Using a red wire, connect the 5 V pin of Arduino board with a line of the breadboard.
2. Connect the Arduino ground to the line near to the black wire. Usually, the red wire is for power and the black for Ground.
3. Install the switch across the slot in the middle of the breadboard.
4. Use a 220 Ohm resistor to connect the power from one side of the switch. On the other side of the button, connect the anode (longer foot) of the LED. Then connect the cathode (short foot) of the LED to Ground using an electrical wire.
5. Connect the USB cable to the Arduino.
6. When everything is ready, press the button and the LED will turn on.

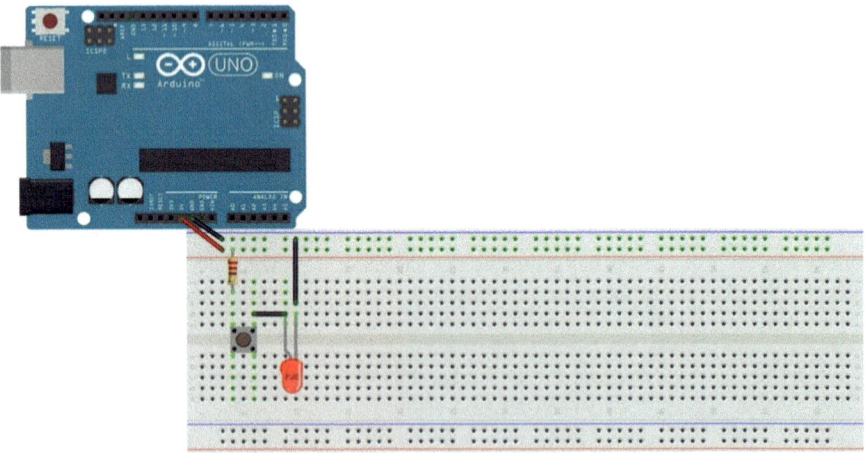

Fig. 6.1 Circuit of Activity #1

6.3.2 Activity #2: Blinking LED

To introduce the algorithm notion, this activity proposes a simple challenge: to build a circuit and a program that allow the LED to blink when the user pushes the spacebar on the keyboard. Starting from the experience in the previous activity, the next circuit can be easily built. The circuit to be produced as output is shown in Fig. 6.2.

What Students Learn
The activity was used to introduce the notion of algorithm. Students built the circuit together with the teacher. Unlike the previous circuit, the LED should blink and should be controlled by the spacebar of the keyboard. In this case, the teacher explained that a short program is required to control the LED. After a brief discussion, students were able to individuate the actions that should be coded in Scratch: press the spacebar, the LED lights up, and after a preset time, it turns off.

How to Build the Circuit
In the previous circuit, the anode of the LED was connected to 5 V pin, and a switch was used to turn the LED on and off. In this case, the LED has to be controlled by the code; thus it has to be connected to pin 13.

The instructions are the following:

1. Use the red wire to connect the anode of the LED with the digital output 13 of Arduino.
2. Connect the cathode of the LED to Arduino Ground (black wire).

Coding with Scratch
The first thing is to define when Arduino should start to execute the code, and then the LED will need to be switched on for a few seconds, and then it will turn off. The algorithm will be the following:

1. When space key is pressed;
2. Switch on pin 13.
3. Wait for 1 second.
4. Switch off pin 13.

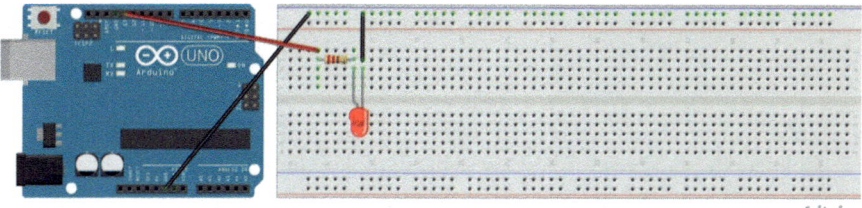

Fig. 6.2 Circuit of activity #2 and activity #3

6.3.3 Activity #3: Blinking LED more than Once

Starting from the algorithm defined in activity #2, the students were asked to build a program able to turn on and turn off the LED more than once. The circuit is the same as in the previous activity (Fig. 6.2).

In the coding activity, the iterative statement "repeat" has to be introduced.

What Students Learn
In this activity the repeat instruction is introduced. The teacher asked the student to modify the previous algorithm to let the LED blink more than once. Students modified the program using the new instruction: Repeat x times.

Coding with Scratch
The algorithm will be the following:

1. When space key is pressed;
2. Repeat the following instructions 10 times:
    (a) Switch on pin 13.
    (b) Wait for 1 second.
    (c) Switch off pin 13.

6.3.4 Activity #4: Turn On and Turn Off the LED

This activity was defined to introduce another key element of structured programming: the if-then-else statement. In this case, the task was to define a circuit and a program that can turn on a LED when a switch is pressed and turn it off when another switch is pressed.

What Students Learn
The activity introduces the if-then-else statement. The teacher explained that in some cases the program must behave differently depending on the different inputs received. In this case, the LED should be turned on or off by two different switches. When Switch1 is pressed the LED should turn on; when Switch2 is pressed the LED should turn off. Students and teachers built the circuit and then define the program in Scratch. To make the topic of the if-then-else statement easier, in this first algorithm, only the "then" branch was used.

How to Build the Circuit
Using the experience gained in the previous activities, it is possible to easily build this circuit that is a little more complex than the previous one (Fig. 6.3):

1. Connect the anode of the LED with the digital output 13 of Arduino. Use a resistor to connect the LED to the board.
2. Connect the cathode of the LED to the Arduino Ground (black wire).

3. Connect one switch to pin 2 of the Arduino board and the other to pin 3. The resistor must be used for these connections.
4. Use the black wire to connect the pin of both the switches to the Arduino Ground.

Coding with Scratch
The algorithm will be the following:

1. If Switch1 is pressed:

    (a) Then turn on pin 13.

2. If Switch2 is pressed:

    (a) Then turn off pin 13.

6.3.5 Activity #5: AND Operator

Starting from the algorithm and the circuit (Fig. 6.3) defined in the previous activity, the students were asked to build a program able to turn on the LED only if both switches are pushed; otherwise the LED will be turned off.

What Students Learn
The activity is useful to acquire knowledge about the AND logic operator that in programming is basic to build complex conditions. The teacher introduced the AND operator using the Italian language. For example, all students that have blonde hair

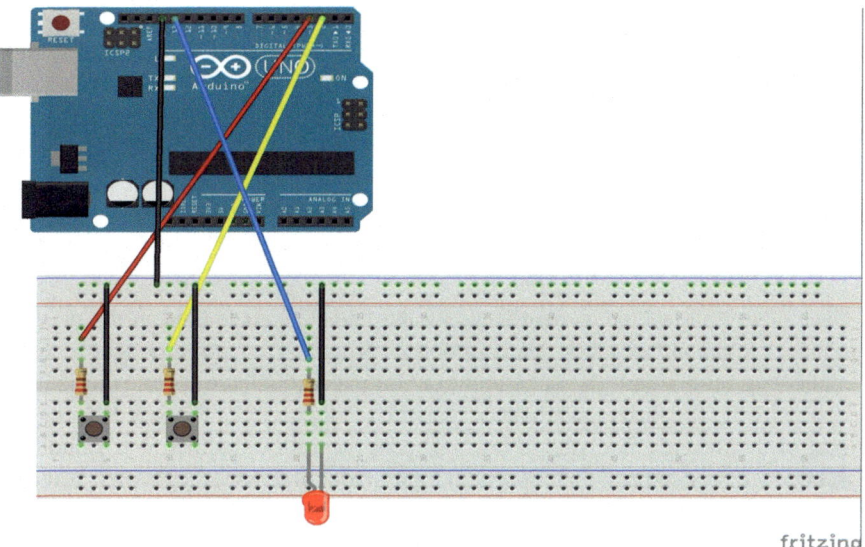

Fig. 6.3 Circuit for activity #4, activity #5, and activity #6

and a blue t-shirt can use the smartphone. Then the teacher asked the students to edit the previous algorithm to turn on the LED if both switches were pressed and turn it off otherwise. In this way, the else statement was introduced.

Coding with Scratch
In this activity the algorithm will be the following:

1. If Switch1 AND Switch2 are pressed:
   (a) Then turn on pin 13.
   (b) Else turn off pin 13.

6.3.6 Activity #6: OR Operator

This activity is very similar to the previous one. It is important in order to allow the students to understand the difference between the two logical operators. In this case the task was to turn the LED on if one of the two switches was pressed.

What Students Learn
After the AND operator, also the OR operator was introduced. Again the teacher gave some examples using the Italian language. For example, the students that have blonde hair or a blue t-shirt can use the smartphone. Then the teacher asked the students to edit the previous algorithm to turn on the LED if one switch was pressed and turn it off otherwise.

Coding with Scratch
In this activity the algorithm will be the following:

1. If Switch1 OR Switch2 is pressed:
   (a) Then turn on pin 13.
   (b) Else turn off pin 13.

6.3.7 Activity #7: The Traffic Lights

This activity allows the student to apply the knowledge acquired in the previous activities to a real task. The idea is to build a program to manage two traffic lights controlling a crossroads. Looking at the circuit in Fig. 6.4 there are two traffic lights T_1 and T_2. The program should turn on the red light of T_1 (Rosso_1) and green light of T_2 (Verde_2). After a few seconds, the yellow light of T_2 (Giallo_2) should be turned on, and then the green light of T_1 and the red light of T_2 should be turned on. The other lights must be turned off.

What Students Learn

The activity was designed to let the student apply all the knowledge and skills acquired in the previous activities. The task was very challenging: simulate a traffic light. This is a very common activity when Arduino is used for education (Plaza et al., 2018). Following the constructionism approach and to make the problem-solving process simpler, a wooden model was used to see its effects on real objects (Fig. 6.5). After a discussion, students define the algorithm to control the traffic light and code it in Scratch.

How to Build the Circuit

The circuit in this activity is composed of two groups of LEDs that have to be connected following the experience made in the previous activities;

1. The anode of LEDs of T_1 should be connected following this pattern:

   (a) Verde_1 with pin 13
   (b) Giallo_1 with pin 12
   (c) Rosso_1 with pin 11

2. The anode of LEDs of T_2 should be connected following this pattern:

   (a) Verde_2 with pin 9
   (b) Giallo_2 with pin 6
   (c) Rosso_2 with pin 5

As usually a resistor should be used for these connections. The cathode of each LED has to be connected to the Arduino Ground.

Coding with Scratch

The algorithm in Activity #7 is very long, since there are many code rows, but basically it is very simple:

1. Repeat 10 times the following instruction:

   (a) Turn on pin 11 (Rosso_1 red light of T_1).
   (b) Turn on pin 9 (Verde_2 green light of T_2).

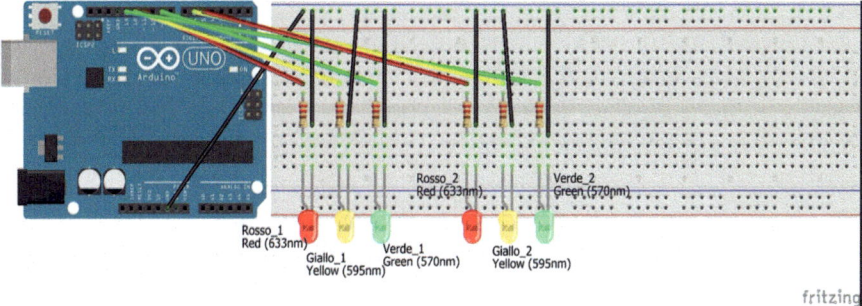

Fig. 6.4 Circuit for Activity #7

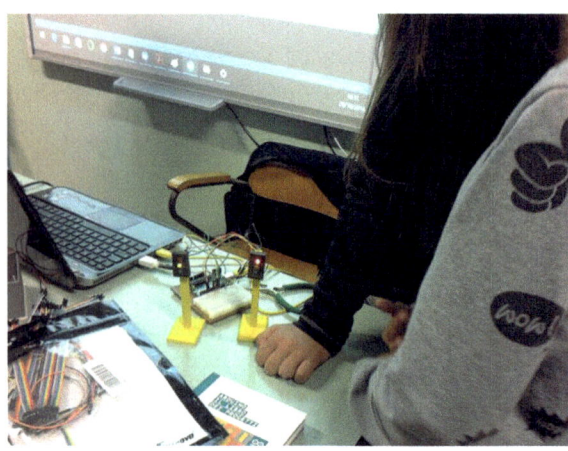

Fig. 6.5 Wooden model of Traffic lights (Rossano et al., 2018)

   (c) Wait for 5 seconds.
   (d) Turn off pin 9 (Verde_2 green light of T_2).
   (e) Turn on pin 6 (Giallo_2 yellow light of T_2).
   (f) Wait for 2 seconds.
   (g) Turn off pin 6 (Giallo_2 yellow light of T_2).
   (h) Turn on pin 5 (Rosso_2 red light of T_2).
   (i) Turn off pin 11 (Rosso_1 red light of T_1).
   (j) Turn on pin 13 (Verde_1 green light of T_1).
   (k) Wait for 5 seconds.
   (l) Turn off pin 13 (Verde_1 green light of T_1).
   (m) Turn on pin 12 (Giallo_1 yellow light of T_1).

This group of instructions will be repeated 10 times or can be repeated until the user presses a button.

6.3.8 Activity #8: Rail Crossing

In order to make the learning process more engaging, another real-world problem was proposed. The aim of Activity #8 is to build a program to control a rail crossing (Fig. 6.6). The scenario is: the user presses a button to close the bar, while the red lights start flashing. When the train has passed, the user presses another button to open the bar. The red lights will continue to blink until the bar is completely open.

What Students Learn
This activity is very complex and allows the student to apply all knowledge and skills acquired in the previous activities. The teacher using the wooden model illustrates how the rail crossing works. When Switch1 is pressed, the bar should be opened; when the Switch2 is pressed, the bar should be closed, and, in both cases, the traffic light has to blink for 10 times.

How to Build the Circuit

The circuit in this activity is the most complex (Fig. 6.7), but to engage students during the learning process, it is necessary to propose challenges with increasing difficulty. The circuit can be built using the following instructions:

1. Connect the switch to open the level crossing bar to pin 3.
2. Connect the switch to close the level crossing bar to pin 2.
3. Connect the positive pole of servo motor to the 5 V pin of Arduino, the negative pole to the Ground, and the controller to pin 8.
4. Connect two LEDs to pins 10 and 11.
5. Connect the Ground to each component using the black wire, as in the previous activities.

Coding with Scratch

The program of this final activity allows the application of all the programming structures used in the previous activities. The aim is to enable students to understand the programmers' work better.

The algorithm of the Activity #8 is the following:

1. Repeat the following instruction ad infinitum:

    (a) If Switch1 is pressed, then:

       (i) Open the level crossing bar.
       (ii) Repeat the following instructions 10 times:

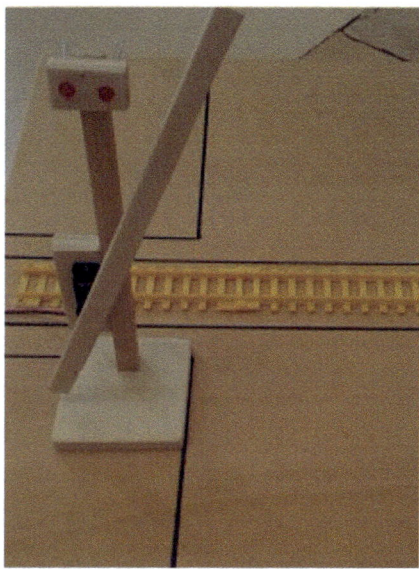
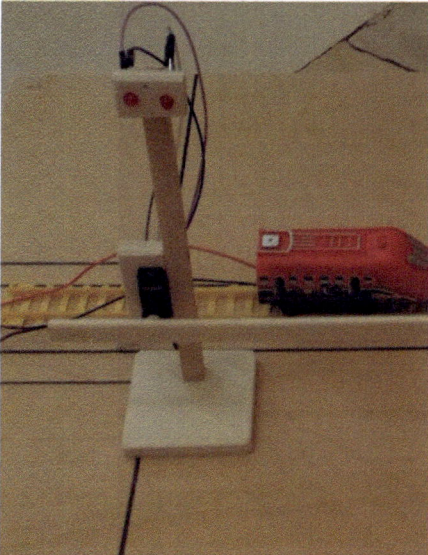

Fig. 6.6 The wooden rail crossing activity model (Rossano et al., 2018)

1. Turn off pin 11.
2. Turn on pin 10.
3. Wait 2 seconds.
4. Turn on pin 11.
5. Turn off pin 10.

(b) If Switch2 is pressed, then:

(i) Close the level crossing bar.
(ii) Repeat the following instructions 10 times:

1. Turn off pin 11.
2. Turn on pin 10.
3. Wait 2 seconds.
4. Turn on pin 11.
5. Turn off pin 10.

Fig. 6.7 Circuit for Activity#8

6.4 The User Test

6.4.1 Instruments

The user test was carried out in the school laboratory using 20 Pentium 4, equipped with Windows XP Professional. The Arduino board was used with all the necessary components listed in Table 6.1. The Scratch 4 Arduino (S4A) tutorial was installed on these machines. Two wooden models used in activity #7 and activity #8 were built before the experiment.

6.4.2 Sample and Design

The study involved 25 students (11 girls and 14 boys) of the third grade of a middle school in Terlizzi, a town near Bari (Italy). All the participants were 13 years old. Together with the teacher, we chose not to inform the participants about the activity in advance, in order to study their reaction and interest. None of the students had ever worked with Arduino and Scratch. A pre-test and post-test design was performed to evaluate the learning effectiveness of the activities; thus, all the participants were exposed to the experimental condition.

6.4.3 Procedure

Initially, all the participants underwent a pre-test consisting of questions to collect both demographic data and exercises to measure background knowledge related to the concepts of algorithm, logical connectives, and coding. The tests were anonymous. At the end of the pre-test, the students participated in the learning activities. The eight learning activities were distributed over 2 weeks. Activities #1, #2, #3, and #4 were completed in the first week and in the second Activities #5, #6, and #7. Activity #8 was only presented to the class, but no actions were required from the student's side. All the activities were presented by a researcher who, using a participatory approach, taught the students how to build circuits, how to build the algorithm using a flowchart, and how to use S4A. The researcher encouraged the students to participate actively, letting them discuss among themselves whenever a decision had to be made.

A few days after the experimental phase, all the participants were given a post-test structured like the pre-test. It was aimed at assessing the improvement in students' knowledge. In addition, some questions were added to measure the students' appreciation of the teaching approach.

6.4.4 Data Collection

The pre-test was composed of 18 questions. The first part of the questionnaire was used to discover the sex and age of the participants, if they have a PC and how much they use it, if they are attracted by technologies, and if they know the programmers' job. The second section consists of six questions aimed at assessing background knowledge about computational thinking and coding. Specifically, there were questions measuring knowledge about algorithm definition and some exercises to measure the ability to build an algorithm. In this case, some algorithms related to daily activities were proposed. For example, the students were asked to put in order a sequence of actions for brushing their teeth and then to write the actions needed to make a phone call with a smartphone. Other questions measured the students' knowledge of logical connectives AND and OR. In this case, using the image of a clown with colorful clothes, students were asked to define the truth values of some statements. Examples of statements were: Has the clown a yellow hat and an orange ribbon? Has the clown a red nose or a blue ribbon? Some other questions were used to measure the students' knowledge about flowchart diagrams.

Like the pre-test, the post-test was composed of two sections. The first one measured the learning improvements in each participant, and the second focused on collecting opinions about the new teaching method used for these activities.

6.4.5 Data Analysis

STEM Interest

As previously mentioned, the first section of the pre-test was composed of questions that let the researcher know the sample.

The pre-test reveals that 24 out 25 students have got a PC at home. Firstly, students were asked to self-assess their ability using a score from 1 to 10. The self-assessment of the e-skills revealed that male students have higher ability in using the PC. Since it is a self-assessment, the values should be taken into consideration carefully, but this pointed out one of the main issues related to the gender gap in STEM (Science, Technologies, Engineering and Math) degree courses (Beede et al., 2011). In our investigation, it seems that girls underestimate their tech skills (Fig. 6.8).

In order to make some qualitative evaluation of this assessment, the next question asked how long students usually spend during the day studying or playing with the PC. The whole mean is 1.5 hours a day. Spreading the results, the male students spend 2 hours, and female students only 1 hour on the PC. This could also explain the self-assessment of PC confidence: the males use the PC more than the females. Another difference between the genders is also seen in the typical uses of the PC; the males answered that they use the PC mainly to play and the females mainly to study.

Many of the students do not like subjects such as mathematics, science, and technology; as a matter of fact, the average scores for the question "On a scale from 1 to 10, how much are you interested in studying mathematics?" was 7.25. Also in this case, the mean of males (7.8) was higher than the mean of females (6.8). The teacher confirmed that their average grade was 5.5/10. As regards programming, only one student knew the binary system, no one knew the programmer's job, and only three students had programmed something. Actually, only one student had used Scratch, other two students had programmed a TV remote control. This means that the word "programming" has been misunderstood by the students.

The gender gap is also evident in the question "On a scale from 1 to 10, how much are you interested in technologies?". The whole mean value was 7.8, but 8.6 for male students and 6.7 for female students. In order to measure whether the proposed learning activities were able to promote interest in STEMs, the post-test asked the same question again. The data analysis revealed that something has changed (Fig. 6.9). The number of students that self-assess the interest in technology with a higher value increases. In the pre-test four students evaluated their interest using a score of 3; all of them improved the evaluation in the post-test assigning a score between 6 and 7. This was confirmed by the average of the score which increased from 7.4 to 8.4.

It is interesting that also the average of females improved, passing from 7.8 to 8.3.

Computational Thinking Skills
Concerning their previous knowledge, students had great difficulty in building the algorithms. Some of them were able to build the algorithm only guided by the tutor and/or the teacher. Both in the pre-test and post-test, exercises of increasing difficulty were proposed to measure the ability to build algorithms. The exercises were defined and evaluated together with the teacher. The results, measured with a score between 0 and 10, are reported in Fig. 6.10.

In the post-test the whole sample obtained assessment between 7 and 10. The average score increased from 5.96 in the pre-test to 8.84 in the post-test. Even the comparison between the background and acquired knowledge about logic

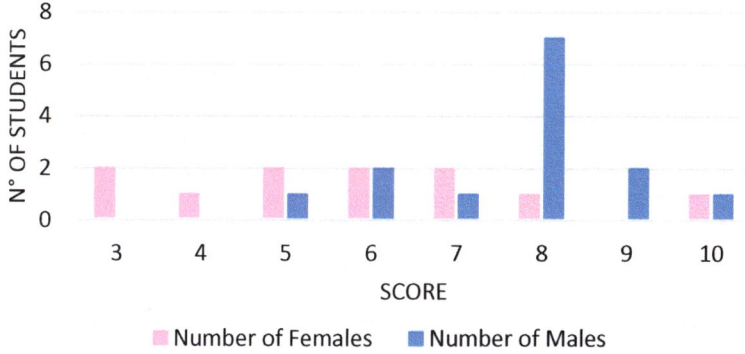

Fig. 6.8 How confident are you using your PC?

connectives was very interesting. As Fig. 6.11 shows, the evaluations in the post-test were higher than the evaluations in the pre-test. The average rises from 5.6 to 9.36.

Splitting the results in terms of males and females, interesting aspects can be seen. The algorithm skills of both males and females improved, but as shown in Fig. 6.12, the females had a better performance in the post-test.

For the logic connectives (Fig. 6.13), the situation is more balanced: both male and female students improved their knowledge, and no significant difference was noted between them.

Teaching Approach Evaluation

The next step of the evaluation focused on understanding if the teaching approach was appreciated by the students. A 3-point Likert scale questionnaire was submitted to the students after the 2 weeks. The use of Arduino was appreciated by 19 out 25 students. The girls were more enthusiastic than the boys (Fig. 6.14).

The data gathered on the other questions, to measure the appreciation of the learning activities (Fig. 6.15), show that almost the whole sample appreciated the method adopted.

Many students, 21 out of 25, stated that they had no difficulties in carrying out the proposed activities thanks to the adoption of learning by doing and tinkering approaches. By contrast, many students stated that using Scratch was hard (Fig. 6.16).

6.5 Conclusions and Discussions

The importance of Computational Thinking at all levels of education has been largely recognized in the recent years. Problem-solving is one of the basic abilities to understand the environment, to identify things that should be changed to improve a situation, and to figure out solutions to face a problem. The Digital Agenda for Europe (DAE) defined 11 actions to support technology use and the development of

Fig. 6.9 The self-assessment of students' interest in technology, measured before and after the proposed activities

digital competences in education (https://ec.europa.eu/education/education-in-the-eu/digital-education-action-plan_en). Among the actions there is the spread of school participation in EU Code Week, which is a community movement which promotes Computational Thinking, coding, and the creative and critical use of digital technologies. This trend was adopted by the Italian Public Education Systems that defined the PNSD (National Plan for Digital Schools) in which coding and CT are listed among the basic skills to be acquired from childhood. In this context, the research aims at introducing CT and coding using the Arduino board. In particular, a learning path composed of eight activities was defined to let students acquire such basic knowledge and abilities. The idea was to use a teaching method that would enable students to be actively involved during the learning process and arouse their interest in technological issues.

The pilot study conducted in a junior high school confirms that the learning activities were engaging and motivating for both the students and the teacher. All the students actively participated in all the proposed tasks; the teacher was surprised by some of them who usually show less interest in all kinds of activities. This confirms that technologies can promote effective interactions and participation in learning activities (Plantamura et al., 2004).

The analysis of the data confirmed that the learning path was effective in terms of knowledge and skill improvement. All the participants learnt basic issues related to programming and circuits. One of the most important results of this experience was the improvement of the students' interest in technologies. The majority of people are interested in using technology since it allows them to simplify process and to make it faster. By contrast, few people are interested in understanding how it works, probably since it is considered too difficult for most of them. The basic idea of this research work is to allow students to interact with circuits and technologies by discovering that they are easy to manage and interesting.

The side effect that the pilot study has highlighted is related to the gender gap. Currently, there is a lack of women in STEM. The scientific communities are studying this phenomenon in order to understand it and fill the gap. In our study, the female students, for example, stated that they were not so confident with the use of

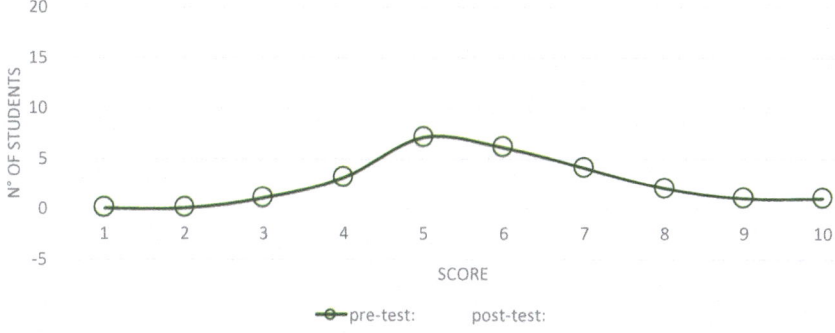

Fig. 6.10 Algorithm-building skills: comparison of the assessment between pre-test and post-test

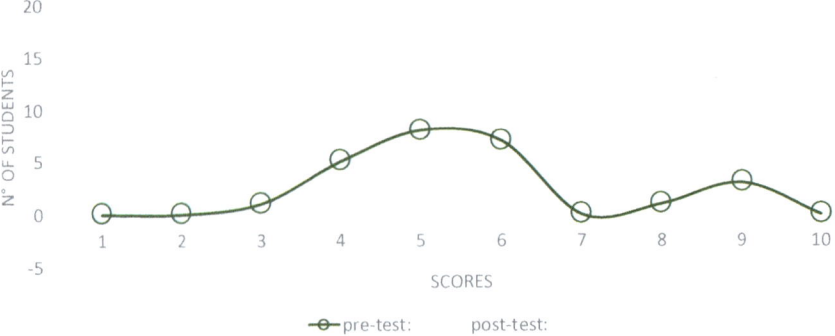

Fig. 6.11 Knowledge of AND and OR: comparison of the assessment between pre-test and post-test

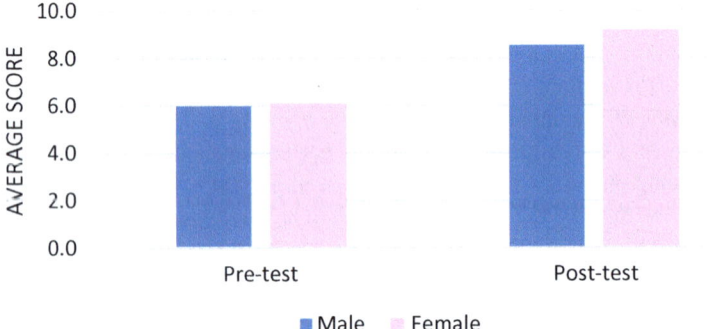

Fig. 6.12 Comparison of the progress of male and female students in acquiring algorithm-building skills

the PC. Probably they are not interested at all in using the PC (Fig. 6.8) since they do not play games. Instead the girls prefer to use the smartphone to access social networks and share contents. After the learning activities, all the participants improved their interest in technologies, but the girls' level of improvement was higher. The comparison of pre-test and post-test exercises reveals that girls obtained better grades. In our opinion, it is essential to encourage female students to study STEM to let them learn technologies during their educational path. This could be a starting point to improve their interest and promote the hope that the number of girls studying scientific disciplines will increase in the near future.

The main limitation of the proposed activity was the strict timetable. The planned lessons path should be carried out in at least 1 month, scheduling two meetings per week. This will enable students to better understand all the matters dealt with and to become autonomous in doing the exercises. Moreover, the engagement and motivation dimensions were not measured with standard questionnaire, such as the UES (O'Brien, Cairns, & Hall, 2018), but only registered by the observer during the experiment.

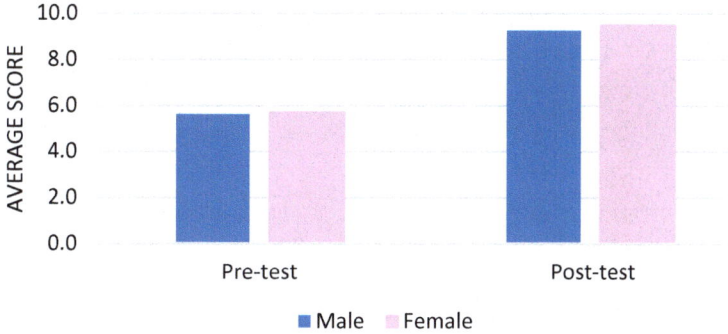

Fig. 6.13 Comparison of the progress of male and female students in acquiring logic connective knowledge

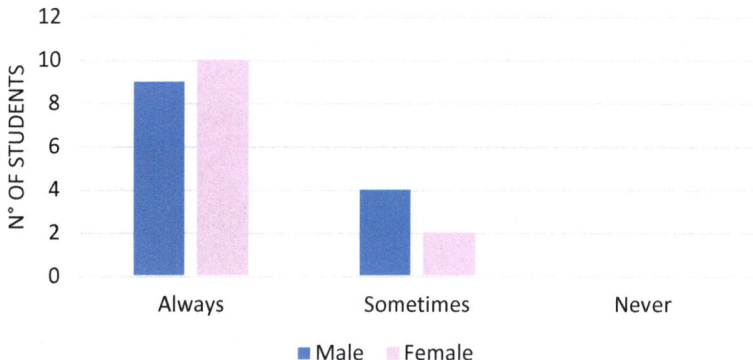

Fig. 6.14 Did you like using Arduino?

The next future investigations would be carried out with a larger sample to measure the effectiveness of the defined learning path without the Arduino board. The expected results should confirm that the use of artifacts and physical devices can improve engagement and motivation and thus learning effectiveness.

Acknowledgements We would like to thank the junior high school "Gesmundo – Moro – Fiore" in Terlizzi (Ba), Italy, in particular the principal Maria Chiapparino, the teacher Silvana Chiapparino, and finally all students involved in the study.

References

Beede, D. N., Julian, T. A., Langdon, D., McKittrick, G., Khan, B., & Doms, M. E. (2011), Women in STEM: A gender gap to innovation. *Economics and statistics administration*, Issue Brief No. 04–11.

Brackmann, C. P., Román-González, M., Robles, G., Moreno-León, J., Casali, A., & Barone, D. (2017). Development of computational thinking skills through unplugged activities in pri-

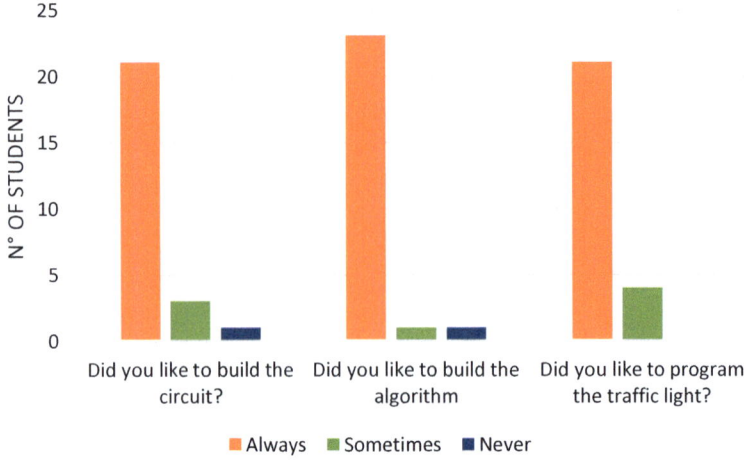

Fig. 6.15 Appreciation of the teaching method

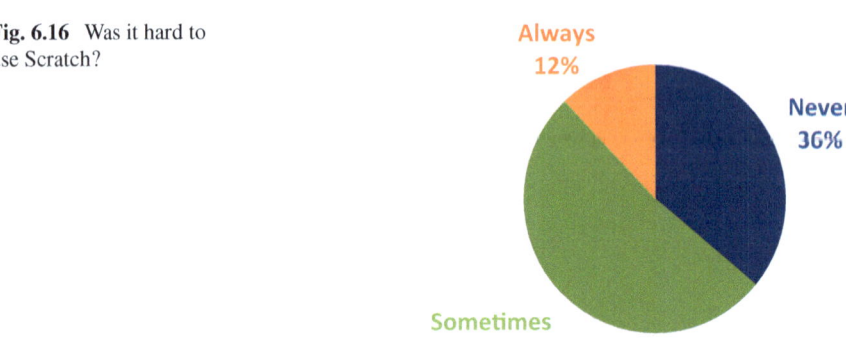

Fig. 6.16 Was it hard to use Scratch?

mary school. In *Proceedings of the 12th workshop on primary and secondary computing education* (pp. 65–72).

Burke, Q. (2012). The markings of a new pencil: Introducing programming-as-writing in the middle school classroom. *Journal of Media Literacy Education, 4*(2), 121–135.

Cabo, C., & Lansiquot, R. D. (2016). Integrating creative writing and computational thinking to develop interdisciplinary connections. In *Proceedings of the 2016 ASEE annual conference & exposition*.

Cho, E., Lee, K., Cherniak, S., & Jung, S. E. (2017). Heterogeneous associations of second-graders' learning in robotics class. *Technology, Knowledge and Learning, 22*(3), 465–483.

Choi, B., Jung, J., & Baek, Y. (2013). In what way can technology enhance student learning? A preliminary study of Technology Supported learning in Mathematics. In R. McBride & M. Searson (Eds.), *Proceedings of SITE 2013—Society for information technology & teacher education international conference* (pp. 3–9). New Orleans, LA: Association for the Advancement of Computing in Education (AACE).

Di Lieto, M. C., Inguaggiato, E., Castro, E., Cecchi, F., Cioni, G., Dell'Omo, M., et al. (2017). Educational robotics intervention on executive functions in preschool children: A pilot study. *Computers in Human Behavior, 71*, 16–23.

Díaz-Lauzurica, B., & Moreno-Salinas, D. (2019). Computational thinking and robotics: A teaching experience in compulsory secondary education with students with high degree of apathy and demotivation. *Sustainability, 11*(18), 5109.

González, Y. A. C., & Muñoz-Repiso, A. G. V. (2018). A robotics-based approach to foster programming skills and computational thinking: Pilot experience in the classroom of early childhood education. In *ACM international conference proceeding series* (pp. 41–45). Association for Computing Machinery.

Haak, V., Abke, J., & Borgeest, K. (2018). Conception of a Lego Mindstorms EV3 simulation for teaching C in computer science courses. In *2018 IEEE global engineering education conference (EDUCON)* (pp. 478–483). IEEE.

Harel, I. E., & Papert, I. S. E. (1991). *Constructionism*. Norwood, NJ: Ablex Publishing.

Israel, M., Pearson, J. N., Tapia, T., Wherfel, Q. M., & Reese, G. (2015). Supporting all learners in school-wide computational thinking: A cross-case qualitative analysis. *Computers and Education, 82*, 263–279.

Lye, S. Y., & Koh, J. H. L. (2014). Review on teaching and learning of computational thinking through programming: What is next for K-12? *Computers in Human Behavior, 41*, 51–61.

Maloney, J., Resnick, M., Rusk, N., Silverman, B. S., & Eastmond, E. (2010). The scratch programming language and environment. *ACM Transactions on Computing Education (TOCE), 10*(4), 16.

Marques, A., Guimarães, C., & Salgado, A. (2019). Scratch 3 – Beginners programming course in 3rd year of primary school. In J. Machado, F. Soares, & G. Veiga (Eds.), *Innovation, engineering and entrepreneurship. HELIX 2018. Lecture notes in electrical engineering* (Vol. 505, pp. 1160–1166). Cham, Switzerland: Springer.

Merino-Armero, J. M., González-Calero, J. A., Cózar-Gutiérrez, R., & Villena-Taranilla, R. (2018). Computational thinking initiation. An experience with robots in primary education. *Journal of Research in Science, Mathematics and Technology Education, 1*(2), 181–206.

O'Brien, H. L., Cairns, P., & Hall, M. (2018). A practical approach to measuring user engagement with the refined user engagement scale (UES) and new UES short form. *International Journal of Human-Computer Studies, 112*, 28–39.

Papert, S. (1980). *Mindstorms: Children, computers, and powerful ideas*. New York: Basic Books.

Papert, S. (1991). Situating constructionism. In I. Harel & S. Papert (Eds.), *Constructionism* (pp. 1–11). Norwood, NJ: Ablex.

Pesare, E., Roselli, T., & Rossano, V. (2017). Engagement in social learning: Detecting engagement in online communities of practice. In *Advances in human factors, business management, training and education* (pp. 151–158). Cham, Switzerland: Springer.

Plantamura, P., Roselli, T., & Rossano, V. (2004). Can a CSCL environment promote effective interaction?. In *IEEE International Conference on Advanced Learning Technologies (ICALT)*. (pp. 675–677). Los Alamitos, CA: IEEE.

Plaza, P., Sancristobal, E., Carro, G., Castro, M., Blazquez, M., & Peixoto, A. (2018). Traffic lights through multiple robotic educational tools. In *2018 IEEE global engineering education conference (EDUCON)* (pp. 2015–2020). Los Alamitos, CA: IEEE.

Resnick, M., Maloney, J., Monroy-Hernández, A., Rusk, N., Eastmond, E., Brennan, K., et al. (2009). Scratch: Programming for all. *Communications of the ACM, 52*(11), 60–67.

Rossano, V., Roselli, T., & Quercia, G. (2018). Coding and computational thinking with Arduino. In *Proceedings of the 15th international conference on cognition AND exploratory learning in the digital age (CELDA 2018)* (pp. 263–269). Lisbon, Portugal: IADIS Press.

Siegle, D. (2017). Technology: Encouraging creativity and problem solving through coding. *Gifted Child Today, 40*(2), 117–123.

Silva, L. R., da Silva, A. P., Toda, A., & Isotani, S. (2018). Impact of teaching approaches to computational thinking on high school students: A systematic mapping. In *2018 IEEE 18th international conference on advanced learning technologies (ICALT)* (pp. 285–289). Los Alamitos, CA: IEEE.

Umbleja, K. (2017). Learning to program with Lego Mindstorms–difference between K-12 students and adults. In *International conference on interactive collaborative learning* (pp. 447–458). Cham, Switzerland: Springer.

Vaca-Cárdenas, L. A., Bertacchini, F., Tavernise, A., Gabriele, L., Valenti, A., Olmedo, D. E., et al. (2015). Coding with scratch: The design of an educational setting for elementary pre-service teachers. In *Interactive collaborative learning (ICL)* (pp. 1171–1177). Los Alamitos, CA: IEEE.

Wing, J. (2006). Computational thinking. *Communications of the ACM, 49*(3), 33–36.

Wing, J. M. (2008). Computational thinking and thinking about computing. *Philosophical Transactions of the Royal Society A: Mathematical, Physical and Engineering Sciences, 366*(1881), 3717–3725.

Wolz, U., Stone, M., Pearson, K., Pulimood, S. M., & Switzer, M. (2011). Computational thinking and expository writing in the middle school. *ACM Transactions on Computing Education (TOCE), 11*(2), 1–22.

Wu, Y., de Vries, C., & Dunsworth, Q. (2018). Using LEGO kits to teach higher level problem solving skills in system dynamics: A case study. *Advances in Engineering Education, 6*(3), n3.

Chapter 7
Learning Through a "Route Planner": Human-Computer Information Retrieval for Automatic Assessment

Michele Fioravera, Marina Marchisio, Luigi Di Caro, and Sergio Rabellino

7.1 Introduction

The need for organizing and dispatching digital contents grows concurrently with the development of educational environments (Steinberger, 2017). This is especially relevant in STEM (science, technology, engineering, and mathematics) education, due to the lack of widely accepted standardizations (Watt, 2016). "Online instructors" (course developers, instructional designers, teachers, tutors) may save time by sharing and reusing e-learning materials, and these savings may activate chances for enhancing individual students' guidance. Guided by supporting agents such as researchers and institutions, they can connect themselves in "virtual communities" to learn new educational supplements for their students, as well as to communicate with peers.

In a virtual community scenario, where learners can take advantage from a variety of educational resources, a "Route Planner" is a system providing additional materials' recommendation – possibly created by different teachers – to students, on top of their scores received from automatic assessment activities. Strategies for enhancing self-paced and self-regulated learning processes via route planning systems integrated to virtual learning communities are discussed in what follows.

Providing students "more" materials means starting to consider the "domain model" before the "learner model" (Bourekkache & Kazar, 2009): the basis for prescribing optimal content should rely primarily on teachers intentions – or, more specifically, on the shared intentions of the instructors' community – that is a

---

M. Fioravera (✉) · M. Marchisio
Department of Mathematics, University of Pisa, Turin (TO), Italy
e-mail: michele.fioravera@unito.it; marina.marchisio@unito.it

L. Di Caro · S. Rabellino
Department of Computer Science, University of Turin, Turin (TO), Italy
e-mail: luigi.dicaro@unito.it; sergio.rabellino@unito.it

"common" framework of learning objectives. To this aim, some techniques from learning analytics, educational data mining, and artificial intelligence may not be feasible solutions for route planning due to the unavailability of "large amount" of information data (developed by teachers). These studies focus primarily on giving instructors information about student performance (Nyland, 2017). Creating an adaptive system may be a further step, which would require an accurate diagnosis of learner characteristics (Shute & Zapata-Rivera, 2012).

Technologies and methodologies for extracting information from online resources shared within online communities are here discussed. In particular, this contribution focuses on the research problem of linking automatic assessment items by analyzing natural language descriptions about students' requirement and learning goals. This research aims at "generating navigable maps", that is "automatically planning routes" choosable by any learning user.

7.1.1 Participating to Virtual Communities

In a virtual community, learners belong to virtual classes held by instructors; these in turn belong to a community of practice, supported by experts in instructional design. Collaboratively working as "learners," instructors realize, interchange, and disseminate educational assets; since they work based on similar learning objectives, students could have high-quality digital contents prepared by more teachers than those who will ever "physically" meet. Nevertheless, such online environment is still affected by downsides related to the "offline communication," which reduce authors' effort in rapidly disseminating (among peers and, consequently, among students) learning objects: the number of contents "reaching" students through virtual classes necessarily depends on the time available to their own teacher for choosing, controlling, and designing coherent learning paths. Moreover, a potential (and paradoxical) problem relates to complexity management of growing repositories: as the number of resources produced and shared increase, it could become more difficult for each teacher to find what "really" needs. For example, two teachers willing to share course units will need to distinguish interesting from irrelevant parts, to translate any subjective notation, and to remove possible duplicates. Complexity of those operations could increase if a raising number of teachers interact with each other.

7.1.2 Moving Learners Through Automatic Assessment

Each learner needs a teacher mentoring to find and select appropriate learning contents, and has different learning habits – which are not completely predictable. An automated assessment system provides instructors with the power of creating and deploying automatically graded tests, which provides feedback moving the learner "forward or backward" (in abstract "learning maps" conceptualized/intended by the teacher/author) according to his/her own live score. New communication means among instructors within a virtual community may radically augment the possibilities for connecting shared materials for automatic assessment without further human supervision. Automatizing this process is referred as "route planning" in the context of formative assessment.

7.1.3 Integrating Technologies to Virtual Communities

Integrations to virtual learning communities can support instructors in sharing and reusing learning assets for automatic formative assessment in STEM education. Recent researches (Barana et al., 2018a) link providers' cooperation (clarification and sharing of reusable learning assets by instructors) with technological-enhanced formative assessment possibilities (automatic generation of learning maps for students' remediation). Those strategies provide students with as more contents as possible and requiring the less possible effort from their own instructor. Three main aspects for realizing such systems are as follows:

- The use of educational references to define learning targets.
- Processing of natural language descriptions related to educational objects.
- E-learning materials clustering based of information encoded in metadata.

7.2 Virtual Learning Communities

The concept of e-learning comprises various forms of learning through Information and Communications Technology (ICT), which are defined in literature by different terms such as borderless education, computer-mediated communication, distributed learning, online instruction, virtual classrooms, web-based learning (Guri-Rosenblit, 2005).

7.2.1 Theoretical Framework for E-learning Systems

Three main components of an information system – participants, services, and technologies – belong to the theoretical framework for a general e-learning system (Aparicio et al., 2016).

- Participants are stakeholders who directly or indirectly interact with the system.
- Technologies enable interactions between different groups of users, support content integration, enable communication, and provide collaboration tools.
- Services integrate all the activities corresponding to pedagogical models and to instructional strategies.

More specifically, in the context of web-based education, stakeholders are entities that are either providing or demanding seamless education from a learner's inquiry to graduation (Aggarwal, 2005). They can be internal (such as students and teachers) and external (e.g., the ministry of education) and may directly or indirectly interact with the system (Romero et al., 2015). Learners, instructors, administrators and education policy committees are stakeholders belonging to virtual learning communities. Here, mapping services can be instantiated on top of instructional strategies related to formative assessment for competence-based education, such as providing automatic assessment and feedback, clarifying goals, and generating learning maps.

7.2.2 Virtual Community System

Virtual learning communities (VLCs) are online systems for learners, held by instructors, managed by administrators, and promoted by an education policy committee. VLC stakeholders belong to the following categories.

- Learners (students): identified as internal stakeholders, they are the ultimate users interacting directly with the system.
- Instructors (content-providing teachers): instructors are internal stakeholders who have both roles of teacher and content provider. They interact directly with the system as responsible for the learners' teaching/learning process, designer of learning objects, and system user.
- Administrators (technology-provider researchers): expert in Information and Communications Technology (ICT) in education and e-learning, they supervise and support instructors' work and collaborate in the development, design, and operational aspects of the system and its related research.
- Education policy committee: this entity is the board which set policies, provide directions and state educational frameworks, affecting all the others stakeholders.

In a VLC, instructors manage one or more online courses for separate groups of learners. Administrators help instructors in experimenting innovative methodologies for teaching, creating digital materials, peer collaborating, sharing resources and best practices, and using advanced tools integrated to the environment that hosts their online courses. The education policy committee defines the framework of learning objectives the learners should achieve at the end of their whole learning process.

7.2.3 Sharing in a Virtual Community

Virtual learning communities (VLCs) foster two fundamental processes:

- Instructors' collaboration. A VLC offers (or integrates) effective means to develop, codify, and share assets with peers teaching subject areas bearing simi-

larities in content and instructional strategies. This overcomes the limits of physical distance and prevents investment lost related to the production of high-quality contents (Krämer, 2008).
- Self-paced formative assessment. Augmenting instruction possibilities with e-learning strategies affects students' motivation (Rajaee Harandi, 2015). VLC is a "trusted" environment where students can become owners of their own learning: they have both just-in-time information and the supervision of "real" instructors.

Figure 7.1 illustrates the idea of the VLC services as areas progressively surrounding the learner, who is at the center: tutoring – namely, instructors training – and sharing among peers in the community lead and connect the participants toward automatic formative assessment.

The community of students can constitute a further actor for continuously improving technology-enhanced teaching and learning processes within the community, if it adopts a framework of common learning objectives.

Regardless the improvements made possible by technological advances, mainly these processes depend on a variable typical of any kind of education: the time available to teachers (Gerry et al., 2014). The importance of this variable is clear when related closely to an effect typical of the digital world, the rapid and continuous growth of available resources. If not carefully guided, instructors risk losing time in efforts related to the creation of "duplicated" e-contents or the retrieval of useful items among a huge amount of "irrelevant" shared materials. The time factor limits the performance of VLCs processes in typically occurring scenarios: instructors searching e-contents shared by peers; learners provided with resources created by teachers different from their own. Instructor's time dedicated to these activities

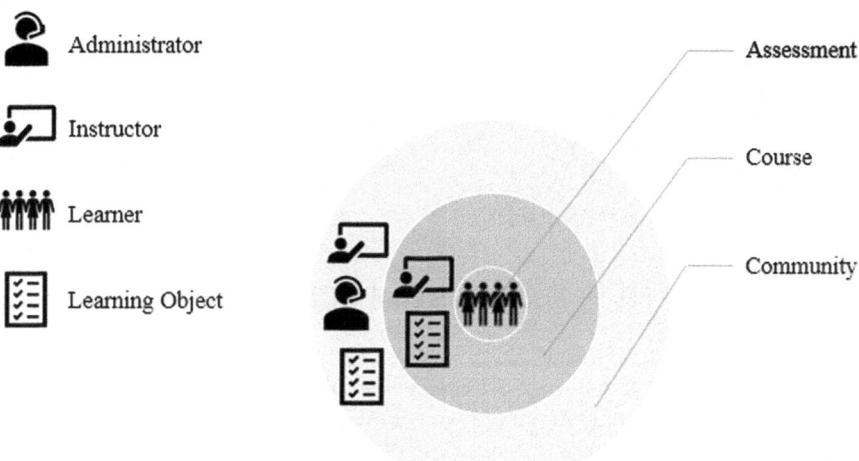

Fig. 7.1 VLC schematic representation

constitutes a "bottleneck" for person-to-person and person-to-learning material interactions. Linearly with the "Semantic Web" conception, VLC participants may benefit from automatically generated "aggregates" of colleagues' works, if provided with metadata about an agreed "meaning" that identifies and puts them in relation.

7.2.4 Examples of Virtual Communities

Examples of VLCs follow, respectively, in local, national, and transnational contexts. They exploit learning management systems (LMSs) integrated with advanced computing environments (ACEs), web conference tools, and automatic assessment system (AASs).

- The service implemented with project School of Homework (Scuola dei compiti) is an example of VLC in a local context. The project aims at reducing scholastic failures (Barana & Marchisio, 2015). It offers remedial actions through tutoring activities supported by new technologies and innovative educational methodologies (Cavagnero et al., 2015).
- The service implemented with project problem posing and solving (PP&S) is an example of nationwide VLC (Barana et al., 2015). PP&S was promoted by the Ministry of Education with the purpose of supporting a strong action aimed at innovating mathematics teaching and learning in the secondary school (Brancaccio et al., 2015). The project proposes to develop an integrated training area that interconnects logic, mathematics, and information technology, to promote problem posing and problem-solving as learning methodologies, and to build an information technology culture (Brancaccio et al., 2014).
- The service implemented with Erasmus+ project SMART (Science and Mathematics Advanced Research for good Teaching) is an example of VLC in a European context (Marchisio et al., 2017). Instructors from different countries collaborated at the development and experimentation of problem-based teaching strategies (Brancaccio et al., 2016).

7.3 Automatic Assessment

Digital testing can play an important role in the provision of timely, targeted and extensive information to learners related to their current situation (Rasila et al., 2015). Automatic assessment allows students to practice wherever and whenever they want and to receive immediate feedback on their level of preparation: indications on the educational material to review based on the results obtained in certain tests. Formative feedback is the outcome of assessment, which aims to improve learning (Ihantola, 2011): continuous practice may enhance the probabilities that monitoring student progresses elicits their difficulties.

7.3.1 Adaptive Teaching

The idea of technology-based adaptive teaching (Snow, 1977) was born from the interest in individual differences among learners, who might show different attitudes toward learning and respond to different forms of instructions in diverse modalities (Jonassen & Grabowski, 1993), possibly changing over time. Instructors should adjust teaching strategies accordingly with the students' progresses (Jonassen et al., 1990), which need to be continuously controlled. To enable automated monitoring of learning outcomes, several online strategies have been experimented (Barana et al., 2017). According to the collection of assessment data, analysis of activities, and feedback, the design of personalized paths can meet the students' needs (Shute & Zapata-Rivera, 2012). The use of Information and Communications Technologies (ICTs) boost the positive effects that the use of adaptive teaching methodologies has on the learners (Phobun & Vicheanpanya, 2010):

- Lessons are engaging, relevant, and interesting.
- The learning environment is comfortable, and learners feel at ease.
- Students do not worry about saying something wrong; in fact mistakes are necessary to inform the teacher about how to adjust and differentiate strategies.
- Learners take increasing responsibility for their own growth (Tomlinson, 2001).

These factors are particularly relevant in contexts of tutoring as key points for the promotion of school success (Mascarenhas et al., 2010).

7.3.2 Adaptive Questioning

A characteristic practice enabled by automatic assessment is the implementation of adaptive questions. It enables students to focus on the reasoning process via differentiated attempts to get to the solution: in case of failure of a first question, a progressively displayed path guides the student's reasoning toward the solution, dividing the proposed problem into successive steps (Barana et al., 2015). Moreover, teachers could implement assignments with different features accordingly to the educational strategy. For instance, "questions chaining" means providing students with a step-by-step solving process, one small question at a time, keeping records about students' responses. Another example would be the provision of test items within a recorded video lecture, steadily stimulating viewers' attention. CAA can enable these services through carefully constructed set of tests, allowing help steps and revealing buttons and random parameters appropriate to the learning level of the student (Beevers & Paterson, 2003).

7.3.3 Microlearning

Microlearning is providing educational content in small well-planned units – requiring relatively short efforts and low degrees of time consumption. It deals with short information units and topics.

Designing and organizing learning involves the planning of small steps and units of content, with structure and classification created by the learner. It can provide better educational results in comparison with the classical approaches when suitably combined and sufficiently interactive (Skalka & Drlík, 2018). Automatic formative assessment implementations (via multiple-choice tests) helped to decrease the number of dropouts and final exam failures (Steen & Richard Movik, 2017). The definition of a learning material into "atomic" components fosters a reflection on multimodal possibilities for implementing automatic assessment. In fact, several distinct types of questions may test an identical learning outcome.

7.4 E-learning Objects and Technologies

Automatic assessment tools integrate with existing web-based technologies and link to diverse e-learning objects. Although it is desirable that future innovative systems will be able to handle any type of e-learning objects, what follows focuses on items for automatic assessment. In particular, the key element proposed for implementing new automatic formative assessment processes is a specific type of semi-structured metadata.

Nowadays advances in computational semantic analysis may enable editors to relax the requirements for structuring competence specifications related to shared resources automating human decisions (such as selecting an appropriate item for a given scenario) can rely on information conveyed in natural language descriptions.

7.4.1 Automatic Assessment Items

Generally, a variety of grading behaviors can be combined and placed anywhere within a formatted HTML that defines a question or a test. For example, it is possible that response areas belong to tables, formatted text, and bulleted lists and include embedded images or media objects (Maple T.A. 10 Online Help, 2015). Today's advances in web technologies are evident in the structure of items for automatic assessment. Question design practice does not start from "question type selection": for instance, the concept of "item containing a multiple choice response area" replaced the one of "multiple choice question." This methodological shift not only makes it possible to quickly duplicate and modify existing questions by changing exclusively the response area, but it is also the principle for providing greater compositional richness to instructors/authors. The conceptualization of a learning item for automatic assessment is a learning object composed by different parts. One of these is the "surface layer." The surface layer is the part of a "learning object" the learner can interact with, before automatic assessment is provided. A surface layer can be composed of intertwined sub-parts with diverse characteristics, such as character formatting, HTML tables, embedded images, and media objects, images, tables, algorithmic variables, inline math expressions.

- The "surface text" is the part of a LO containing natural or mathematical language the learner is able to read.
- The "response area" is the part of a LO the learner must use to input an answer in the system.

Some components may be included in an automatic assessment item's definition and (eventually) interact with students after a grading: feedback, information fields, and question details. Others execute before the item displays to the student, such as the algorithmic part generating variables for differentiating the surface layer appearance. The surface layer of a single item may thus vary.

7.4.2 Learning Object

The concept of e-learning object presents several definitions in literature. Learning object is often referred as synonym of "learning material," "learning item," "learning resource," "educational material," "educational resource," and "educational content." Chiappe et al., (2007) early alerted the research community about the risks of obsolescence related to the excessive management of the technical issues (standards, metadata, repositories, etc.). They gave the following definition: a learning object (LO) is a digital, self-contained, reusable entity with a clear learning aim that contains at least three internal changing components – content, instructional activities, and context elements.

As a complement, the learning object should have an external component of information that helps its identification, storage, and recovery: the metadata.

7.4.3 Metadata

Metadata is human constructed data about data (Gartner, 2016). Nowadays methodologies suggest composing semi-structured free text metadata. Natural language metadata usually appear in domains lacking precise metadata requirements (Barker & Campbell, 2010), while the use of established metadata standards (such as IEEE LOM and Dublin Core metadata) presents technical issues related to their maintenance (Dietze et al., 2013).

Structured metadata record machine-readable resource descriptions. Resource description based on a standard's compliance is an approach typical of the age of monolithic systems, in contrast with today's shift toward service-oriented architectures and distributed components. The traditional practice of creating catalogs of self-contained stand-alone metadata records that fully describes the resource did not really take hold, in comparison with the approach of augmenting web resources with semantically informative metadata to assist search engines in their discovery (Barker & Campbell, 2016).

Recent e-learning trends attempt to standardize competency definitions, to help interchange and processing by machines (De Marcos et al., 2007). It is unrealistic to expect that a unified metadata standard emerge to describe all e-learning resources uniformly, as different people sometimes interpret the same things in different ways, or use different words to describe them. Semantic web introduces approaches and technologies to solve this issue – referred as semantic heterogeneity problem (Ivanova & Ivanova, 2011): if knowledge is semantically represented through the use of ontologies, automatic reasoning agents might then manipulate not words or sentences but thoughts senses, helping users in and integrating educational materials from different sources.

7.5 Learning Management Systems and Integrations

Learning management systems (LMSs) host virtual learning communities (VLCs). They offer a set of functions oriented to transmit, trace, inform, and manage learning objects, as well as students' progresses and their interaction with contents (Romero et al., 2015). Main LMS functionalities follow.

- Management. The environment provides facilities for user enrollment and accesses, activities, accessed content, assessment scores, reports, and statistics.
- Communication and collaboration. Different channels enable synchronous and asynchronous communication: chat, web conference tools, help desk, blogs, advertisement board, and forums.
- Customization. Users may customize virtual spaces according to their capacities and necessities.
- Interoperability. External software integrates with the LMS; examples are automatic assessment systems, web conferencing tools, and advanced computing environments.

7.5.1 Automatic Assessment Systems

Automatic assessment systems can improve the practice of formative assessment, especially for the immediacy of feedback and the flexible solutions for questioning (Barana et al., 2018). An automatic assessment system (AAS) consists of the following parts (Rasila et al., 2007):

- User identification.
- Student interface for taking assignments.
- Teacher interface for authoring new questions and assignments.
- Database for storing user and data information (questions, results, etc.).
- Computer algebra system to grade students answers.
- Gradebook where the results are stored.

An LMS is a container for courses (organized in categories); every course has a teacher, and some students enrolled into it. AAS-VLC integrations can map gradebook, database data, and user interfaces within the course setting (Barana et al., 2015).

7.5.2 Advanced Computing Environments

An advanced computing environment (ACE) is a system capable of performing numeric and symbolic computation and interactive geometrical visualizations in 2D and 3D, embedding of interactive components where students can change the parameters and explore the varying situation, and automatizing computations through algorithms and procedures (Barana et al., 2017). It is a complete environment for hosting problem-solving processes (Barana & Marchisio, 2018). The use of an ACE empowers problem-solving in that it offers several possibilities for representation and it frees users from manual computations, allowing them to focus on strategy. ACE's engine is a computer algebra system, useful for implementing an AAS. Thanks to its capabilities, it is possible to create complex elements such as the following:

- Variables based on algorithms.
- Random mathematical formulas.
- Graphics.

Furthermore, open mathematical response area (RA) might have customized grading algorithms. These enable to test different competences focusing on complex cognitive processes (Barana & Marchisio, 2016).

7.5.3 Retrieval Systems

Instructors from different levels of expertise demand to find reusable resources to integrate them into their individual courses. The time-consuming effort of learning resource creation is not the unique factor leading this demand: in several cases, appropriate resources might already exist. While web search engines make access easy, the vastness of available resources could make it very challenging to find the appropriate ones. Systems developed and refined through the years help communities of e-instructors, facilitating the tasks of finding, sharing, reusing, and analyzing educational contents to address specific student needs. Technological strategies for disseminating e-learning objects include:

- Institutional repositories and websites, such as Wisc-Online (https://www.wisc-online.com).
- Content-type-specific repositories, such as SlideShare (https://www.slideshare.net), dedicated to share specific types of content.
- Global repositories, such as Merlot (https://www.merlot.org), which are not limited by subject or resource type and include links to several peer-reviewed educational resources.

Traditional methods for retrieving learning objects (LOs) include alphabetical indexing, keyword-based searching, and extracting information from on surface features (title, location, publication date, etc.). New strategies address semantic issues via artificial intelligence techniques (Martín & León, 2012).

Repository integration into VLC systems strengthens teachers' awareness and use of educational resources: a central search across several repositories is available within the environment; peer collaboration enables to better define essential learning resource criteria; community administrators provide further support for finding content of appropriate educational use and quality.

7.5.4 Recommender Systems

Recommender systems form a conceptual representation of an electronic collection, calculate the measure of thematic proximity between documents by using this representation, and output a list of documents reflecting the user interests (Elizarov et al., 2016). For automatic assessment purposes, recommender systems represent missed requirements that – according to the judgment of the person who created the resource / metadata – are necessary to answer correctly, as well as learning objectives. Proximity regards the alignment between objectives and requirements of different items.

Figure 7.2 provides a schematic representation of recommendation in automatic assessment contexts: an object for learning ("Feedback" path) can redirect ("Recommendation") a learner toward a different learning path ("Remedial" path) where to answer a new item whose objectives match the requirements of the first one.

7.6 Route Planning for Self-Paced Learning

Formative assessment focuses on achieving goals rather than determining if a goal was or was not met, and one of the ways it does so is by helping to clarify learning targets and standards for both teachers and students (Greenstein, 2010). The fea-

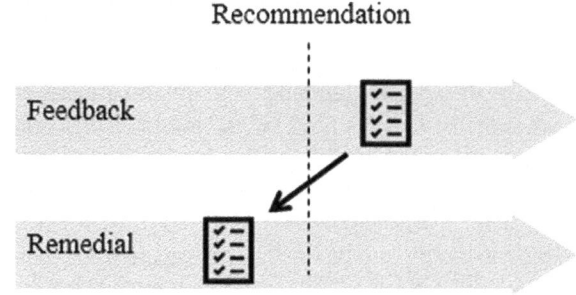

Fig. 7.2 Schema of learning objects recommendation

tures of an assignment reflect the educational strategy chosen by the instructor. Whatever the features, clarifying, sharing, and understanding learning intentions and criteria for success are fundamental factors for activating learners' reasoning on their own achievements (formative assessment) and for stimulating the students to undertake appropriate learning paths (proactive assessment) (Trinchero, 2017).

7.6.1 Learning Outcomes and Learning Targets

The presence of descriptions associated to learning materials helps instructors in developing an instructional strategy, selecting proper materials, and constructing tests and other instruments for assessing and then evaluating students' outcomes (Dooley et al., 2006). There is a dominant definition of the term learning outcome. Nevertheless, several alternatives exist, often referring to the concept of learning objective (Proitz, 2010).

- Learning outcome. A learning outcome is the description of knowledge, skills, and competences that a learner acquires because of a learning activity (European Commission, 2012).
- Learning target. A learning target is the description – in language that students understand – of a bite-sized chunk of information, skills, and reasoning processes that students will come to know deeply and thoroughly.

A learning target describes the intended micro-sized learning outcome and the nature of evidence that will determine mastery of that outcome from a student's point of view. In this sense, it is important to stress the difference between a learning target and an instructional objective: the latter describes an intended outcome and the nature of evidence that will determine mastery of that outcome from a teacher's point of view, containing content outcomes, conditions, and criteria. A learning target contains the immediate learning aims for a single micro-lesson (Moss & Brookhart, 2012).

7.6.2 Learning Maps

A correctly designed learning target refers to a larger "route" – the planned learning path. Teacher designs not a single unit but a coherent series of learning challenges ("goals") toward an overarching outcome. The "learning path" concept is referred as a cognitive model in the sense that it is used to represent how a person's knowledge may be organized, containing descriptions of component pieces of knowledge and connections among them to indicate how understanding develops in a specified domain (Gierl et al., 2008). Various authors described cognitive models, including learning maps, learning trajectories, and learning hierarchies (Adjei et al., 2016).

- Learning progression is a linear sequence of learning goals (Popham, 2011).
- Learning trajectory includes a learning goal, a developmental progression defining the levels of thinking that students pass through as they work toward the defined goal, and a set of learning activities or experiences that assist students in reaching the defined goal (Clements & Sarama, 2004).
- Learning hierarchy models prerequisite knowledge components in hierarchies, allowing multiple pathways to extend from one prerequisite skill to multiple learning goals (Gagné, 1968).
- Learning map represents knowledge as a network of component skills and connections, allowing for multiple paths from prerequisites to learning goals (Confrey et al., 2017).

Learning maps – usually designed by domain experts – extend the notion of learning hierarchies by adding complexity to the cognitive model. This characteristic makes the learning map appropriate to represent multiple pathways generated by a broad range of individual differences or learning preferences (Rao & Meo, 2016).

7.7 Technologies for Online Generation of Learning Maps

The following technologies have promising e-learning applications for route planning within virtual learning communities (VLCs).

7.7.1 Ontologies

An ontology can be defined as "an explicit specification of a conceptualization" (Gruber, 1994) or as "a formal specification of a shared conceptualization" (Borst, 1997). It is a machine-readable abstract model of a phenomenon, obtained through the identification of concepts, properties, and relevant constraints that characterize it, the explicit definition of these elements, and the sharing with a group of people who express their consent on them (Guarino et al., 2019). Ontologies differ from other formalizing knowledge resources by their degree of formalization (Mitkov & Navigli, 2016). Ontology building requires the effort of knowledge engineers and domain experts (Fernández-López et al., 1997). Several methodologies for ontology development (De Nicola et al., 2009) have been refined through the years (Noy & Mcguinness, 2001), as well as automatic ontology learning (Humm & Ossanloo, 2017) methods to speed up manual work (Mousavi et al., 2014).

7.7.2 Natural Language Processing

Natural language processing (NLP) refers to the function of computer systems which analyze spoken or written language. Linguistic analysis of texts typically involves subsequent steps: documents are broken up into paragraphs, paragraphs into sentences, and sentences into words; words turn into stems or part of speech tags. Hence, the analysis involves most of the following operations (Jackson & Moulinier, 2003).

- Sentence delimitation: determining the scope of sentences and identifying their constituents.
- Tokenization: segmenting characters' streams into meaningful units ("tokens").
- Stemming: associating terminological variants with a root form according to morphological analysis.
- Part of speech tagging: labelling each word in a sentence with its appropriate tag.
- Noun phrasing: identifying part of speech patterns that include a noun.
- Named entity recognition: identifying proper names in documents.
- Parsing: determining the syntactic structure of a text by analyzing its constituent words with respect to an underlying grammar.

7.7.3 Semantic Analysis

Processing natural languages computationally involves text representation (Zhang et al., 2017). Approaches to represent ("embed") words into vectors have been proposes, based on the main idea that words of semantically similar meaning should have similar vectors. Embedding documents as vectors of term weights has been very fruitful for retrieval and clustering tasks. A well-established method for computing term weights is the term frequency and inverse document frequency (tf-idf) model. Tf-idf function returns the weight of a term by considering the term frequency (tf) component – which depends upon the frequency with which a term occurs in a given document – and the inverse document frequency (idf) component, which measures the relative rarity of a term (Sarasu & Thyagharajan, 2014).

7.7.4 *Mathematical Language Processing*

Employing an analysis of natural language to enrich the information content of formulae is a new approach, which Pagael and Schubotz (2014) termed mathematical language processing (MLP). Mathematical formulae are essential in science but face challenges of ambiguity, due to the use of a small number of identifiers to represent an immense number of concepts. Nearly all of the mathematical literature is online and mostly in natural language form: math content processing presents some same challenges faced in NLP (Youssef, 2017). Corresponding to word sense disambiguation in NLP, mathematical identifiers can be disambiguated by regarding formulae and natural text as one monolithic information source (Schubotz et al., 2016).

7.7.5 *Clustering*

Clustering is the task of finding underlying patterns and grouping objects together (in clusters) based on their similarity. It differs from classification, which is the task of grouping objects into predefined classes created with prior knowledge. Classification is often performed with supervised machine learning against a known standard; on the contrary, since rarely there is a standard to learn against, clustering typically uses unsupervised machine learning (Zhang et al., 2017). The following principles define clustering (Jain & Dubes, 1988):

- Objects in the same cluster must be similar as much as possible.
- Objects in different clusters must be as much different as possible.
- Measurement for similarity and dissimilarity must be clear and have the practical meaning.

Many clustering algorithms have been proposed in literature (Xu & Tian, 2015), intersecting diverse research fields (Dietze et al., 2013), and growing concurrently with the development of modern computer technology (Maniriho & Effendi, 2018).

7.8 Route Planning for Students' Remediation

Sequencing problem concerns arranging specific learning objects (units, questions, videos, etc.) in a suitable succession for a particular learner. Instructors usually perform sequencing, but several researches tried to automate part of their task. De Marcos et al. (2007) proposed a technique for learning object automated sequencing using e-learning standards about competencies: definitions of prerequisites-outcomes relations between learning items help solving the sequencing problem as a permutation problem.

Tugsgerel et al., (2010) proposed learning processes personalization via learning object (LO) sequencing: their example consists of a framework that matches LOs metadata and the learner profiles. A learning management system mediates learning processes: it acts as a repository of metadata published by providers. The LMS can also generate automatically a learning path on behalf of a learner and determine the schedule of the learning process. The proposed learning path generation relies on the combination of metadata and learner profile. This approach is limited to the standardization of these elements.

Defining richer sets of semantics provided by ontologies could broaden and refine the impact of personalization. Chen, Peng, and Shiue (2008) proposed a curriculum-sequencing scheme based on a generated ontology-based concept map, automatically constructed by a large amount of learners pre-test results. Shmelev et al., (2015) used a simplified ontology to identify connections between prerequisite subjects and the outcome subjects. Their approach utilizes ontology and a revised version of Bloom's taxonomy for creating learning paths and an algorithm for choosing the most appropriate.

Strategies based on natural language processing (NLP) help overcoming the problems that can occur in e-learning systems where human experts solely determine learning paths. In order to plan appropriate routes for individual learners, Tam et al., (2014) proposed an e-learning system framework based on information extracted from the concerned course materials descriptions.

Wang et al. (2015) showed how external domain knowledge might help filtering noisy texts and organize a corpus of digital materials: their knowledge representations of lecture videos facilitated online learners in designing their learning strategies and searching for the target concepts.

A technology applied to educational data mining by Ignatov (2015) facilitates route planning: formal concept analysis (FCA). If input data describe relationship between a set of objects and a set of attributes, FCA produces two kinds of output: a graph clustering (the concept lattice) and a set of dependency rules (the attribute implications). The former is a collection of formal concepts in the data – namely, particular clusters that represent natural human-like concepts – hierarchically ordered by a subconcept-superconcept relation. The latter are particular dependencies found among data. Mathematical foundations of FCA were thoroughly treated by Ganter and Wille (1997). Skopljanac Macina and Blaskovic (2014) proposed simple and effective ways of applying FCA in the area of teaching and computer-aided learning: they helped instructors with the preparation of exam materials by providing FCA-based methods for checking how a given set of questions covers specific concepts. Questions represent the input data: FCA provides teachers with a visual overview (the concept lattice) of the proposed exam structure and key information about found concepts. The use of a concept lattice can support the analysis of exam results; furthermore, the direct acyclic graph representing the concept lattice enables topological sorting algorithms to lead toward questions order optimization. The authors also discussed the possibility of using concept lattices as a starting point for building educational ontologies.

7.9 Use of Educational References to Define Learning Targets

In the area of competency-based education, operational strategies have been proposed (Trinchero, 2017) to support teachers in clarifying and sharing learning intentions, especially by:

- Defining observable indicators for the skills being trained.
- Building learning paths.
- Designing a teaching that is based on national guidelines goals but insists on a plurality of cognitive processes, educational activities and assessment, tests, and certification of competence.
- Defining mastery levels to be included in the final certification forms.

European projects have been activated to help instructors deciding which assessment strategies to use in their online courses (Soeiro et al., 2014), to foster learning objects sharing in an open perspective (Ravotto et al., 2011), and to align learning outcomes with assessment methods (Gil-Jaurena & Softic, 2016). Actions to facilitate sharing and e-learning assets and clarifying their usability often exploit popular educational references, but lack of capabilities able to automate teachers work. Semantic web approaches may boost the effectiveness of such strategies for disseminating educational resources (Steinberger, 2017).

Semantic technologies enable the organization of "semantically structured" learning objects. Structuring educational references as semantic technologies is strategic for identifying when two authors express identical concepts with different terms from the domain vocabulary. Ontologies provide shared understanding of a domain to overcome differences in terminology (Guo, 2009).

7.9.1 Educational References

Educational references may support outcome-based approaches to teaching and learning. In the context of cognitive domains, several published taxonomies have been largely used, especially involving the design and interpretation of achievement tests (Webb, 2014). Examples are Bloom's taxonomy (Bloom, 1956), which is one of the most recognized educational references published in the twentieth century, TIMSS 2003 Mathematics framework (Mullis et al., 2003), and Anderson and Krathwohl's revision of Bloom's taxonomy. Anderson et al., (2001) shifted the focus from learning products (objects of the classification proposed by Bloom) to cognitive processes, which applies to different types of knowledge. At the school/university level and considering students of Mathematics, objective test questions may test all cognitive levels. However, the use of educational objectives levels has been subject of discussion particularly when related to problem-solving and skills assessment: Bloom's taxonomy is not for identifying which levels of learning are involved a posteriori but as a design guideline (Beevers & Paterson, 2003).

7.9.2 Ontology-Based Educational Systems

The development of automated systems relates to disciplinary areas inherent to information technology and in the context of higher education. The availability of huge amounts of educational data existing in learning environments may confuse learners instead of helping them to choose pertinent contents. Researches in digital humanities highlight how the knowledge transmitting process from the author to learners does not require only the providing of a simple learning content but also a set of information about the content (metadata) to ensure an accurate learning process (Bourekkache et al., 2015).

Semantic web is a promising technology to make the educational content easily accessible: "semantic description" of learning objects may accelerate communication between human agents and machines, especially facilitating the delivery of adaptive contents to learners.

Ivanova (2011) proposed an adaptive e-learning system for finding, manipulating, describing, and organizing new content in the domain of programming environment. The system can analyze HTML and plain text resources, determine their structure and components using ontologies, break them in smaller parts, supply parts with required metadata, and propose them as potential further learning resources. It helps professionals in understanding learner needs, saving time and efforts in searching and analyzing external materials, and promoting active participation of learners in the process of learning and resource development. It also ensures the enrichment of its underlying semantic schema by using interactive ontology learning. Written and used in the domain of programming environment, the system's main parts are domain-independent, except for the ontology.

The development of specific purpose ontologies is a fundamental step for ontology-based educational systems.

- Curriculum ontologies may define a set of basic concepts and structure of distance-learning courses.
- Test ontologies provide validation and comparison of tests offered by instructors to assess students' knowledge as well as relevance of the curriculum structure.
- Library ontologies are used for saving and storage of information about requires and/or suggested readings (Mouromtsev et al., 2013).

Several research projects studied how ontologies may be used in every stage of e-learning: authoring, tutoring, and assessment. Ivanova and Ivanova (2011) reviewed ontology-based approaches and proposed a model of shareable educational ontologies to make learning contents reusable and machine-readable. They highlighted how ontology building is a difficult and time-consuming task and suggested that community-driven ontology management approaches and tools may facilitate the ontology development process.

7.9.3 Ontologies for STEM

In the domain of science, technology, engineering, and mathematics (STEM), students and scientists would especially profit from systems that are able to manage not only texts but also formulae (Youssef, 2017). Terminological resources – such as vocabularies, datasets, thesauri, and ontologies – have been developed and used for the descriptions of mathematical knowledge objects (Pagael & Schubotz, 2014) in computer systems. The following are examples of high-level resources (ontologies) proposed in literature:

- Open Mathematical Documents (OMDoc) (Heras et al., 2009).
- MathLang Document Rhetorical Ontology (Kamareddine & Wells, 2008).
- Mocassin Ontology (Solovyev & Zhiltsov, 2011).
- OntoMathPRO (Nevzorova et al., 2014).

These newly available ontologies enabled the implementation of new technologies for mathematical knowledge management (MKM) (Elizarov et al., 2016) relying on knowledge-based measures: recommender systems (Elizarov et al., 2014) and information retrieval systems (Schubotz et al., 2016). One of the difficulties that a user might experience is to formulate an effective retrieval request. Ontology-based retrieval systems simplify the task of finding correct information by building a search system based on the meaning of keyword instead of the keyword itself (Elangovan & Nirmala, 2016). One of the obstacles in the propagation of ontological approaches is the laboriousness of the development of models for each knowledge domain separately. In literacy there is still not a single widely accepted formalism for "computer mathematics," even though mathematics is full of formalisms. The need for a more computable mathematics with robust and standardized representation led to the proposal of increasing the interoperability between existing systems and languages (Ion et al., 2016).

7.10 Research Directions

Aligning contents, requirements, and educational objectives might not only connect learners to appropriate educational materials but also foster reflections among instructors about the effectiveness of digital-based methodologies adopted (Di Caro et al., 2018b). Enriching automatic assessment resources with free-text annotations enables to target route planning through the combination of techniques typical of formal concept analysis (FCA) and natural language processing (Di Caro et al., 2018a).

Newly developed models for structuring shared resources respond to a need for quality. Nevertheless, innovative methodologies for creating metadata related to intended competences might be both useful and prone to misconceptions (Di Caro et al., 2017). Further investigations could provide structured knowledge supporting resource sharing in a community: contrary to what exists for learning objectives, there are no well-established educational references for the definition of learners' performance. Taxonomies designed as linguistic resources for text processing are key elements from which to link learning materials.

Integrating online communities with semantic-capturing technologies opens up possibilities for further implementations of adaptive systems for automatic formative assessment (Di Caro et al., 2018c). Experts' supervision of resources shared by teachers (and peer-reviewed) guarantees the quality of a "community repository": similar practices might lead future research on automated tests creation through the combination of natural and algorithmic language. Linking learning material descriptors with taxonomic levels generates a dataset from which machine learning techniques may infer concrete occurrences of named entities (Barana et al., 2018b), facilitating human effort in realizing ontological knowledge.

Fostering the use of VLCs helps overcoming difficulties in implementing solutions based on semantic technologies: projects involving numerous teachers and students may be set up to experiment adaptive mechanisms for personalized learning (Barana et al., 2018c). Benefits brought by technology are both in terms of saving time and quality of the educational offer: this factor promotes the willingness of participating to online communities.

7.10.1 Final Remarks

Last decades registered the constantly growth of the role of technology in every area of life and work, accompanied by international surveys and recommendations highlighting the importance of competence-based education (Council of the European Union, 2006). A society with a high degree of mobility demands for innovative teaching and learning strategies, and this request can be met by the possibilities opened up by the technological revolution that brought the demand itself (Council of the European Union, 2018).

Teaching and assessment strictly relate to the content to which they refer: competence (Comoglio, 2018). Competence-based education indicates a shift from content of teaching and training paths to the learning outcomes, which students will achieve and can use in either the further education path, the world of work, or any other social context. The development of competence does not produce evidence of sudden changes, and therefore frequent testing is not necessary to obtain significant information on its acquisition. Nevertheless, autonomous and independent continuous practice is a key factor for fostering student's activeness and meta-cognitive experiences, which are parts of competence development.

Online teaching could still require at least as much effort by human teachers as classroom teaching: not only must the teacher prepare materials and make them available by computer, the teacher have also to motivate and guide each student, through ongoing interaction and a sense of social presence (Ravotto et al., 2011). Hopefully, processing of natural language descriptions related to educational objects – as well as and e-learning materials clustering based of information encoded in metadata – will help in rapidly developing e-learning strategies to support teachers and trainers in understanding new educational systems that are based on learning goals and competences (Gerry et al., 2014).

References

Adjei, S., Botelho, A., & Heffernan, N. (2016). Predicting student performance on post-requisite skills using prerequisite skill data: An alternative method for refining prerequisite skill structures. In *Proceedings of the sixth international conference on Learning Analytics & Knowledge, LAK '16* (p. 25).

Aggarwal, A. (2005). Stakeholders in web-based education. In *Encyclopedia of distance learning* (Vol. 19). Hershey, PA: Idea Group Inc (IGI).

Anderson, L., Krathwohl, D., & Bloom, B. (2001). *A taxonomy for learning, teaching, and assessing: A revision of Bloom's taxonomy of educational objectives*. New York, US: Longman.

Aparicio, M., Bacao, F., & Oliveira, T. (2016). An e-learning theoretical framework. *Journal of Educational Technology Systems, 19*(1), 292–307.

Barana, A., Brancaccio, A., Marchisio, M., & Pardini, C. (2015). L'efficacia della metodologia del "problem posing and solving" con l'utilizzo delle tic nella didattica della matematica e delle materie tecnico-scientifiche. *Bricks, 5*(3), 106–126.

Barana, A., Conte, A., Marchisio, M., Fioravera, M., & Rabellino, S. (2018). A model of formative automatic assessment and interactive feedback for STEM In *Proceedings of the 2018 IEEE 42nd annual computer software and applications conference, COMPSAC 2018* (pp. 1016–1025).

Barana, A., Di Caro, L., Fioravera, M., Marchisio, M., & Rabellino, S. (2018a). Developing competence assessment systems in e-learning communities. In *Proceedings of EDEN 2018 annual conference* (pp. 879–888).

Barana, A., Di Caro, L., Fioravera, M., Marchisio, M., & Rabellino, S. (2018b). Ontology development for competence assessment in virtual communities of practice. In *Proceedings of the 19th international conference on artificial intelligence in education, AIED 2018* (pp. 94–98).

Barana, A., Di Caro, L., Fioravera, M., Marchisio, M., & Rabellino, S. (2018c). Sharing system of learning resources for adaptive strategies of scholastic remedial intervention. In *Proceedings of the 4th international conference on higher education advances, HEAd'18* (pp. 1495–1503).

Barana, A., Fioravera, M., & Marchisio, M. (2017). Developing problem solving competences through the resolution of contextualized problems with an advanced computing environment. In *Proceedings of the 3rd international conference on higher education advances, HEAd'17*, (pp. 1015–1023).

Barana, A., Fioravera, M., Marchisio, M., & Rabellino, S. (2017). Adaptive teaching supported by ICTs to reduce the school failure in the project "Scuola Dei Compiti". In *Proceedings of the 2017 IEEE 41st annual computer software and applications conference, COMPSAC 2017* (pp. 432–437).

Barana, A., & Marchisio, M. (2015). "Testi digitali interattivi" per il recupero nella matematica nel progetto per la riduzione della dispersione scolastica "Scuola Dei Compiti". *Form@re – Open Journal per la formazione in rete, 15*, 129–142.

Barana, A., & Marchisio, M. (2016). Ten good reasons to adopt an automated formative assessment model for learning and teaching mathematics and scientific disciplines. *Procedia – Social and Behavioral Sciences, 228*, 608–613.

Barana, A., & Marchisio, M. (2018). Developing problem solving competences with CLIL methodology through innovative technologies. In *Proceedings of EM&M ITALIA 2018 multi conference* (pp. 30–37).

Barana, A., Marchisio, M., & Rabellino, S. (2015). Automated assessment in mathematics. In *Proceedings of the 2015 IEEE 39th annual computer software and applications conference (COMPSAC)* (pp. 670–671).

Barker, P., & Campbell, L. (2010). Metadata for learning materials: An overview of existing standards and current developments. *Technology, Instruction, Cognition and Learning.* (vol. 7(3–4), pp. 225–243).

Barker, P., & Campbell, L. (2016). Technology strategies for open educational resource dissemination. In P. Blessinger & T. Bliss (Eds.), *Open Education: International Perspectives in Higher Education*, Cambridge, UK: Open Book Publishers.

Beevers, C., & Paterson, J. (2003). Automatic assessment of problem-solving skills in mathematics. *Active Learning in Higher Education, 4*, 127.

Bloom, B. (1956). *Taxonomy of educational objectives.* New York, US: Longmans, Green.

Borst, W. (1997). *Construction of engineering ontologies for knowledge sharing and reuse, Enschede*, NL: Centre for Telematics and Information Technology (CTIT).

Bourekkache, S., & Kazar, O. (2009). Agent-based approach for e-learning. *International Journal of Emerging Technologies in Learning (iJET)* (vol.4(4), pp.57–63).

Bourekkache, S., Kazar, O., Kahloul, L., Aloui, A., & Benharkat, A.-N. (2015). Semantic annotation approach using ontology for e-learning. In *Proceedings of the 5th international symposium ISKO-Maghreb knowledge organization in the perspective of digital humanities: Researches and applications.*

Brancaccio, A., Demartini, C., Marchisio, M., Pardini, C., & Patrucco, A. (2014). Il progetto pp&s. informatica a scuola. *Mondo Digitale,* 565–574.

Brancaccio, A., Esposito, M., Marchisio, M., & Pardini, C. (2016). L'efficacia dell'apprendimento in rete degli immigrati digitali. l'esperienza smart per le discipline scientifiche. *Mondo Digitale, 15*, 803–821.

Brancaccio, A., Marchisio, M., Palumbo, C., Pardini, C., Patrucco, A., & Zich, R. (2015). Problem posing and solving: Strategic Italian key action to enhance teaching and learning mathematics and informatics in the high school. In *Proceedings of the 2015 IEEE 39th annual computer software and applications conference (COMPSAC)* (vol. 2, pp. 845–850).

Cavagnero, S., Gallina, M., & Marchisio, M. (2015). Scuola dei compiti. didattica digitale per il recupero dell'insuccesso scolastico. *Mondo Digitale, 14*, 834–843.

Chen, C.-M., Peng, C.-J., & Shiue, J.-Y. (2008). Ontology-based concept map for planning personalized learning path. In *Proceedings of the 2008 IEEE conference on cybernetics and intelligent systems* (1337–1342).

Chiappe, A., Segovia Cifuentes, Y., & Yadira Rincón Rodríguez, H. (2007). Toward an instructional design model based on learning objects. *Educational Technology Research and Development, 55*, 671–681.

Clements, D., & Sarama, J. (2004). Learning trajectories in mathematics education. *Mathematical Thinking and Learning, 6*, 81.

Comoglio, M. (2018). *Insegnare e valutare competenze, proceedings of the seminar "valutare e certificare le competenze" in la valutazione degli apprendimenti* (3a ed.).

Confrey, J., Gianopulos, G., McGowan, W., Shah, M., & Belcher, M. (2017). Scaffolding learner-centered curricular coherence using learning maps and diagnostic assessments designed around mathematics learning trajectories. *ZDM: The International Journal on Mathematics Education, 49*, 717–734.

Council of the European Union. (2006). *Recommendation of the European parliament and of the Council of 18 December 2006 on key competences for lifelong learning.* [Online; last accessed 2019, March 31] https://eur-lex.europa.eu/legal-content/EN/ALL/?uri=celex:32006H0962

Council of the European Union. (2018). *Council recommendation of 22 may 2018 on key competences for lifelong learning (text with EEA relevance).* [Online; last accessed 2019, March 31] https://eur-lex.europa.eu/legal-content/EN/TXT/?uri=CELEX:32018H0604(01)

De Marcos, L., Pagés, C., Martínez, J., & Mesa, J. (2007). Competency-based learning object sequencing using particle swarms. In *Proceedings of the 19th IEEE international conference on tools with artificial intelligence* (pp. 111–116).

De Nicola, A., Missikoff, M., & Navigli, R. (2009). A software engineering approach to ontology building. *Information Systems, 34*(2), 258–275.

Di Caro, L., Fioravera, M., Marchisio, M., & Rabellino, S. (2017). A model for structuring shared learning materials within a virtual community. In *Proceedings of EM&M ITALIA 2018 Multi conference* (pp. 613–621).

Di Caro, L., Fioravera, M., Marchisio, M., & Rabellino, S. (2018a). A model for enriching automatic assessment resources with free-text annotations. In *Proceedings of the 15th international conference CELDA 2018, Budapest, Hungary* (pp. 186–193).

Di Caro, L., Fioravera, M., Marchisio, M., & Rabellino, S. (2018b). Alignment of content, prerequisites and educational objectives: Towards automated mapping of digital learning resources. In *Proceedings of the 14th international scientific conference eLearning and software for education, eLSE 2018* (pp. 335–342).

Di Caro, L., Fioravera, M., Marchisio, M., & Rabellino, S. (2018c). Towards adaptive systems for automatic formative assessment in virtual learning communities. In *Proceedings of the 2018 IEEE 42nd annual computer software and applications conference, COMPSAC 2018* (pp. 1000–1005).

Dietze, S., Sanchez-Alonso, S., Ebner, H., Yu, H., Giordano, D., Marenzi, I., & Pereira Nunes, B. (2013). *Interlinking educational resources and the web of data – a survey of challenges and approaches*. Emerald Program: Electronic Library and Information Systems.

Dooley, K., Linder, J. R., & Dooley, L. M. (2006). Advanced methods in distance education: Applications and practices for educators, administrators and learners, chapter VII (pp. 118–131)

Elangovan, D., & Nirmala, K. (2016). Semantic search of e-learning documents using ontology based system. *International Journal of Business Intelligents, 5*, 25.

Elizarov, A., Kirillovich, A., Lipachev, E., Nevzorova, O., Solovyev, V., & Zhiltsov, N. (2014). Mathematical knowledge representation: Semantic models and formalisms. *Lobachevskii Journal of Mathematics., 35*, 348.

Elizarov, A., Zhizhchenko, A., Zhil'tsov, N., Kirillovich, A., & Lipachev, E. (2016). Mathematical knowledge ontologies and recommender systems for collections of documents in physics and mathematics. *Doklady Mathematics, 3*(2), 231–233.

European Commission. (2012). *Press release – commission presents new rethinking education strategy*. [Online; last accessed 2019, March 31] http://europa.eu/rapid/press-release_IP-12-1233_en.htm

Fernández-López, M., Gomez-Perez, A., & Juristo, N. (1997). *Methontology: From ontological art towards ontological engineering*. Engineering Workshop on Ontological Engineering (AAAI97).

Gagné, R. (1968). *Learning hierarchies*. Classic Writings on Instructional Technology

Ganter, B., & Wille, R. (1997). *Formal concept analysis: Mathematical foundations*. Springer.

Gartner, R. (2016). *Metadata: Shaping knowledge from antiquity to the semantic web*. Springer.

Gerry, S., Koschmann, T., & Suthers, D. (2014). *Computer-supported collaborative learning, chapter XIV* (pp. 479–500). Cambridge University Press.

Gierl, M., Changjiang, W., & Jiawen, Z. (2008). Using the attribute hierarchy method to make diagnostic inferences about examinees' cognitive skills in algebra on the sat©. *The Journal of Technology, Learning, and Assessment* (vol. 48(2), pp. 165–187).

Gil-Jaurena, I., & Softic, S. (2016). Aligning learning outcomes and assessment methods: A web tool for e-learning courses. *International Journal of Educational Technology in Higher Education, 13*, 17.

Greenstein, L. (2010). *What teachers really need to know about formative assessment*. Alexandria: ASCD.

Gruber, T. (1994). Toward principles for the design of ontologies used for knowledge sharing. *International Journal of Human-Computer Studies* (vol. 43(5–6), pp. 907–928).

Guarino, N., Oberle, D., & Staab, S. (2019). *What is an ontology? chapter I* (pp. 1–17). Springer Science & Business Media.

Guo, W. (2009). An ontology-based e-learning scenario. In *Methods and applications for advancing distance education technologies: International issues and solutions*.

Guri-Rosenblit, S. (2005). 'Distance education' and 'e-learning': Not the same thing. *Higher Education, 49*, 467.

Heras, J., Pascual, V., & Rubio, J. (2009). Using open mathematical documents to interface computer algebra and proof assistant systems. In *Proceedings of intelligent computer mathematics. CICM 2009. Lecture notes in computer science* (Vol. 5625, pp. 467–473).

Humm, B., & Ossanloo, H. (2017). Cost-effective semi-automatic ontology development from large domain terminology. In *Proceedings of collaborative European research conference, CERC 2017*.

Ignatov, D. (2015). Introduction to formal concept analysis and its applications in information retrieval and related fields. In *Proceedings of the Russian Summer School in Information Retrieval, RuSSIR 2014*.

Ihantola, P. (2011). *Automated assessment of programming assignments: Visual feedback, assignment mobility, and assessment of students' testing skills*. PhD thesis, Department of Computer Science of Aalto University.

Ion, P., Trott, M., Weisstein, E., & Wiedijk, F. (2016). *White paper – Semantic representation of mathematical knowledge workshop*. [Online; last accessed 2019, March 31] http://www.fields.utoronto.ca//sites/default/files/whitepaper.pdf

Ivanova, T. (2011). Adaptive open corpus e-learning and authoring, using collaborative ontology learning. In *Proceedings of the 9th IEEE international conference on Emerging E-learning Technologies and Applications, ICETA 2011*.

Ivanova, T., & Ivanova, M. (2011). Ontology-driven e-learning system in support of knowledge gathering. In *Proceedings of the 7th international scientific conference E-learning and software for education*.

JJackson, P., & Moulinier, I. (2003). Natural language processing for online applications: Text retrieval, extraction and categorization. *Computational Linguistics* (vol. 29(3), pp. 510–511).

Jain, A. K., & Dubes, R. C. (1988). *Algorithms for clustering data*. New York, US: Pearson College Div.

Jonassen, D., Grabinger, S., & Harris, N. (1990). Analyzing and selecting instructional strategies and tactics. Originally published in 1991, PIQ 4.2. *Performance Improvement Quarterly* (vol. 10(1), pp. 34–54).

Jonassen, D., & Grabowski, B. (1993). *Handbook of individual differences, learning and instruction*. Abingdon-on-Thames, UK: Routledge.

Kamareddine, F., & Wells, J. (2008). Computerizing mathematical text with mathlang. *Electronic Notes in Theoretical Computer Science, 205*, 5.

Krämer, B. (2008). Campus content: An infrastructure for sharing and reuse of teaching experience and e-content. *Journal of Lifelong Learning Society* (vol. 4, pp. 133–156).

Maniriho, P., & Effendi, A. (2018). Examining the performance of k-means clustering algorithm. International *Journal of Research in Engineering, Science and Management* (vol. 1, pp. 1–5).

Maple T.A. 10 Online Help. (2015). *Maple T.A. Instructor help – Question designer*. [Online; last accessed 2019, March 31] https://www.maplesoft.com/support/help/MapleTA2017/MapleTAInstructor/ch04s03.aspx#ManagingContent_QuestionDesigner

Marchisio, M., Barana, A., Fioravera, M., Brancaccio, A., Esposito, M., Pardini, C., & Rabellino, S. (2017). Problem solving competence developed through a virtual learning environment in a European context. In *Proceedings of the international scientific conference E-learning and software for education, eLSE 2017* (pp. 455–463).

Martín, A., & León, C. (2012). An intelligent e-learning scenario for knowledge retrieval. In *Proceedings of the 2012 IEEE global engineering education conference, EDUCON 2012* (pp. 1–6).

Mascarenhas, A.; Parsons, S., & Cohen Burrowbridge, S. (2010). Preparing teachers for high-needs schools: A focus on thoughtfully adaptive teaching. *Bank Street Occasional Papers*.

Mitkov, R., & Navigli, R. (2016). Ontologies. In *The Oxford handbook of computational linguistics*. Oxford, UK: Oxford University Press.

Moss, C., & Brookhart, S. (2012). Learning targets: *Helping students aim for understanding in today's lesson*. Alexandria, VA: ASCD.

Mouromtsev, D., Kozlov, F., Parkhimovich, O., & Zelenina, M. (2013). Development of an ontology-based e-learning system. In P. Klinov & D. Mouromtsev (Eds.) *Knowledge Engineering and the Semantic Web. KESW 2013. Communications in Computer and Information Science* (vol. 394, pp. 273–280). Heidelberg, GE: Springer.

Mousavi, H., Kerr, D., Iseli, M., & Zaniolo, C. (2014). Harvesting Domain Specific Ontologies from Text. In *the Proceedings of 2014 IEEE International Conference on Semantic Computing* (pp. 211–218).

Mullis, I., Martin, M., Smith, T., Garden, R., Gregory, K., Gonzalez, E., et al. (2003). *2003 TIMSS assessment frameworks and specifications* (2nd ed.). Chestnut Hill, MA: International Study Center, Lynch School of Education, Boston College.

Nevzorova, O., Zhiltsov, N., Kirillovich, A., & Lipachev, E. (2014). OntoMathPRO ontology: A linked data hub for mathematics. In *Proceedings of the 5th international conference on knowledge engineering and the semantic web, KESW 2014*.

Noy, N., & Mcguinness, D. (2001). *Ontology development 101: A guide to creating your first ontology*. Knowledge Systems Laboratory.

Nyland, R. (2017). A review of tools and techniques for data-enabled formative assessment. *Journal of Educational Technology Systems, 46*(4), 505–526.

Pagael, R. and Schubotz, M. (2014). Mathematical language processing project. In *Proceedings of the MathUI, OpenMath and ThEdu Workshops and Work in Progress track at CICM 2014*.

Phobun, P., & Vicheanpanya, J. (2010). Adaptive intelligent tutoring systems for e-learning systems. *Procedia – Social and Behavioral Sciences, 2*(2), 4064–4069.

Popham, J. (2011). *Transformative assessment in action: An inside look at applying the process*. Alexandria, VA: ASCD.

Proitz, T. (2010). Learning outcomes: What are they? Who defines them? When and where are they defined? Educational Assessment. *Evaluation and Accountability, 22*(2), 119–137.

Rajaee Harandi, S. (2015). Effects of e-learning on students' motivation. *Procedia – Social and Behavioral Sciences* (vol. 181, pp. 432–430).

Rao, K., & Meo, G. (2016). Using universal design for learning to design standards-based lessons. *SAGE Open, 6*, 215824401668068.

Rasila, A., Harjula, M., & Zenger, K. (2007). Automatic assessment of mathematics exercises: Experiences and future prospects. *The second RefleKTori 2007 symposium of Engineering Education*.

Rasila, A., Malinen, J., & Tiitu, H. (2015). On automatic assessment and conceptual understanding. *Teaching Mathematics and its Applications, 34*, 149.

Ravotto, P., Fulantelli, G., & Oprea, L. (2011). *Preparing the teachers for a competence-based education system*. Galati, RO: Europlus Publishing.

Romero, L., Ballejos, L., Gutiérrez, M., & Caliusco, M. (2015). Stakeholder's analysis in e-learning software process development. *EAI Endorsed Transactions on e-Learning, 2*(5), 1–8.

Sarasu, R., & Thyagharajan, K. K. (2014). Concept-based annotation and retrieval of e-learning materials. *WIT Transactions on Information and Communication Technologies, 60*, 393–399.

Schubotz, M., Grigorev, A., Leich, M., Cohl, H., Meuschke, N., Gipp, B., Youssef, A. S., & Markl, V. (2016). Semantification of identifiers in mathematics for better math information retrieval. In *Proceedings of the 39th international ACM SIGIR conference* (pp. 135–144).

Shmelev, V., Karpova, M., & Dukhanov, A. (2015). An approach of learning path sequencing based on revised bloom's taxonomy and domain ontologies with the use of genetic algorithms. *Procedia Computer Science, 66*, 711.

Shute, V., & Zapata-Rivera, D. (2012). Adaptive educational systems. In P. Durlach & A. Lesgold (Eds.), *Adaptive Technologies for Training and Education* (pp. 7–27). Cambridge, UK: Cambridge University Press.

Skalka, J., & Drlík, M. (2018). Conceptual framework of microlearning-based training mobile application for improving programming skills. In *Proceedings of the 11th international conference on interactive collaborative learning* (pp. 213–224).

Skopljanac Macina, F., & Blaskovic, B. (2014). Formal concept analysis - overview and applications. *Procedia Engineering, 69*, 1258–1267.

Snow, R. (1977). Individual differences and instructional theory. *Educational Researcher, 6*, 11.
Soeiro, A., Lossenko, J., Softic, S., & Gil-Jaurena, I. (2014). Time to assess learning outcomes in e-learning (TALOE) – e-assessment practices. In *Proceedings of EDEN 2014 annual conference*.
Solovyev, V., & Zhiltsov, N. (2011). Logical structure analysis of scientific publications in mathematics. In *Proceedings of the international conference on web intelligence, mining and semantics, WIMS 2011*.
Steen, A., & Richard Movik, H. (2017). Atomized feedback, an approach to automatic formative assessment. In *Proceedings of the 10th annual international conference of education* (pp. 5206–5214).
Steinberger, C. (2017). In search of reusable educational resources in the web. In *Proceedings of the 3rd international conference on higher education advances, HEAd'17* (pp. 1–8).
Tam, V., Lam, E., & Fung, S. (2014). A new framework of concept clustering and learning path optimization to develop the next-generation e-learning systems. *Journal of Computers in Education, 1*, 335.
Tomlinson, C. (2001). *How to differentiate instruction in mixed ability classrooms*. New York, US: Pearson College Div.
Trinchero, R. (2017). *Costruire e certificare competenze con il curricolo verticale nel primo ciclo*. Milano, IT: Rizzoli Education.
Tugsgerel, B., Anane, R., & Theodoropoulos, G. (2010). An integrated approach to learning object sequencing. In *Proceedings of the 10th IEEE international conference on advanced learning technologies, ICALT 2010* (pp. 105–109).
Wang, F., Li, X., Lei, W., Huang, C., Yin, M., & Pong, T.-C. (2015). Constructing learning maps for lecture videos by exploring Wikipedia knowledge. Proceedings of the Pacific Rim conference on Multimedia, PCM 2015, pages 559–569.
Watt, S. (2016). How to build a global digital mathematics library. In *2016 18th international symposium on symbolic and numeric algorithms for scientific computing (SYNASC)* (pp. 37–40).
Webb, D. (2014). Bloom's taxonomy in mathematics education. In *Encyclopedia of mathematics education* (pp. 63–68). Dordrecht, NE: Springer.
Xu, D., & Tian, Y. (2015). A comprehensive survey of clustering algorithms. *Annals of Data Science, 2*, 165.
Youssef, A. (2017). Part-of-math tagging and applications. In *Proceedings of the international conference on intelligent computer mathematics 2017* (pp. 356–374).
Zhang, C., Kwon, Y., Kramer, J., Kim, E., & Agogino, A. (2017). Concept clustering in design teams: A comparison of human and machine clustering. *Journal of Mechanical Design, 139(11)*.

Chapter 8
Orchestrating Outdoor Location-Based Learning Activities

Kadri Mettis and Terje Väljataga

8.1 Introduction

Various technologies available for educational purposes can provide resources for teachers to plan, orchestrate and support cooperation and creativity. For example, computer technology has several functions for helping orchestration (Kollar, Hämäläinen, Evans, De Wever, & Perrotta, 2011), although the use of technology always challenges a teacher's work (Arvaja, Hämäläinen, & Rasku-Puttonen, 2009). The effectiveness of mobile learning in outdoor learning has been studied previously, and various ways have been proposed to reduce the burden of orchestration (Lai, Lai, Chuang, & Wu, 2015; Munoz-Cristobal, Gallego-Lema, Arribas-Cubero, Martínez-Mones, & Asensio-Perez, 2017), but in all of these studies, the main creator and designer of the learning process is a teacher. Crompton, Burke, Kristen and Gregory (2017) point out that in most mobile learning studies, students are ready-made consumers of knowledge and are not exploiting the full potential of mobile devices. Ishtaiwa, Khaled and Dukmak (2015) survey showed that mobile learning has different pedagogical uses; however, it tends to focus on certain activities. Crompton and others (2017) have concluded that a large proportion of mobile learning studies have been conducted in a formal education environment, that is, in a classroom or school district. The use of mobile learning in a non-formal environment (Crompton et al., 2017), for example, in a park, a zoo and a botanical garden, should be explored. The goal of this study is to explore the challenges of orchestrating outdoor learning in two different types of learning scenarios and to understand the potential of SmartZoos and Avastusrada applications to orchestrate outdoor learning activities.

K. Mettis (✉) · T. Väljataga
Tallinn University, Tallinn, Estonia
e-mail: kadrimet@tlu.ee; terjev@tlu.ee

© Springer Nature Switzerland AG 2020
P. Isaias et al. (eds.), *Technology Supported Innovations in School Education*, Cognition and Exploratory Learning in the Digital Age,
https://doi.org/10.1007/978-3-030-48194-0_8

8.2 Orchestration

Many educators and researchers have used the word "orchestration" to design and manage real-time classroom activities, learning processes and teaching activities (Dillenbourg & Fischer, 2007; Gravier, Fayolle, Noyel, Leleve, & Benmohamed, 2006). An orchestration does not indicate that the lecture is more intense or that the teacher has to make a show. Orchestration refers more to the meaning of "teacher's central constructivism". Students need to learn through activities, but teachers have a role as manager in the whole scenario (Dillenbourg & Jermann, 2010). Furthermore, very often mobile learning brings along a set of personal devices, which fosters learning experiences to be designed more learner-centered and learner-controlled in complex distributed settings. Pedagogical concepts such as knowledge building and knowledge creation metaphor (Paavola, Engeström, & Hakkarainen, 2012), learning through authoring of user-generated content (Fitzgerald, 2012; Klopfer & Sheldon, 2010, etc.), learning through making (Hsu, Baldwin, & Ching, 2017) and learner as a creator and designer (Lim, 2008; Sorensen & Levinson, 2014; Väljataga, Fiedler, & Laanpere, 2015, etc.) become central in mobile learning design. Following these concepts while designing learning experiences has a great potential to influence orchestration of learning experiences in distributed outdoor settings. Quite likely teacher-centered approaches, in which a learner follows a predesigned scenario, and student-centered approaches, in which a learner acquires knowledge through creating artefacts, ideas, models, experiences, etc., have a different effect on orchestration challenges and needs.

Prieto, Dlab, Gutiérrez, Abdulwahed and Balid (2011) have suggested 5 + 3 aspects in their literature review about orchestrating learning that have emerged from different studies. The five main aspects are *design*, the preparation and organization of learning activities; *management*, classroom management, time management, group management and workflow management; *awareness*, the perceptual processes aimed at modelling what is happening in the learning situation; *adaptation*, the adaptations to the designed/planned learning activities, to cope with unexpected or extraneous events, take advantage of emergent learning opportunities or adapt to student learning progress; and *role of the teacher and other actors*, the identification of who performs the previous four aspects and what the relationship is between the actors (e.g. a teacher, a technological system, students themselves and researchers). Other three aspects are *theory*, the mental models that different actors have about how the scenario should be orchestrated; *pragmatism*, the intrinsic and extrinsic contextual constraints that the actors have to cope with compliance with the mandatory curriculum, limited amount of time available for a lesson, need for discipline in the classroom, available economic resources and so on; *synergy*, how the multiple elements present in the scenario (new technologies and legacy tools, learning activities at different social levels, students' prior knowledge and learning styles) can be aligned by the orchestrators to achieve effective learning. These aspects can be helpful for planning evaluation for orchestration process and tools (Prieto et al., 2011).

8.2.1 Instrumental Orchestration

Instrumental orchestration is defined as the intentional and systematic organization of various digital artefacts by the teacher to guide students (Drijvers, Doorman, Boon, Reed, & Gravemeijer, 2010). In instrumental orchestration, three elements can be distinguished: didactic design or how different means are related to the environment, the way in which the teacher decides to use the didactic design and the didactic presentation or how the selected didactic design and presentation are actually used, such as how to link student questions to the context or how to cope with emerging problems (Drijvers et al., 2010). Coordinating the academic environment of an IT environment in recent years has been a source of interest in research communities engaged in studying technology learning (Dillenbourg, Järvelä, & Fischer, 2009; Roschelle, Dimitriadis, & Hoppe, 2013). Since the first problem faced by teachers in carrying out such activities as the creation and preparation of a scenario, several studies have recommended the use of a special environment that allows linking all other tools in one place (Munoz-Cristobal et al., 2014; Ternier, Klemke, Kalz, van Ulzen, & Specht, 2012). In these environments, however, there are restrictions on orchestration: (1) most environments have limited or even no opportunity to regulate the flexibility of students' work; this is especially important in the case of the use of librarianship environments that may require partial orchestration burden for students (Sharples, 2013); (2) many environments do not allow the integration of technologies that teachers already use, which reduces the use of these methods by teachers (Cuendet, Bonnard, Do-Lenh, & Dillenbourg, 2013; Prieto, Wen, Caballero, & Dillenbourg, 2014); and (3) most environments do not allow the use of surrounding or context where learning takes place which is an important factor in achieving unobtrusive learning (Milrad et al., 2013).

In addition to the limitations described above, in the case of out-of-school education, the real dispersal of students must also be taken into account, which makes it very difficult for the teacher to monitor and support the learning process. Due to the high workload of teachers, it is difficult to put in place new methods and tools that would be needed to implement new learning pathways. In order to solve this problem, reducing the burden on teachers' orchestration, for example, by allowing for mobile applications where a large proportion of the planning would be distributed to students, might be an option. This in turn requires changes in teachers' mindset regarding learning design, i.e. to accept the view that learning through creating has a pedagogical value. In addition, it would be wise to develop an easy-to-use technological solution that helps orchestrate learners in dispersed environments.

8.3 SmartZoos and Avastusrada Learning Apps

Mobile learning could help teachers to conduct outdoor education by involving learners in the creation and orchestration of a learning process. For that it is necessary to know how to arrange, orchestrate and monitor such diversified forms of learning in a systematic and technical manner. In pursuit of the goal to support teachers' orchestration in outdoor settings, to reduce teachers' workload and to share part of the orchestration load (in this case planning) to students, location-based outdoor learning apps Avastusrada and SmartZooswere used. The used applications are very similar web-based mobile learning tools, which provide structure and frame to create and follow learning tracks with various location points, help to set learning goals and organize sequence of the activities. In both applications the users can follow the chosen track and move from one location to another with the guidance of their phone, and in specific location points, they need to solve various tasks. The tasks can be different types of questions like information, one correct answer, multiple correct answers, free-form answer, match pairs, making an embedded content question or photo task. It is possible to set also other parameters like language, distance from the location point in order for the task to be open, location of the task, etc. (Fig. 8.1).

The main idea and the design of the two applications are the same; differences occur in some features (Table 8.1). While SmartZoos is a location-based tool developed for the use at zoos, Avastusrada can be used anywhere and is not restricted by location. Avastusrada has teachers' view where it is possible to track users' locations and submitted answers, which is not possible in SmartZoos. SmartZoos on the other hand gives an opportunity for everyone to create tracks (Fig. 8.2), which is currently not an option in Avastusrada.

8.4 Method

The current chapter takes a closer look at teachers' orchestration challenges and load in two different learning scenarios: (1) teacher-created learning tracks, in which students' role was to follow the tracks with the help of Avastusrada application, and (2) students as creators who learned a topic through creating tracks themselves with SmartZoos application. Conducted studies were a part of a bigger research, which follows a design-based research with the aim to develop outdoor learning applications and appropriate learning designs for authentic learning experiences. The piloting sessions described in this chapter focused on testing the suitability of SmartZoos and Avastusrada applications and understanding further development needs of the applications for outdoor learning and investigating teachers' experience and orchestration challenges in two different scenarios.

In the first study, 12 teachers who had experience in using Avastusrada during the period of 1 year were interviewed. These teachers had developed and tested several learning tracks in Avastusrada for K-12 students of various age. In these learning scenarios, students' role was to follow the track designed by their teacher. The students got clear and concrete instructions in every track without any option to be creative. In addition to Avastusrada and personal mobile phones, a number of various Vernier sensors were used. In some of the location points, the students were asked to carry out measures about environmental conditions (temperature, pH,

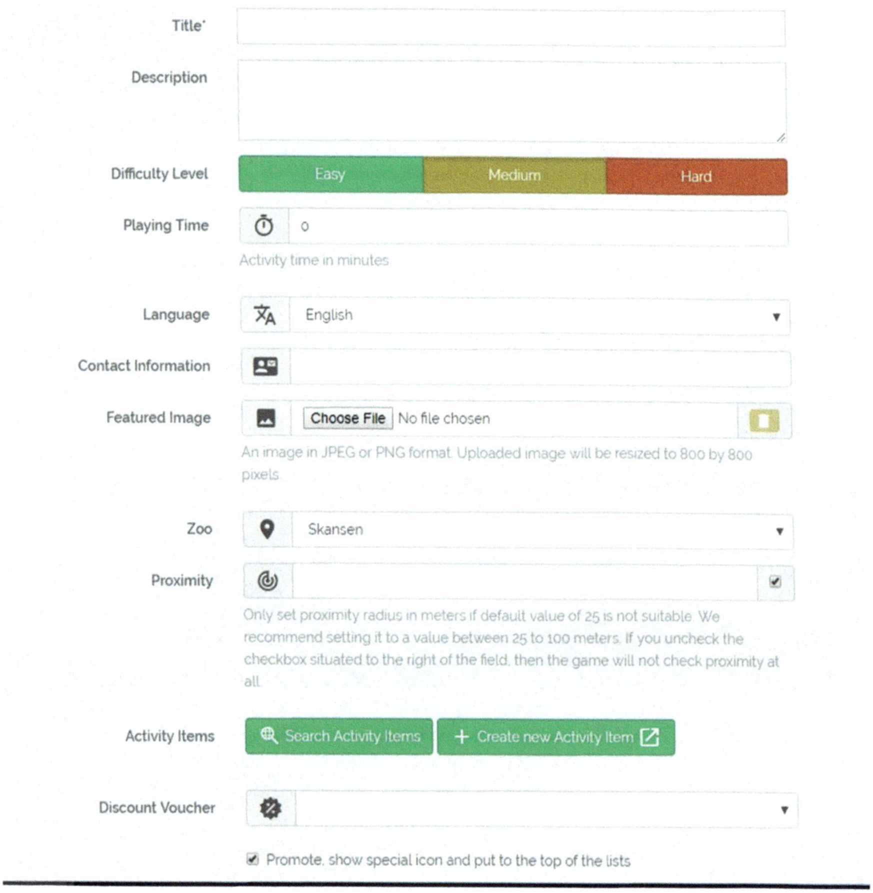

Fig. 8.1 Screenshot of a creation process in SmartZoos application, similar process appears in Avastusrada application, but creation feature in Avastusrada is not opened to every user

water turbidity, etc.). The common goal in these scenarios was to integrate various subjects to provide students real-life learning situations.

In the second study, nine K-12 students and three teachers conducted an experiment with the SmartZoos application. Together with the teachers and the Zoological Gardens pedagogues, activities were planned, where the learner could acquire the knowledge through playing and creating learning tracks in the zoo. First, the students followed the track in the zoo created by their teachers to get an understanding of the tool and what kind of tasks are possible to create in every location point. After that the students were asked to create a track in groups for other student groups to follow. This task was given as homework; thus, the students were left alone to deal with the task and occurring challenges.

For the data collection, a focus group interview method was used to study teachers' experience and orchestration challenges while using Avastusrada

Table 8.1 Comparison of SmartZoos and Avastusrada features

Features	SmartZoos	Avastusrada
Users can follow the chosen track	Yes	Yes
Every user can create tracks	Yes	No
Question types (information, one correct answer, multiple correct answers, freeform answer, match pairs, making an embedded content question or photo task)	Yes	Yes
Location	Restricted	Can be used anywhere
Teachers' view	No	Yes
Possibility to track players	No	Yes
Possibility to see players' answers	No	Yes
Location based	Yes	Yes
Simple user statistics	Yes	Yes

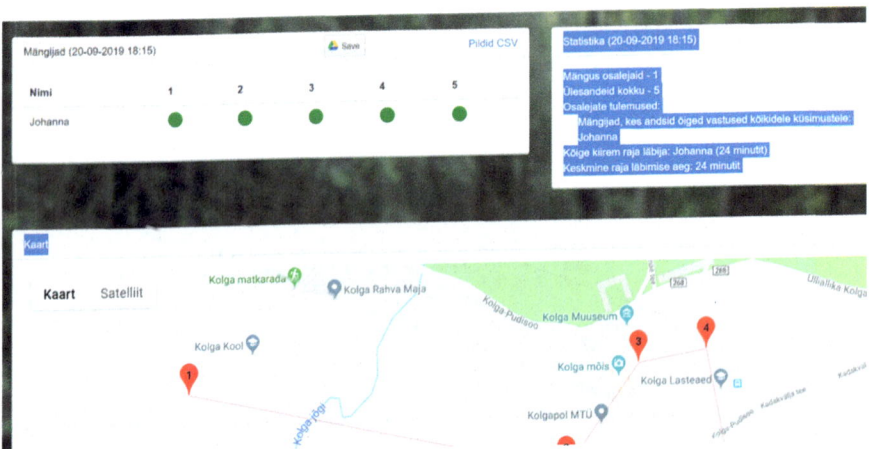

Fig. 8.2 Teachers' dashboard in Avastusrada. This feature is missing from SmartZoos application

(teacher-centered approach) and SmartZoos (student-centered approach) application. 12 teachers who participated in the first study were from 6 different schools which were partners in one of the projects that aimed to develop technology-enhanced outdoor learning scenarios, and during 1 year they had experience in designing and conducting activities with Avastusrada. Participants in the second experiment were nine tenth graders from one K-12 school and three biology teachers who had experience in using SmartZoos.

All the focus group interviews were grouped and categorized into first five categories based on the orchestration aspects. Prieto et al. (2011) define in their 5 + 3 orchestration framework (Prieto et al., 2011). The formed categories were planning/design (planning, often referred to as learning design), regulation/management (issues related to class, time, workflow and group management), adaptation/flexibility/intervention (changing and adapting the design/plan to both the local context of the classroom and the emergent occurrences during the enactment of learning activities), awareness/assessment (awareness of what is happening in the classroom and within the learners' minds, assessment) and roles of the teacher and other actors. Results were compared and discussed together.

8.5 Results

The aim of conducting the focus group interviews was to get a deeper understanding of the teachers' experiences and challenges while using mobile learning applications for outdoor learning, their need for support to reduce their orchestration load and potential further development needs of the applications Avastusrada and SmartZoos. Students' experiences and opinions about the application features and learning designs were studied with a questionnaire. As the aim of this study was to focus on teachers, then these results are described elsewhere (Mettis & Väljataga, 2018).

First, the interview focused on teachers' attitudes and previous experiences in using technology for learning. All the teachers consider the use of technology as a very important part of learning, and they have tried to find different ways to use digital technology in their classrooms. The reason to do it is mostly derived from local curricula, which aim to develop students' digital competences. One of the teachers claimed: "Nowadays the digital competences development is very important. When students can create learning experiences on their own then that is a big plus". The participating teachers have the same approach for using mobile devices in their lessons. They want to make use of existing students' devices and make lessons more interactive or supporting students' self-study. The teachers acknowledge that the schools have more equipment than before which is giving more possibilities. This is nicely reported by one of the teachers: "There are new tablet sets at the school, we only had one laptop set before. Two tablet sets and WiFi router. And it goes well, I use much more this year. We also have technical support at school who checks if everything is okay, batteries full and programs installed. If the technological side is okay, then it goes nicely". All the teachers allow their students use smartphones in their lessons, for example, electronic tests or searching for information. They also have used mobile devices in outdoor learning, for example, plant and lichen determinants and Avastusrada, to make discovery tracks around the schoolhouse or park. There exists a big motivation to use more technology in outdoor settings, but there are certain limitations, for example, location, weather and a lot of work with preparation. To conclude, the participating teachers were already rather familiar with mobile technologies and have some experience in implementing them in their lessons.

The interview results presented below will be structured according to Prieto et al.'s (2011) framework to understand the different orchestration aspects in distributed outdoor learning settings.

Design/Planning All the teachers point out that preparing for just outdoor learning activities without any technology and subject integration is already very time-consuming. In the studies presented in this chapter, first, the teachers need to learn and prepare the necessary technology they are planning to use, and they also need to know the area where they plan to conduct the activity. For example, one teacher described that she planned to use Vernier sensors for outdoor learning activity, and it took her 1 year to find a solution how to connect it with computers. On the other hand, some teachers suggested that teachers' preparation time could be reduced by engaging some students with preparation, for example, programming some devices in the lesson. The teachers from the second study pointed out that preparing an outdoor activity at the zoo can be even more time-consuming than near the school. This idea is illustrated by the one of the teachers: "Teachers will need 2 days for preparation. One day for walking and planning at the zoo, the other day for completing the track. Teachers would prefer already composed tracks most likely". They also mentioned that the time expenditure of course depends on how well the teachers know the particular zoo.

To make teachers' life easier, the teachers from the second study suggest that the questions and tasks in the applications should already exist beforehand. Questions should contain meta-info about the grade and the topic to make searching easier, so it would be possible to filter and use what is suitable for a particular purpose. They also suggest that there is a need for a place where to change the experiences and ideas with other teachers like a forum or the possibility to evaluate tracks so that other users would know what kind of tracks to choose. They refer to similarity in social media that good rating is trusted. The teachers point out that it is necessary to give a possibility for students to create the questions and tracks. This would take away the need for teachers to prepare, and it would give students the chance to be creative. On the other hand, it raises new issues, like how to monitor the quality and the process of creating task. As the best design for this kind of outdoor learning activity, the teachers from the second study suggest a project day type of solution where students create questions/tasks and tracks directly at the zoo and play each other's tracks later. The activity would be longer for students, but at the same time it would free teachers from preparing the tracks and questions.

Although both applications provide structure and scripting of the learning design to a certain degree, designing integrated learning activities with technology out of the classroom is rather time-consuming for teachers, and they prefer to have some content already created by professional content providers, which is rated, and the teachers can choose according to their particular needs. In general, the teachers have to make a choice whether they prepare more themselves and win in lesson time, which is crucial for filling the curricula, or they engage students into preparation and share part of their role to students losing in lesson time and quality. As it is seen, this opens up another box of challenges for teachers. However, at the same time, students definitely gain more from doing themselves, because they will have to take responsibility and handle problems independently.

Regulation/Management Time allocation was problematic for most of the teachers in both studies, because of the school's everyday schedules and the teachers' underestimation of students' orienteering skills. Thus, the whole activities took longer as planned. In practice, it needs cooperation within the school so that these activities could have more time. New ways of learning and new instruments and applications mean extra time for introducing them to students and getting acquainted with them. The teachers from the first study emphasized that planning the lessons and rearranging schedules for outdoor learning activities are essential. Due to some school regulations (such as there should be at least two teachers with students if a plan is to leave the school territory), teachers' busy timetable, etc., going outside with students needs a lot of organizing. Nevertheless, the teachers also state that the more they do these kind learning projects, the easier it gets from the organizing side as well.

Based on the aforementioned teachers' experiences, organization of outdoor activities is one of the biggest challenges for teachers requiring good communication and management skills.

Furthermore, as the applications have different affordances to manage and monitor students' workflow, the teachers' experiences were different in these studies. The teachers from the first study had an option to keep track on students' progress by following teacher's dashboard in Avastusrada with students' submitted answers and their locations. All the teachers who used SmartZoos application complained about this missing option as it leaves the teachers sitting in the dark, not knowing how their students are managing and not able to provide support and help whenever needed. Thus, the feature, which allows teachers to communicate via the application with the students, was considered essential by the teachers from both studies. This thought can be illustrated by one of the teachers: "I'm responsible, I have to know that they are safe. It is very important. Would be good to see where they are".

To conclude, regulating learning process (both external and facilitating self-regulation) and student activities is not currently well supported in either application, and additional features need to be developed. Some sort of automated management and regulation of the learning process by mobile applications can be an option.

Adaptation/Flexibility/Intervention The missing features in Avastusrada and SmartZoos applications discussed previously influence also orchestration-related adaptations. Under the adaptation category, the teachers' experiences related to adapting with the sudden changes while dealing with outdoor learning were gathered. It is important that environments that support orchestration would enable fast changes whenever needed. The teachers from both studies mentioned that the applications allow to change questions easily, so the teacher can interrupt and change tasks or information quickly which helps to adapt the activity to the current situation. One of the teachers explained: "Once I was too busy to go there and I used only website. And they didn't find the answers. You have to put much effort into it, but you can change questions here easily". A similar situation was described by another teacher from the first study, who conducted an activity where students had to distinguish species of water invertebrates. She noticed that the students can't remember the names themselves, but if they see the correct name in the list, they will recognize it. The teacher added all possible species in the list as correct answers, and the students could choose from what they saw.

Of course, being aware of the students' progress and their location would allow teachers to react to emergent occurrences during the enactment of learning activity faster and more efficiently. The same applies to the next aspect of orchestration – being aware of what is happening in the learning situation, especially if it is distributed, irregular and in a new context.

Awareness/Assessment In addition to awareness of what is happening outside the classroom, the current applications do not support assessment very well. One of the teachers from the second study explains the problem quite nicely: "Right now SmartZoos is not supporting assessment. I don't see summary report. I don't know how the students performed. It is not possible to grade. They can go through the track and complete... well... they played...so? nice? How did you like? liked! What did you learn? I only get to know if I ask them afterwards". Some of the teachers also mentioned that it is not that important to know where the students are but more essential is the possibility to give timely feedback and assess as discussed already in the previous sections. One of the teachers from the second study adds: "I have no idea what students are doing, and if they are doing at all". This applies for both while students follow the track (scenario 1) and create one themselves (scenario 2). The teachers want to be able to interrupt students for guidance to avoid acquiring misconceptions. They reported that they didn't have the overview of what their students were doing, but in their opinion it was important to monitor the students' work progress. On the other hand, one teacher also noted that it is not good to monitor the students too much; the students' creativity and joy will be restricted.

The teachers from the first study who used Avastusrada had a feature for monitoring students' progress and location during the learning activity. Nevertheless, currently the summary of the submitted answers is not supporting teachers' needs. As the answer sheet in the system wasn't exactly as usable as teachers would have expected, they preferred to use other methods, which were not related to the used applications. In case of Avastusrada, it is possible to use feedback email, which sums up all the results for both students and teachers, but during the study some technical issues emerged with this feature.

In general the teachers emphasize that reflection and feedback are important, and they shouldn't be skipped, but the students' tasks do not have to be graded. As already mentioned before, some of the important awareness mechanisms of the applications are currently poorly designed or completely missing, which would support well-orchestrated learning scenarios.

Roles The teacher's role in orchestrating a learning process is crucial, even if the learning scenario has been designed as a learner-centered activity. In this case the teacher may seem not to be the main "conductor". The teachers from the second study were greatly supporting the idea of sharing orchestration load to students and through that giving the role of a teacher partially to the students. They see it as a more effective way of learning, which does not mean that the teacher is not needed anymore. This learner-driven orchestration may happen on different levels. In the case of our second study, the teachers still orchestrated the whole process providing the general goals and frames for the activity and only partially gave away their roles and tasks. But at the same time the teachers also note the risks with this kind of scenarios. The quality of the tracks created by the students and the possibility of students not taking the task seriously are presented. However, it must be noted that this is also a learning process and mistakes should be accepted. The teachers from the first case emphasize that the students certainly should be engaged into preparation of an activity (setting up equipment, programming devices if these are planned to use). The more they are familiar with the devices and systems used during the lessons, the more independent they will get. Our second study demonstrated very well that the students were able to work on their own (create a track as homework) and solve problems by themselves be it technical or content related.

A summary of the features in the used applications about the five main orchestration aspects is provided in Table 8.2.

Orchestrating learning activities outside the classroom needs practice and answering many pragmatic questions such as: "What is the situation with technology in the school?" "What kind of technology?" "When is available?" For instance, the teachers from the first study used besides Avastusrada additional Vernier sensors for carrying out a set of various environmental measurements. They recognized that the schools have a limited number of devices and the teachers need to be very creative to make use of the devices with the greatest potential. They had to decide whether

Table 8.2 Description of application features of Avastusrada and SmartZoos according to Prieto's 5 + 3 framework

Features	Avastusrada	SmartZoos
Design/planning	Teacher plans all activities and creates the track. Very time-consuming	Teacher can direct students to create content. Less time allocated for preparation but loss in content quality
Regulation/time management	Teachers can keep track on students' progress. Teachers can adjust the plan according to the situation or help a group who has a problem. Communication possibility is missing	Teachers don't have overview about students' progress. Communication possibility is missing
Adaptation/flexibility/intervention	Possible to interrupt and make quick adjustments	Possible to interrupt and make quick adjustments
Awareness/assessment	Some awareness is provided but designed poorly	Not supporting assessment. Students get a summary email with the answers only
Roles	Teacher is leading and creating everything. Orchestration load is not shared with students	Teacher is in lead of everything but can decide to share some orchestration load to students

to use students' devices or school equipment and what is the level of digital competence of the students. Obviously, there are many practical questions teachers have to ask and find answers; however, the teachers reported that through constant practicing, the problems and issues get solved faster and with less effort. Also, the students get more confident every time they use technology. Despite the constantly occurring challenges and problems, the teachers point out that outdoor learning is very refreshing and there are less problems every time. They mention that the best place to learn about nature is in nature, and it is important to emphasize using different senses, discussions and discoveries while learning. As a positive side while using mobile devices, they point out motivation, support for students natural need to discover and purposeful use of device. One of the teachers claimed: "It is a very big plus that students can investigate and try themselves".

From the orchestration perspective, it is very important that different environments and activities would be combined smoothly and would support each other. Based on the interview data, we can report that SmartZoos and Avastusrada enabled combining physical and virtual spaces, helping students to learn and engage more. Both of the tools allow designing in the learning scenario some playful elements, for instance, competition. One of the teachers from the second study reported: "I like that students are active and need to show initiative. Guys were engaged. I was surprised. One was facetiming with a boyfriend, but others were engaged... It was fun, like Pokemon Go. Boys liked it. Even though there were problems with GPS, it was still fun for them. It was like catching the Pokemon".

8.6 Conclusion

The goal of this study was to explore teachers' orchestration challenges in outdoor learning settings and understand the applicability of the used applications SmartZoos and Avastusrada for orchestration purposes. In general, the teachers from both studies were positively minded about using this kind of learning tool and learning setting despite the fact that planning and designing learning activities outside the classroom with mobile technologies is very time-consuming and challenging. They acknowledged that the applications have the potential to orchestrate learning activities in distributed outdoor settings; however, they need additional features in order to facilitate teachers' work. The teachers' main concerns were related to the possibility to access and monitor students' playing and creating process and communicate with students directly through the applications. Based on the focus group interview, we can claim that implementing these two different scenarios brings along rather similar orchestration challenges for the teachers. However, the results from the second study showed that these tools could be successfully used with some additional features in activities, where more responsibilities are given to students. Sharing orchestration load to students actually creates a condition for students to be more creative, independent and self-directed and at the same time be a successful solution for reducing teachers' preparation time. This of course presumes that the implemented pedagogical designs need to be reconsidered from teacher-centered to more student-centered approaches. Furthermore, from awareness, assessment and management perspectives, it is necessary for well-orchestrated learning experiences to add learning analytics features for teachers. Because of the small sample size, the results can't be generalized. However, the findings from this study are a good start for developing tools that would support teachers while planning, conducting and sharing orchestration load in outdoor learning.

Acknowledgements This project is partially funded by SmartZoos, CB64, Central Baltic Programme 2014–2020, and the European Union's Horizon 2020 Research and Innovation Programme, grant agreement No. 669074 and by the project "TU TEE – Tallinn University as a promoter of intelligent lifestyle" (nr 2014–2020.4.01.16-0033) under activity A5 in the Tallinn University Centre of Excellence in Educational Innovation.

References

Arvaja, M., Hämäläinen, R., & Rasku-Puttonen, H. (2009). Challenges for the teacher's role in promoting productive knowledge construction in computer-supported collaborative learning contexts. In J. O. Lindberg & A. D. Olofsson (Eds.), *Online learning communities and teacher professional development: Methods for improved education delivery* (pp. 263–280). Hersey: IGI Global.

Crompton, H., Burke, D., Kristen, H., & Gregory, K. H. (2017). The use of mobile learning in PK-12 education: A systematic review. *Computers & Education, 110*, 51–63.

Cuendet, S., Bonnard, Q., Do-Lenh, S., & Dillenbourg, P. (2013). Designing augmented reality for the classroom. *Computers & Education, 68*, 557–569.

Dillenbourg, P., & Fischer, F. (2007). Basics of computer-supported collaborative learning. *Zeitschrift für Berufs- und Wirtschaftspädagogik., 21*, 111–130.

Dillenbourg, P., Järvelä, S., & Fischer, F. (2009). The evolution of research on computer-supported collaborative learning. In N. Balacheff, S. Ludvigsen, T. Jong, A. Lazonder, & S. Barnes (Eds.), *Technology-enhanced learning* (p. 3e19). Dordrecht: Springer Netherlands.

Dillenbourg, P., & Jermann, P. (2010). Technology for classroom orchestration. In: Khine, M.S., Saleh, I.M. (eds.) New science of learning: cognition, computers and collaboration in education, 525–552. Springer, Dordrecht.

Drijvers, P., Doorman, M., Boon, P., Reed, H., & Gravemeijer, K. (2010). The teacher and the tool: Instrumental orchestrations in the technology-rich mathematics classroom. *Educational Studies in Mathematics, 75*, 213–234.

Fitzgerald, E. (2012). Creating user-generated content for location-based learning: an authoring framework. *Journal of Computer Assisted Learning, 28*(3), 195–207.

Gravier, C., Fayolle, J., Noyel, G., Leleve, A., & Benmohamed, H. (2006). Distance learning: Closing the gap between remote labs and learning management systems. In *Proceedings of IEEE first international conference on E-learning in industrial electronics, Hammamet, Tunisie, 18–20 December* (pp. 130–134).

Hsu, Y.-C., Baldwin, S., & Ching, Y.-H. (2017). Learning through making and maker education. *TechTrends, 61*(6), 589–594.

Ishtaiwa, F. F., Khaled, A., & Dukmak, S. (2015). Faculty members' perceptions of the integration, affordances, and challenges of Mobile learning. *International Journal of E-learning & Distance Education, 30*(2), 1–20.

Klopfer, E., & Sheldon, J. (2010). Augmenting your own reality: Student authoring of science-based augmented reality games. *New Directions for Youth Development, 128*, 85–94.

Kollar, I., Hämäläinen, R., Evans, M., De Wever, B., & Perrotta, C. (2011). Orchestrating CSCL – More than a metaphor? In H. Spada, G. Stahl, N. Miyake, & N. Law (Eds.), *Connecting computer-supported collaborative learning to policy and practice: CSCL2011 conference proceedings* (Vol. II, pp. 946–947). International Society of the Learning Sciences, Hong Kong, China.

Lai, A., Lai, H.-Y., Chuang, W.-H., & Wu, Z.-H. (2015). Developing a mobile learning management system for outdoors nature science activities based on 5e learning cycle. *International Conference e-Learning*, 2015, pp. 59–65.

Lim, C. P. (2008). Spirit of the game: Empowering students as designers in schools? *British Journal of Educational Technology, 39*(6), 996–1003.

Mettis, K., & Väljataga, T. (2018). Get out! Helping teachers orchestrate outdoor game-based learning activities. In D. G. Sampson, D. Ifenthaler, & P. Isaías (Eds.), *CELDA2018 cognition and exploratory learning in digital age: CELDA2018, Budapest, Hungary, 21–23 October* (pp. 3–10). IADIS, Budapest, Hungary. https://www.celda-conf.org/wp-content/uploads/2019/04/CELDA_2018.pdf

Milrad, M., Wong, L.-H., Sharples, M., Hwang, G.-J., Looi, C.-K., & Ogata, H. (2013). Seamless learning: An international perspective on next-generation technology-enhanced learning. In Z. L. Berge & L. Y. Muilenburg (Eds.), *Handbook of mobile learning* (p. 95e108). Abingdon: Routledge.

Munoz-Cristobal, J. A., Prieto, L. P., Asensio-Perez, J. I., Martínez-Mones, A., Jorrín-Abellan, I. M., & Dimitriadis, Y. (2014). Deploying learning designs across physical and web spaces: Making pervasive learning affordable for teachers. *Pervasive and Mobile Computing, 14*, 31e46.

Munoz-Cristobal, J. A., Gallego-Lema, V., Arribas-Cubero, H. F., Martínez-Mones, A., & Asensio-Perez, J. I. (2017). Using virtual learning environments in bricolage mode for orchestrating learning situations across physical and virtual spaces. *Computers & Education, 109*, 233–252.

Paavola, S., Engeström, R., & Hakkarainen, K. (2012). Trialogical approach as a new form of mediation. In A. Moen, A. I. Morch, & S. Paavola (Eds.), *Collaborative knowledge creation: Practices, Tools, Concepts* (pp. 1–14), Sense publishers, Rotterdam.

Prieto, L. P., Dlab, M. H., Gutiérrez, I., Abdulwahed, M., & Balid, W. (2011). Orchestrating technology enhanced learning: A literature review and a conceptual framework. *International Journal of Technology Enhanced Learning, 3*(6), 583–598. Inderscience.

Prieto, L. P., Wen, Y., Caballero, D., & Dillenbourg, P. (2014). Review of augmented paper systems in education: An orchestration perspective. *Journal of Educational Technology & Society, 17*(4), 169e185.

Roschelle, J., Dimitriadis, Y., & Hoppe, U. (2013). Classroom orchestration: Synthesis. *Computers & Education, 69*, 523e526.

Sharples, M. (2013). Shared orchestration within and beyond the classroom. *Computers & Education, 69*, 504e506.

Sorensen, B. H., & Levinson, K. T. (2014). Digital production and students as learning designers. *Designs for Learning, 7*(1), 54–73.

Ternier, S., Klemke, R., Kalz, M., van Ulzen, P., & Specht, M. (2012). ARLearn: Augmented reality meets augmented virtuality. *Journal of Universal Computer Science, 18*(15), 2143–2164.

Väljataga, T., Fiedler, H. D. S., & Laanpere, M. (2015). Rethinking digital textbooks: Students as co-authors. In F. W. B. Li, R. Klamma, M. Laanpere, J. Zhang, B. F. Manjon, & R. W. H. Lau (Eds.), *Advances in web-based learning – ICWL2015. LNCS proceedings 9412* (pp. 143–151). Springer-Verlag Heidelberg, Romania.

Part III
Teachers' Professional Development

Chapter 9
Online Professional Learning Communities for Developing Teachers' Digital Competences

Sabine Seufert, Josef Guggemos, and Eric Tarantini

9.1 Introduction

One would be hard-pressed to find a topic of current debate in education policy and educational practice that is as exhaustively discussed as the (proper) handling of the digital transformation (e.g. "standing conference of the ministers of education and cultural Affairs" KMK, 2016; Blossfeld et al., 2018). A widely shared perception is that a more intensive use of digital media in the classroom will improve learning effectiveness, facilitate greater orientation to the future needs of learners and support accompanied personality development in a digital society. The sweeping pressure to make changes is marked with a high degree of uncertainty regarding the use and benefits of digital media in schools (Bach, 2016).

Teachers addressing digital skills, such as the competent handling of online information, are often entering uncharted territory in their respective fields (media education). In this context, teachers are increasingly asking for inclusion of media-specific qualification objectives. However, the kind of competences teachers need to possess or to acquire remains somewhat vague and is largely limited to the use and operation of computer applications and digital content media (Blömeke, 2003; Blömeke, 2005). Furthermore, it may be evident that formal seminars, such as 1-day training workshops on how to use ICT, are neither sufficient nor effective for developing teachers' (digital) competences (Sorge & Russell, 2000). Rather, successful support initiatives to develop teachers' competences have to be rooted in their particular context and simultaneously embedded in innovation strategies and quality

---

S. Seufert (✉) · J. Guggemos · E. Tarantini
Institute of Business Education and Educational Management, University of St. Gallen, St. Gallen, Switzerland
e-mail: sabine.seufert@unisg.ch; josef.guggemos@unisg.ch; eric.tarantini@unisg.ch; https://www.alexandria.unisg.ch/persons/Sabine_Seufert; https://www.alexandria.unisg.ch/persons/7932; https://www.alexandria.unisg.ch/persons/7494

development processes in their respective schools (Schneider & Mahs, 2003). The conceptualisation and design of suitable training measures for teachers requires a systematic approach to the professional development of teachers at vocational schools. Developing professional communities among teachers to underpin the benefit of learning together and from each other is of high importance (Hord, 1997). Learning communities that make use of the potential of digital information and communication technology are becoming increasingly important as a means of continuously fostering teachers' digital competences. However, there is a research gap in the promotion of digital competences for teachers (Büsser, 2017, p. 15). Against this backdrop, this chapter addresses two research questions:

1. How can digital competences of teachers be defined and captured?
2. How can measures and interventions to foster online professional learning communities (online PLC) be designed and evaluated for a systematic development of teachers' digital competences?

The chapter consists of four parts. In the first part, we consolidate relevant theoretical considerations. The second part outlines the research methodology. The third part presents results of the research conducted and discusses implications for designing online PLCs. The fourth and final section provides a perspective for further research.

9.2 Review of the Literature

9.2.1 Digital Competences of Teachers

Baumert and Kunter (2006); Kunter, Klusmann and Baumert (2009); and Kunter et al. (2011) presented a highly regarded model of professional teaching competence, which comprises professional knowledge and believes in the sense of personally influenced basic orientations, values, motivational orientations and self-regulation (for empirical findings on professional knowledge in the context of vocational education and training, see Seifried & Wuttke, 2015). Professional knowledge comprises content knowledge, pedagogical content knowledge and pedagogical knowledge. This division can be traced back to Shulman (1986, 1987). Koehler and Mishra (2009) added technological aspects to these facets of professional knowledge and included technological knowledge as a new, disparate type of knowledge.

Moreover, approaches for developing media skills (Aufenanger, 1997; Baacke, Kornblum, Lauffer, Mikos, & Thiele, 1999; Mayrberger, 2012; Schorb, 2009; Tulodziecki, 2004) might be taken into account. In this vein, Blömeke's (2003) model is an approach that refers to teacher training. It distinguishes five areas of competence: "didactic media competence", "educational media competence", "socialisation-related competence", "school development competence" and "personal media competence".

The demands faced by schools due to digital transformation cannot be tackled through the efforts of single individuals. In that case, the individual teachers would quickly feel overworked (Seufert & Scheffler, 2016). In light of digital transformation, appropriate advisory and organisational knowledge regarding cooperation in teams and networks can thus be regarded as a relevant facet of competence for the joint development of teaching practices and the school as a system.

For vocational education and training, the official competence framework of the European Union (Carretero, Vuorikari, & Punie, 2017) is leading the way because it defines cross-vocational digital competences (in the sense of "digital literacies"), which can be specified in the Europass European Skills Passport[1] in the form of self-evaluations. In Germany, the KMK strategy in 2016 follows a similar path, identifying six areas of competence for education in the digital world – comparable to the EU competence framework (KMK, 2016). However, the implications for professional teaching skills have remained (as yet) vague.

Empirical findings on technology-mediated learning (TML) indicate that affective-motivational characteristics of the instructor are a decisive factor influencing the educationally effective use of digital media in the classroom (Gupta & Bostrom, 2009). Teachers have widely divergent views regarding the extent to which teaching itself should undergo digital change (Schmid, Goertz, & Behrens, 2017).

In sum, professional competence can be conceptualised as a "bundle of occupation-related characteristics" (Voss, Kunina-Habenicht, Hoehne, & Kunter, 2015, p. 4), which are central prerequisites for observable professional behaviour (Blömeke, Gustafsson, & Shavelson, 2015; Shavelson, 2013). Professional knowledge is thereby acknowledged as a key aspect of professional competence (Baumert & Kunter, 2006; Voss et al., 2015). At the classroom level, it comprises content knowledge, pedagogical content knowledge and pedagogical knowledge. However, these facets have an extended meaning in the context of digital transformation. For instance, a part of pedagogical knowledge could be teachers' knowledge about how to foster students' interdisciplinary digital skills. At the school level, advisory and organisational knowledge to contribute to the digital transformation of the entire school might be a facet. Pertinent to both levels are teachers' instrumental skills and knowledge in handling digital media as well as affective-motivational characteristics. For more details, see Seufert, Guggemos, Tarantini and Schumann (2019).

---

[1] The Europass aims to provide a way to present qualifications and competences in a way that is transparent and understandable throughout Europe, cf. https://europass.cedefop.europa.eu/de.

9.2.2 Online PLCs for the Professional Development of Teachers

Teacher training and its effectiveness is a field of research that has great untapped potential (Terhart, Bennewitz, & Rothland, 2014).

Multiple studies have shown that teachers develop their skills mainly in the informal context of their professional practice, i.e. in exchange with colleagues or through individual, critical reflection (Hoekstra, Korthagen, Brekelmans, Beijaard, & Imants, 2009; Jurasaite-Harbison, 2009; Meirink, Meijer, Verloop, & Bergen, 2009). As a result, international research literature on teacher education and training is especially focused on "integrated learning at the workplace", which is increasingly aimed at informal learning and reflective dialogue among the teaching staff (Meirink et al., 2009). For this reason, strong learning environments are based on design principles from a socio-constructivist perspective in the context of informal learning theories.

Team- and community-based learning may be considered as a highly effective learning method in this context. Against this backdrop, the construct of professional learning communities (PLC) should be mentioned. According to Hord (1997), PLCs involve groups of teachers or the entire teaching staff at a school that are jointly and constantly seeking ways to increase the effectiveness of their teaching, sharing what they have learned, attempting to put new ideas into actual practice, systematically testing these ideas and reflecting on them (Höfer, 2006). New competence requirements in the wake of increasing digitalisation necessitate ongoing (further) education that is marked by a high degree of speed and innovation dynamic. Teachers can no longer implement these changes individually and in isolation from one another in their day-to-day school routine. Bonsen and Rolff (2006, p. 170) therefore propose "the combination of community and professionalism" in times of turbulent change. In general, experimental testing of new approaches is risky. Hence, it requires continuity and a stable framework for developing common value patterns (Bonsen & Rolff, 2006, p. 170). Effectiveness studies on PLCs have produced key success factors: shared practice (Hord, 2004, p. 7), reflective dialogue, deprivatisation of teaching (teaching is a personal, but not a private matter), common focus on students' learning (shifting the focus from teaching to learning) and fundamentally reinforced cooperation (Newmann, 1994).

Learning communities that make use of the potential of ICT are becoming increasingly important as a means of fostering teachers' digital competences. The advantages of online environments are evident, especially in terms of time and location flexibility for cooperation as well as the availability of knowledge gained through specific experience. The learning community is no longer restricted to a single school. Cooperation across schools is possible, which facilitates knowledge spill overs. For instance, teachers may share good practices how their schools address the digital transformation process. Teachers' perception of the usefulness of online PLG is reportedly high. Duncan-Howell (2010) surveyed 98 teachers who participated in online communities. Among them 87% regarded a participation in such a community as meaningful. The success factors of learning communities in an online setting (such as coherence, transparency and quality of moderator performance) have been examined in numerous studies (particularly noteworthy is the meta-study [comparison of 64 studies] by Arnold, 2005; Carlén & Jobring, 2007; Dückert, 2003; Hew, 2009; Lazar & Preece, 2002; Seufert, Lechner, & Stanoevska, 2002; and Wegener & Leimeister, 2012). Similar results have been obtained in studies that investigate professional learning communities for the teaching profession supported by digital media (Huffman & Hipp, 2003). In the following section, we will point out key success factors for online PLC that Wegener and Leimeister (2012, pp. 389–391) lined out in their literature review.

Facilitation and Presence of the Instructor The instructor or moderator should initiate discussions and encourage them by reacting to the contributions of participants. He or she is also responsible for creating a psychological safe environment where the participants are willing to bring in their thoughts.

Face-to-Face Meetings Pure online learning settings should be enriched by real-life meetings. Those are primarily necessary to build up trust among the participants. Against this backdrop, they might be of special importance at the early stage of establishing an online PLC.

Well-Structured Small-Group Assignments Besides discussing about topics, learning takes place by collaboratively performing tasks. Those tasks should be authentic and dedicated to teachers' needs (Duncan-Howell, 2010). Specific tasks might also increase the commitment to the community. Asking for a product to be produced by the group may enhance the self-regulation processes of the group. For example, the teachers that participate in the online PLG could be split up into groups. Each group is asked to create an online course module. Putting together the modules would yield a complete online course. In the process of creating the course modules, the groups should receive guidance and support by the moderator or instructor.

Online PLC also faces challenges (Wegener & Leimeister, 2012). It is important to be aware of these obstacles and to address them appropriately. Teachers' motivation for participating in an online PLC plays an important role. They have to invest a considerable amount of time. Hence, the return on this investment has to be clear. A benefit could be time-saving due to access to teaching material and tools for more efficient assessment of students. Moreover, the success of the community highly depends on the level of trust within the group. If the participants were afraid of making mistakes and giving or receiving feedback, the learning outcome would be suboptimal. This is a crucial point because teachers indeed might be reluctant to openly speak about their professional experiences. Technical issues constitute a further challenge in an online environment. In light of this, teachers have to be equipped with appropriate tools for an effective and efficient online collaboration. Moreover, teachers need to be trained to use these means.

9.3 Method

9.3.1 Design

After having delineated professional competences of teachers in the context of digital transformation, we aim at systematically differentiating our framework. In this phase of instrument development, it is imperative to take into account the purpose of the measurement and the intended use of the results (AERA, APA, & NCME, 2014, p. 75f.). The purpose of the measurement is to assess teachers' digital knowledge, skills and attitudes for formative purposes. The results should serve to identify potential for improvements and to design appropriate support measures. With this in mind, we have designed a self-assessment tool that has been validated using confirmatory factor analyses. Since the aim of our research is to identify adequate professional development measures, which is within teachers' own interest, we regard a self-assessment instrument as suitable.

In collaboration with five partner schools from German-speaking Switzerland, we have developed items that capture the constructs described in Sect. 9.2.1 (see Table 9.1). This process was informed by the findings of 14 expert interviews. The experts show a diverse background: training representatives of companies, researcher in the field of digitalisation, school principals, educational policy makers and federation representatives. Finally, we carried out five focus group discussions with the school management team of the five partner schools.

To evaluate teachers' competences and to identify promising fields for improvement, we utilised an importance-performance map analysis (IPMA) (Ringle & Sarstedt, 2016). IPMA, though not yet widely used, enables a comprehensible and theoretically justified presentation of the results for a baseline evaluation. It is a way of presenting the results of structural equation modelling and shows how a target construct is shaped by other constructs. To this end, it takes direct and indirect effects into account. IPMA comprises two dimensions. The first dimension (importance [I]) depicts for each construct or item (see Table 9.1) its impact on the target construct by means of unstandardised path coefficients. In our case, we utilise frequency of use (measured on a five-point rating scale) as the target construct (see Table 9.2). For instance, $I = 0.1$ for "pedagogical knowledge" would indicate that an increase in this construct by one unit on the rating scale increases the expected frequency of digital media use by 0.1 units (considering direct and indirect effects). It enables us to identify measures that are potentially most conducive in terms of increasing the frequency of use. The second dimension (performance [P]) places each construct or item on a standardised scale from 1 to 100, indicating how pronounced the construct or item is among the teachers studied with respect to a 7-point scale of rating. A value that is low compared to other constructs or in absolute terms may indicate a potential for improvement. After having calculated importance and performance, I (on x-axis) and P (on y-axis) are plotted for all facets of teachers'

Table 9.1 Facets of teachers' digital competences including sample questions

Professional knowledge (classroom level and school level) with respect to digitalisation	Instrumental skills and knowledge in handling digital media	Affective-motivational characteristics related to digitalisation
Classroom-oriented professional knowledge Content knowledge: 1. General knowledge about digitalisation (e.g. "My basic knowledge about decisive principles of digitalization is…") 2. Business knowledge about digitalisation (e.g. "My knowledge about digital value chains is…") Pedagogical content knowledge: 3. Knowledge about digitalisation as a school subject (e.g. "My knowledge about teaching digital value chains is…") *Pedagogical knowledge:* 4. General knowledge of digital media (e.g. "I am able to use digital assessment tools for students' summative assessment") 5. Promoting students' interdisciplinary digital skills (e.g. "I am able to foster my students' digital skills to use online information") 6. Media didactics (e.g. "I am able to select adequate learning videos for students' knowledge creation") *Professional knowledge at the school level* 7. advisory and organisational knowledge (e.g. "I am able to support my colleagues to improve professional practice in terms of digital content and digital media use")	8. Digital skills Handling digital information (e.g. "I can efficiently use search strategies to find online information") Creating digital content (e.g. "I can create learning videos") Digital collaboration (e.g. "I can efficiently use digital communication tools") Ensuring digital security (e.g. "I regularly check my security settings of my digital devices and/or applications") Digital problem solving (e.g. "I can regularly keep up-to-date my skills in handling digital media/ tools") Specific applications (e.g. "I can use profession-specific applications")	9. Positive attitudes (e.g. "I like using digital media/tools in my instruction") 10. Negative attitudes (e.g. "I am afraid of making mistakes when using digital media/tools in my instruction")

Table 9.2 Target construct "frequency of use" including sample items

Facet	Sample items
Use of digital content: digitalisation as a class subject (professional, interdisciplinary)	"How often do you consider digital related topics in your instruction?" "How often do you foster students' competences when dealing with digital media (e.g. dealing with online information)?"
Use of digital media	"How often do you use blended learning scenarios (e.g. flipped classroom)?" "How often do you use digital learning arrangements in your instruction?"

digital competences and corresponding items. When selecting interventions, the focus should be on constructs that have a comparatively strong impact on the target construct and are not (yet) close to the maximum. We discuss IPMA results in focus groups with school administrations and specialist representatives from the partner schools. Based on this, we worked out focal points for fostering digital competences within the framework of an online PLC.

9.3.2 Development and Validation of Instruments

The final instrument for capturing teachers' digital competences consists of 86 items covering 11 constructs (10 facets of digital competences, see Table 9.1, and frequency of use, see Table 9.2). For obtaining the sample for the quantitative analysis, we contacted all vocational schools in the commercial domain in German-speaking Switzerland. Besides the five partner schools, four more schools participated in the study.

For validating the instrument, we rely on confirmatory factor analysis by means of the R-package "lavaan" 0.5–12.1097 (Rosseel, 2012). To determine the suitable method of data analysis, we conduct a Shapiro-Wilk test. The null hypothesis of this test is that the data are normally distributed. In case of non-normality, we will utilise a robust maximum likelihood estimator (MLR) because it is moderately robust against violations of the assumption of normally distributed data (Li, 2016). Moreover, we carry out Little's Missing Completely At Random (MCAR) test taking into account all context variables. The null hypothesis of this test is that the missing data is Missing Completely At Random (MCAR). In case of MCAR, we could apply Full Information Maximum Likelihood Estimation to handle the missing values (von Hippel, 2016). To check for outliers, we use Mahalanobis distances.

Table 9.1 provides an overview of the ten competence facets measured on a seven-point rating scale: from "very low" to "very high" (content knowledge, pedagogical content knowledge) and from "does not apply at all" to "applies very strongly" for all other facets (see Table 9.1).

Table 9.2 shows the two facets of the target construct "frequency of use". The items are measured on a five-point scale of rating: never, infrequently (one to two times per semester), occasionally (three to five times per semester), frequently (every month) and very frequently (every week).

Overall, we consider our instrument suitable for a comprehensive and valid formative assessment of digital competences. This assertion is based on the expert interviews and the focus group discussions that we carried out. Moreover, our empirical validation indicated decent fit values. The instrument may be useful for assessing the development of teachers' competences in the context of digital transformation.

9.4 Results

9.4.1 Instruments and Data Analysis

Our sample comprises 215 teachers nested in 9 schools. The proportion of females equals 50%. On average, the persons in our sample are aged 45 years (SD = 6 years) and have 18 (SD = 10) years of teaching experience. Overall, 3.9% missing values occurred. Due to the absence of a normal distribution for all our items (Shapiro-Wilk test: $p <.05$), we utilise an MLR estimator. Moreover, since we do not reject the hypothesis of MCAR ($\chi^2 = 3616$, df = 3297, $p = 1$), we rely on Full Information Maximum Likelihood. We did not exclude any observation based on the outlier analysis. The confirmatory factor analyses generally yielded good values for all 11 constructs (CFI > .980, TLI > .969, RMSEA <.093, SRMR <.036). Furthermore, the measures are reliable, indicated by Cronbach's alpha and composite reliability above .70. Convergent validity is established as all standardised factor loadings exceed .70. Hence, for every construct, the average variance extracted (AVE) is greater than .50, which indicates convergent validity. Discriminant validity is ensured because the square roots of AVE are always higher than the correlations among the constructs (Fornell-Larcker criterion). Measurement invariance analyses demonstrate the instrument's suitability for assessing competence development as well as group comparisons in terms of gender, age and teaching expertise. The findings on the prognostic validity of the instrument are positive. Frequency of use can be adequately explained using the facets of digital competence: 36% of the variance of digital content use and 34% of digital media use.

The results of the structural equation models reveal that, in general, all competence facets are important for the use of digital content and digital media in teaching. "Negative attitudes" are the exception. This may indicate that it is not necessary to address negative attitudes. Rather, positive attitudes may be put into focus.

It might be important to view the facets of competence in context and to systematically foster all of them. However, developing all facets of competence at the same time would likely overtax the teaching personnel. Therefore, the next step will be to concentrate on selected competence facets within the framework of an online PLC. In line with the IPMA (baseline evaluation), these would primarily encompass the following:

- *Media didactics:* This facet of competence exhibits both a low self-assessment and a high impact on the frequency of digital media use. Furthermore, the findings show that digital media is primarily used for instructional knowledge acquisition (e.g. use of learning videos) but less for constructivist and cognitive processes, such as for discussion, reflection or forms of action-oriented teaching and learning (e.g. simulations and multimedia applications).
- *Pedagogical knowledge:* General interdisciplinary knowledge of digital media also shows a rather high importance and a moderate performance. In this area, competence diagnostics using digital means in particular constitutes a knowl-

edge gap for many teachers (this is accompanied by the relatively low values for formative and summative self-assessments in the competence facet of media didactics, which basically represents the concrete implementation level).

- *Fostering students' digital skills:* Teachers' self-assessment of their knowledge to promote students' digital skills is on a rather low level. Against the requirements in vocational education and training, this finding is alarming and illustrates how pressing the need for action to develop the skills of teachers in this area is.
- *Instrumental skills and knowledge in handling digital media:* This competence facet also has a relatively strong impact on the use of digital content and digital media use. The importance of the inclusion of digitalisation-related topics in the classroom is even higher than that of the use of digital media in the classroom. A teacher who seems to be more active in the "digital world" is more likely to recognise the necessity and become familiar with concrete application possibilities in order to integrate digitalisation topics into the classroom in a meaningful way.

In sum, media didactics has a particularly positive influence on the use of digital learning arrangements. There is potential for improvement, particularly in the digital assessment of learners' competences (summative and formative).

9.4.2 Developing Teachers' Digital Competences in Online PLC

We discussed the results of the study with the school administrators of the nine schools in the sample. In this process, we addressed focal points for the ongoing promotion of digital competences within the framework of cross-school online PLC. The design of the online PLC as a social construct for a continuous set of measures was conceptually established, and access to the technological platform was regulated. Table 9.3 describes the elements of the online PLC.

Our online PLC considers the success factors outlined in Sect. 9.2.2. A moderator will be present at the communication platform and during the webinar series in order to create an atmosphere that is conducive to learning. During the blended learning modules, the participants of the online PLC meet each other in person. Teachers are asked to work out examples of good practices in small groups and to present their concepts in the webinars. In an introductory seminar, all the functionalities of the WordPress platform and the webinar software ZOOM (https://zoom.us/) are explained to the participants. The introductory course will be recorded; this allows teachers to easily join the online PLC also at a later point of time.

In terms of content, we focus on those facets that we have identified in the performance map analysis as most promising, i.e. that have relatively high importance and at the same time a relatively low performance. Namely, we address media didactic skills in the form of assessment with digital means. Besides, this, we aim at

Table 9.3 Interventions for developing digital competences within online PLC

Online PLC	Objectives	Implementation
Communication platform (continuously expanded)	Theme-based channel for digitalisation (blog with comment functionality) Collection of good practices (webinar recordings, teaching materials)	Portal structure with access to online PLC WordPress platform Moderator present on platform
"Good Practices" webinar series, approx. 2 hours per session	Moderated good practice sessions in an online setting: five webinars within 1 year; each participating school hosts one webinar	Teacher input, moderated reflection; virtual classroom (with ZOOM software)
Blended learning courses over 8 weeks	One blended learning course in 1 year with three course components: 1. Learning with digital media (subject area "Interdisciplinary Competences") 2. Testing with digital media (subject areas "Economy and Society", "Consolidating and Networking") 3. Digital school development (everyday school life: joint cooperation among different places of learning)	Three-phase concept: 1. Preparation phase (building on existing experience, providing new impetus) 2. Presence phase (experimenting) 3. Transfer phase with learning assignment Moodle platform (access via portal website)

fostering teachers' knowledge about how to shape the digital transformation process at their schools. Our online PLC may also act as a role model how such a community can be established. Teachers receive a certificate issued by our institute that may contribute to a favourable incentive structure.

9.5 Conclusion and Outlook

Our research project yielded a framework of digital competences of vocational education and training teachers in the field of business. In terms of professional knowledge, there are two building blocks of digital competences: (1) instructional level, designing classroom situations, and (2) school level, shaping school development. Drawing on this framework model, we were able to operationalise the 10 facets of digital competence in an instrument that we validated with 215 teachers from 9 schools. It may be promising to use the instrument also in other countries and to carry out measurement invariance analyses, i.e. to evaluate whether there is a common understanding of teachers' digital competences across countries. The psychometric quality criteria of the instrument are generally high, allowing the results to be used as a baseline evaluation for subsequent research projects.

Furthermore, it was possible to acquire insight into how these digital competences can be effectively fostered among teachers by means of online PLC. To this end, we presented success factors for online PLC. The aim is not only to examine the effectiveness of the support models but also to explore which factors influence teachers' use of digital learning opportunities. In this way, it will also be possible to ascertain potential ways to increase the effectiveness of the support models.

For one thing, the significance of reflected documentation of effective learning episodes in the form of interactive knowledge among the faculty became evident (in which the descriptions of knowledge are differentiated into the dimensions of content knowledge, pedagogical content knowledge and media didactics) (Fried, 2003; Mishra & Koehler, 2005). This interactive knowledge seems to be of particular relevance for restructuring and innovating teaching development in terms of self-produced knowledge coupling in the area of practice (Fried, 2003). Since the questionnaire for the framework model of digital competences of teachers in the field of business is already very extensive, the open questions for the qualitative survey of interactive knowledge in the following three contexts were not yet included: (1) any teacher in any subject, (2) a colleague teaching the same subject and (3) an individual learning episode. These areas of knowledge are to be included in a follow-up project as a further facet of competence based on a qualitative research design. This also offers the advantage that institutional framework conditions (e.g., support structures, cultural development at schools) can be analysed using a qualitative evaluation design.

A limitation of our study is the reliance on self-assessments. This could result in two different types of bias: teachers deliberately give inaccurate answers or are not able to provide a valid self-assessment. We regard the first bias as unlikely because the survey was voluntary and anonymous. Irrespective of this, based on the impressions gained during the qualitative phase of the research project, we can attest that the teachers are highly self-reflective. This indicates that the second type of bias may also be inapplicable. Moreover, since we use survey data, we cannot make causal claims. Furthermore, our sample is restricted because it comprises only 215 teachers from vocational schools from German-speaking Switzerland.

The results of the empirically validated instrument for assessing the digital competences of vocational education and training teachers and the baseline evaluation involving 215 teachers provide a basis for the follow-up project. In this context, we intend to assess the online PLC in a longitudinal study. Furthermore, we would like to embed the concept of online professional learning concept into a larger context. To this end, we regard digital ecosystems as a promising approach (Seufert, Guggemos, & Tarantini, 2018).

Acknowledgements The instruments were developed as part of the project "Digi Comp to Teach" funded by the Swiss State Secretariat for Education, Research and Innovation.

References

AERA, A. P. A., & NCME. (2014). *Standards for educational and psychological testing*. American Educational Research Association: Washington, D.C.

Arnold, P. (2005). Kooperative Lerngemeinschaften. Gestaltungsdimensionen und -prinzipien. In L. Burkhard & E. Bloh (Eds.), *Online-Pädagogik, Band 3: Referenzmodelle und Praxisbeispiele* (pp. 98–107). Schneider-Verlag Hohengehren: Baltmannsweiler, Germany.

Aufenanger, S. (1997). Medienpädagogik und Medienkompetenz. Eine Bestandsaufnahme. In: Bonn: Deutscher Bundestag (Hrsg.). *Medienkompetenz im Informationszeitalter* (S. 15–22). Bonn, Germany: Deutscher Bundestag.

Baacke, D., Kornblum, S., Lauffer, J., Mikos, L., & Thiele, G. A. (Eds.). (1999). *Handbuch Medien. Medienkompetenz – Modelle und Projekte*. Bonn, Germany: Bundeszentrale für Politische Bildung.

Bach, A. (2016). Nutzung von digitalen Medien an berufsbildenden Schulen – Notwendigkeit, Rahmenbedingungen, Akzeptanz und Wirkungen. In: J. Seifried, S. Seeber, & B. Ziegler (Hrsg.), *Jahrbuch der berufs- und wirtschaftspädagogischen Forschung 2016* (S. 107–123). Opladen, Leverkusen: Verlag Barbara Budrich.

Baumert, J., & Kunter, M. (2006). Stichwort: Professionelle Kompetenz von Lehrkräften. *Zeitschrift für Erziehungswissenschaft, 9*(4), 469–520.

Blömeke, S. (2003). Neue Medien in der Lehrerausbildung. Zu angemessenen (und unangemessenen) Zielen und Inhalten des Lehramtsstudiums. *Zeitschrift für Theorie und Praxis der Medienbildung, (Occasional Papers)*, 1–29.

Blömeke, S. (2005). Medienpädagogische Kompetenz. In A. Frey, R. S. Jäger, & U. Renold (Eds.), *Berufspädagogik: Bd. 5. Kompetenzdiagnostik. Theorien und Methoden zur Erfassung und Bewertung von beruflichen Kompetenzen* (pp. 76–97). Empirische Pädagogik e.V: Landau.

Blömeke, S., Gustafsson, J.-E., & Shavelson, R. J. (2015). Beyond dichotomies: Competence viewed as a continuum. *Zeitschrift für Psychologie, 223*(1), 3–13.

Blossfeld, H.-P., Bos, W., Daniel, H.-D., Hannover, B., Köller, O., Lenzen, D., et al. (2018). *Digitale Souveränität und Bildung*. Münster, Germany: Waxmann.

Bonsen, M., & Rolff, H. (2006). Professionelle Lerngemeinschaften von Lehrerinnen und Lehrern. *Zeitschrift für Pädagogik, 52*(2), 167–184.

Büsser, B. (2017). Zwischen digital und analog. In*: Bildungsdirektion Kanton Zürich* (Hrsg.). Schulblatt 6/2017 – Digitalisierung. *Wo stehen Schulen*. Zürich, Switzerland: Staempfli.

Carlén, U. & Jobring, O. (2007). Perspectives on the sustainability of activities within online learning communities. *International Journal of Web Based Communities, 3*(1), 100–113.

Carretero, S., Vuorikari, R., & Punie, Y. (2017). *DigComp 2.1: The digital competence framework for citizens with eight proficiency levels and examples of use*. Luxembourg, Europe: European Union (EU).

Dückert, S. (2003). Treffpunkt Wissensnetzwerk. *Wissensmanagement, 8*, 20–22.

Duncan-Howell, J. (2010). Teachers making connections: Online communities as a source of professional learning. *British Journal of Educational Technology, 41*(2), 324–340.

Fried, L. (2003). Pädagogisches Professionswissen als Form und Medium der Lehrerbildungskommunikation – empirische Suchbewegungen. *Zeitschrift für Pädagogik, 49*(1), 112–126.

Gupta, S., & Bostrom, R. P. (2009). Technology-mediated learning. A comprehensive theoretical model. *Journal of the Association for Information Systems, 10*(9), 686–714.

Hew, K. F. (2009). Determinants of success for online communities. An analysis of three communities in terms of members' perceived professional development. *Behaviour & Information Technology, 28*(5), 433–445.

Hoekstra, A., Korthagen, F., Brekelmans, M., Beijaard, D., & Imants, J. (2009). Experienced teachers' informal workplace learning and perceptions of workplace conditions. *Journal of Workplace Learning, 21*(4), 276–298.

Höfer, C. (2006). Unterrichtsentwicklung als Schulentwicklung. In H. Buchen & H.-G. Rolff (Eds.), *Professionswissen Schulleitung* (S. 752–788). Weinheim, Germany: Beltz.

Hord, S. M. (1997). *Professional learning communities. Communities of continuous inquiry and improvement*. Austin, TX: Southwest Educational Development Laboratory.

Hord, S. M. (2004). *Learning together, leading together. Changing schools through professional learning communities*. New York: Teachers College Press.

Huffman, J. B., & Hipp, K. K. (2003). *Restructuring schools as professional learning communities*. Lanham, MD: Scarecrow Education.

Jurasaite-Harbison, E. (2009). Teachers' workplace learning within informal contexts of school cultures in the United States and Lithuania. *Journal of Workplace Learning, 21*(4), 299–321.

KMK. (2016). *Strategie der Kultusministerkonferenz "Bildung in der digitalen Welt"*. Abgerufen unter http://www.kmk.org/fileadmin/Dateien/pdf/PresseUndAktuelles/2016/Entwurf_KMK-Strategie_Bildung_in_der_digitalen_Welt.pdf.

Koehler, M. J., & Mishra, P. (2009). What is technological pedagogical content knowledge? *Contemporary Issues in Technology and Teacher Education, 9*(1), 60–70.

Kunter, M., Baumert, J., Blum, W., Klusmann, U., Krauss, S., & Neubrand, M. (2011). *Professionelle Kompetenz von Lehrkräften. Ergebnisse des Forschungsprogramms COACTIV*. Münster, Germany: Waxmann.

Kunter, M., Klusmann, U., & Baumert, J. (2009). Professionelle Kompetenz von Mathematiklehrkräften: Das COACTIV-Modell. In O. Zlatkin-Troitschanskaia, K. Beck, D. Sembill, R. Nickolaus, & R. Mulder (Eds.), *Lehrprofessionalität. Bedingungen, Genese, Wirkungen und ihre Messung* (pp. 153–166). Beltz: Weinheim, Germany.

Lazar, J., & Preece, J. (2002). Social considerations in online communities. Usability, sociability, and success factors. In H. Van Oostendorp (Ed.), *Cognition in the digital world*. Lawrence Earlbaum: Mahwah, NJ.

Li, C.-H. (2016). Confirmatory factor analysis with ordinal data: Comparing robust maximum likelihood and diagonally weighted least squares. *Behavior Research Methods, 48*(3), 936–949.

Mayrberger, K. (2012). Medienpädagogische Kompetenz im Wandel – Vorschlag zur Gestaltung des Übergangs in der Lehrerbildung am Beispiel mediendidaktischer Kompetenz. In R. Schulz-Zander (Ed.), *Jahrbuch Medienpädagogik* (pp. 389–412). Wiesbaden, Germany: Springer VS.

Meirink, J., Meijer, P., Verloop, N., & Bergen, T. (2009). How do teachers learn in the workplace? An examination of teacher learning activities. *European Journal of Teacher Education, 32*(3), 209–224.

Mishra, P., & Koehler, M. J. (2005). What happens when teachers design educational technology? The development of technological pedagogical content knowledge. *Journal of Educational Computing Research, 32*(2), 131–152.

Newmann, F. M. (1994). School-wide professional community. *Issues in Restructuring Schools, 6*, 1–3.

Ringle, C. M., & Sarstedt, M. (2016). Gain more insight from your PLS-SEM results. *Industrial Management & Data Systems, 116*(9), 1865–1886.

Rosseel, Y. (2012). lavaan: An R Package for Structural Equation Modeling. *Journal of Statistical Software, 48*(2), 1–35.

Schmid, U., Goertz, L., & Behrens, J. (2017). *Monitor Digitale Bildung. Die Schulen im digitalen Zeitalter*. Gütersloh, Germany: Bertelsmann Stiftung. Retrieved from http://www.bertelsmann-stiftung.de/digi-monitor.

Schneider, P., & Mahs, C. (2003). Kontinuierliche und Kooperative Selbstqualifikation und Selbstorganisation (KoKoSS) der Ausbilder. In: Euler, D. (Ed.), *Handbuch der Lernortkooperation. Band 2: Praktische Erfahrungen* (S. 298–312). Bielefeld, Germany: Bertelsmann.

Schorb, B. (2009). Gebildet und kompetent. Medienbildung statt Medienkompetenz? *merz, 53*(5), 50–56.

Seifried, J., & Wuttke, E. (2015). Was wissen und können (angehende) Lehrkräfte an kaufmännischen Schulen? – Empirische Befunde zur Modellierung und Messung der professionellen

Kompetenz von Lehrkräften. In: Schumann, S. & Eberle, F. (Hrsg.). Ökonomische Kompetenzen in Schule, Ausbildung und Hochschule. Empirische Pädagogik, 29, H. 1, Themenheft. Landau, 125–145.

Seufert, S., Guggemos, J., & Tarantini, E. (2018). Digitale Transformation in Schulen – Kompetenzanforderungen an Lehrpersonen. *Beiträge zur Lehrerinnen- und Lehrerbildung, 36*(2), 175–193.

Seufert, S., Guggemos, J., Tarantini, E., & Schumann, S. (2019). Developing and validating a framework of digital competencies for teachers in the commercial domain. *Zeitschrift für Berufs- und Wirtschaftspädagogik, 115*(2), 312–339.

Seufert, S., Lechner, U., & Stanoevska, K. (2002). A reference model for online learning communities. *International Journal on E-Learning (IJEL), 1*(1), 43–54.

Seufert, S., & Scheffler, N. (2016). Developing digital competences of vocational teachers. *International Journal of Digital Literacy and Digital Competence (ILDLDC), 7*(1), 50–65, ISSN 1947-3944.

Shavelson, R. J. (2013). On an approach to testing and modeling competence. *Educational Psychologist, 48*(2), 73–86.

Shulman, L. S. (1987). Knowledge and teaching. Foundations of the new reform. *Harvard Educational Review, 57*(1), 1–23.

Shulman, L. S. (1986). Those Who Understand: Knowledge Growth in Teaching. *Educational Researcher, 15*(2), 4–14.

Sorge, D. H., & Russell, J. D. (2000). A strategy for effective change in instructional behavior: Staff development that works. *Educational Technology, 40*(6), 46–48.

Terhart, E., Bennewitz, H., & Rothland, M. (2014). *Handbuch der Forschung zum Lehrerberuf* (2. Auflage ed.). Münster, Germany/New York: Waxmann Verlag.

Tulodziecki, G. (2004). *Mediendidaktik. Medien in Lehr- und Lernprozessen*. Stuttgart, Germany: Klett-Cotta.

von Hippel, P. T. (2016). New confidence intervals and bias comparisons show that maximum likelihood can beat multiple imputation in small samples. *Structural Equation Modeling: A Multidisciplinary Journal, 23*(3), 422–437.

Voss, T., Kunina-Habenicht, O., Hoehne, V., & Kunter, M. (2015). Stichwort Pädagogisches Wissen von Lehrkräften. Empirische Zugänge und Befunde. *Zeitschrift für Erziehungswissenschaften, 18*(2), 187–223.

Wegener, R., & Leimeister, J. M. (2012). Virtual learning communities: Success factors and challenges. *International Journal of Technology Enhanced Learning, 4*(5/6), 383.

Chapter 10
Experiences of Multimodal Teaching Through a Serious Game: Meanings, Practices and Discourses

Petros Lameras and Vasiliki Papageorgiou

10.1 Introduction

This chapter elucidates on secondary school teachers' experiences of multimodal teaching through a serious game. We have developed a serious game called STEAM as a digital medium to help teachers to understand the concept of multimodality for teaching and learning. Serious games have been perceived as a medium for instigating playful learning aligned with rich-mediated content to achieve in-game learning goals. The overarching aim of such games is to infuse learning content amalgamated with teaching models, frameworks assessment and feedback in-game representations for discerning a more constructive, reflective and memorable learning experience (Bellotti et al., 2012; Boot, Kramer, Simons, Fabiani, & Gratton, 2008; Del Blanco et al., 2012).

There is an increasing body of evidence, which suggests that multimodality is an activity-based and student-centred approach to teaching and learning in which a series of different tools, technologies, resources and environments are deployed for helping learners during the meaning-making process (Cope & Kalantzis, 2020; Haniya et al., 2019; Jewitt, 2008; Sun, 2015). The essence of multimodality, therefore, is to instantiate teaching using an array of different resources and pedagogies for stimulating learning in meaningful ways (Antonietti & Giorgetti, 2006) within and across disciplines. This is directly relevant to the way teachers attempt to teach and deliver subject-content knowledge in terms of understanding how the use of a

---

P. Lameras (✉)
School of Computing, Electronics and Mathematics, Coventry University, Coventry, UK
e-mail: ab3430@coventry.ac.uk

V. Papageorgiou
Centre for Higher Education Research and Scholarship, Imperial College London, London, UK
e-mail: v.papageorgiou18@imperial.ac.uk

plethora of different learning resources, technology and tools would likely influence students' learning. Multiple modes of representation are central for adopting a multimodal approach to teaching that combines print with visual images and interactive resources. Multimodality is not a new concept as it has been developed in early 2000s (Kress & Van Leeuwen, 2001). Connected concepts may embrace literacy-related terms, such as multiliteracy or multimodal literacy, which transcends the basic idea of reading and writing to multiple forms of mixed-print representations (Miller & McVee, 2013).

There is a widespread view from different commentators (e.g. Cope & Kalantzis, 2009; Cowan & Cipriani, 2009) that school teachers seem to be overwhelmed by the plethora of teaching representations such as digital tools, resources and pedagogies that may be used for enacting teaching in more activity-oriented ways. This, in principle, would allow to design activities that encourage students to be actively involved in situated learning instances in or out of the classroom. Multimodality is indeed an ill-defined concept encompassing social and cultural shaped resources with an emphasis on the inherently social negotiated character of meaning (Lave, 1991). To support teachers' efforts to understand a complex and ill-defined phenomenon such as multimodality, we decided to design STEAM as a multimodal digital artefact for discerning richer, context-orientated and visual-based representations of multimodal teaching as experienced by teachers whilst interacting the game.

The following sections start by presenting the aims and research questions underpinning this study. Then, we discuss the tenets of multimodality as a learning and teaching strategy and its variations in meaning-making processes driven by how meaning is conveyed from a multimodal perspective. The design of the STEAM game encompassing analysis of high-level goal, scenarios and learning objectives is then described. Following, we present the adopted methodology and our study's findings. The chapter concludes by providing a discussion on game design considerations and implications for multimodal learning and teaching, study limitations and future research directions.

The aim of this study was to contemplate on how school teachers understand multimodality through playing a serious game. The following research questions were identified from the literature:

1. What are teachers' experiences of multimodal teaching and learning through interacting with a serious game?
2. What are the implications of teachers' in-game experiences of multimodality for practicing multimodal teaching in the classroom?

Despite increasing interest into how multimodality is conceived and practiced for amplifying teaching and learning, there is no empirical evidence that explores multimodal teaching through playing a multimodal serious game. Current impetus is on how multimodal teaching is perceived and developed through traditional teaching professional development programs or more recently through massive open online courses (MOOCs). These training programs typically focus on teacher development from a more universal viewpoint encompassing broad aspects of teaching and not specifically from a multimodal standpoint focusing on amalgamating and aligning pedagogies, teaching strategies, technology and different learning spaces. We hence take a different stance in developing teachers' understandings of multimodality by perpetuating the development of a game acting as the environment in which teachers' views and beliefs of multimodality are constructed and developed.

10.2 Variation in Multimodal Meaning-Making Processes

We argue that multimodality draws on the process of creating meaning through connecting and combining teaching modes (e.g. in-class and out of class teaching), semiotic resources (e.g. multimedia types such as video, audio, images, animation, interactive content), teaching approaches (e.g. inquiry- and problem-based learning) and immersive technologies (e.g. games, simulations, online learning platforms). Meaning inferences may be perceived as social actions triggered by experiences, beliefs and practices situated in specific contexts. Jewitt (2013) identifies three meaning variations: (1) ideational meaning, dealing with choices related to how people interpret content meanings, (2) interpersonal meaning, employing the resources being used to represent the social relations between communicators, and (3) textual and organisational meaning, representing decisions on choice or resources as means to understand a text's structure or the nature of an interaction between two people.

The proliferation of digital technologies (personal, mobile, networked) may supplement or enhance conventional non-digital activities. From administrative-level tasks such as organising and storing content (e.g. Schoorman, Mayer, & Davis, 2007) or via transferring information to students for content accommodation and assimilation (e.g. Mayer, 2001) to more knowledge construction processes, such as conducting research or for skills development (Greenhow, Robelia, & Hughes, 2009), technology seems to be used in varied ways to accommodate different puroses and outcomes. Multimedia tools in these environments may include, for example, interactive videos, recorded lecture presentations, online quizzes, discussion forums, digital storytelling and visual representations of student data to depict progress. This increasing use of multimedia in teaching and learning may lead to presenting multiple representations of content (e.g. text, images, video, audio, pervasive media) to accommodate different teaching strategies, learning outcomes, assessment methods and feedback mechanisms. It has also been argued that by incorporating multimedia learning, students may be encouraged to develop a more flexible and research-based approach to learning as activities are designed towards encouraging discovery through information literacy skills, critical thinking and inquiry-led investigations. Studies into multimodal composition have revealed enhanced learning experiences and outcomes (e.g. Crook & Crook, 2017; Miller & McVee, 2013) as well as enabling students to identify and express their personal identity (e.g. Thibaut & Curwood, 2018). Shah and Freedman (2003) identified a series of benefits of using visualisations, as representational modes, for improving learning outcomes such as (1) providing external representations of information, (2) deeper learning and (3) triggering student's attention and concentration by making information more comprehensive, hence simplifying ill-defined concepts and ideas.

10.2.1 Multimodality as a Meaning for Teacher-Directed Teaching

In more traditional classroom settings, oral communication modes are predominantly and directly linked with a teacher-centred approach to teaching. Reinforcement, memorisation and repetition of desired actions underpinned teachers' actions as 'sage on the stage'. The main written communication mode is the textbook covering the standard-based curriculum predefined by the institution or country. The students are producing written texts (e.g. written assignments or tests), and they are evaluated predominantly via a quantitative score. Less emphasis is given to student's own interests, needs and prior knowledge because it is important for the teacher to cover the curriculum and transmit the information prescribed. Student's development of social skills and the utilisation of peer interaction for participatory and collaborative learning are not encouraged; hence transmissive teaching with unimodal, noninteractive tools for content transfer and basic skills acquisition is the focus of attention.

We are not asserting that teacher-directed approaches to multimodality are not appropriate for multimedia learning as it has been shown that unimodal and noninteractive practices may be used in schools. Indeed, such practices may help build a knowledge-rich subject domain, particularly for students with special needs or disadvantaged backgrounds (e.g. Lerkkanen et al., 2016).

The STEAM game design employs different multimodalities and semiotic resources to exemplify the inclusiveness and totality of different paradigms, models and strategies needed for achieving the necessary outcomes as defined by the teacher and external influences such as context, institutional or policy educational developments.

10.2.2 Multimodality as a Meaning for Active and Student-Centred Learning

Multimodality is inherently connected to activity-led learning, in which students are autonomous and self-directed and they construct knowledge through processing prior learning experiences and knowledge as well as through empathising, ideating, discovering and producing. Students may select relevant words and images and organise them into coherent verbal and visual models. In the teaching and learning spectrum, a different range of semiotic tools and resources are being used to facilitate students to apply, analyse, evaluate and create new knowledge. The central focus is extracting meaning though using visual representation techniques for understanding, linking and negotiating ideas and concepts with the teacher and peers. Arguably, we may observe a shift into students' role from knowledge consumers to knowledge producers (Cope, Kalantzis, & Abrams, 2017). Technology and tools may involve among others serious games, virtual reality and virtual learning environments. Teaching and learning can go beyond the boundaries of the classroom and may be combined with visits to (open air) museums, science centres and library spaces as a way of extending the learning process in other contexts where information is directly linked to specific artefacts or tangible objects. Such modes and semiotic resources help students to create, apply and transfer meaning within their own social context. This may also signify the importance of stretching teaching and learning practice beyond the potentialities and constraints of the normal classroom. In addition, such technologies may enable to extend the standard forms of written and spoken language to connect with the culturally and linguistically diverse landscapes and the multimodal texts mobilised across these landscapes (Jewitt, 2008).

The main assumption is that multimodality is the vehicle for students to design, implement, share and reuse/repurpose semiotic resources and multimodal ensembles (e.g. Greenhow et al., 2009). For example, students are constructing learning through content and resources found online and offline, in various places such as in the school, in field trips, in the library, in museums and in science centres. This blend of learning spaces between formal and informal enables the participation of actors with different experiences and learning settings (e.g. museum curators, scientists, researchers and business experts) having the role of the facilitator and thereby helping the students to experience a multitude of opinions and ideas. This more active approach to learning where the students are constantly looking for new ways of learning from diverse perspectives, spaces and educators from different disciplines and sectors may infer to the notion of multiple intelligences (e.g. Picciano, 2009). Such diverse multimodal learning activities do not exist as a linear equation of 'yes' or 'no' but within a continuum of naive to more coherent ways of learning influenced by the learning environment (formal and informal), prior knowledge, design of learning and the subject-content domain. It is perceived, therefore, that multimodality with active, student-centred learning is aligned in terms of designing learning in multisensory modes and delivered via an array of distinctive semiotic resources.

10.3 Design of the STEAM Game

The aim of the STEAM serious game is to stipulate teachers' awareness on experiencing multimodality for teaching and learning as a process inherently connected with rich-mediated pedagogies, a variety of tools and multiple learning environments. The main impetus is to help teachers to understand both the conceptual and practical manifestations of designing and implementing learning and teaching activities with multiple media, instigating different teaching strategies and by 'exploiting' distinct modes of teaching.

STEAM is a simple point-and-click game that is played through a web browser. A game design and usability study of the STEAM game revealed that it balances game mechanics with multimodal learning elements as means to offer a semiotic resource that may help teachers to understand the different meanings of multimodality (e.g. Lameras, Philippe, & Oertel, 2019). The game play represents non-linear dialogues with a non-player character (NPC) visualising a set of choices for the player to choose from. Complementing the dialogue game, there is a mini card game for players to select card combinations for establishing a multimodal teaching environment of their choice.

10.3.1 Goals and Outcomes

The game's narrative sets the player to have the role of a newly appointed teacher interested to learn more about multimodality and how (e.g. resources, pedagogies, modes, technology) it can be practiced. The main in-game goal, therefore, is to create an awareness of what is multimodality and how it can be enacted to enhance students' leaning experience. The player commences the game as having the fictional character of 'Mary' a newly appointed mathematics teacher at Charles Darwin School that attempts to transcend theory and practice as means to enhance teaching by using multimodal tools, pedagogies and strategies. Interactions with the students and ways of delivering content are influenced by the dialogue responses given by the player, which in turn enable the collection of game cards for designing lesson plans.

10.3.2 In-Game Scenarios

To situate multimodality into a learning context, we have designed three chapters encompassing four learning scenarios in which multimodal teaching challenges are presented to the player. The flow of each scenario determines the in-game sequence aligning the dialogue and cards game mechanics and the actions of the player. Each chapter may be played as a way of introducing the player to three multimodal in-game objectives following the subject content and flow of each scenario. When the player loops out of the introduction sequence, then the scenario starts by introducing the *narrative sequence* as a means for the in-game *dialogue mechanic* to engage the player with the teacher NPC. This is for getting information about what multimodality is and to highlight that it reflects a range of pedagogies, digital tools and resources amalgamated together to form an interacting and multimodal learning experience within and beyond the classroom context. Then, the *game cards*, the next core game mechanic, are combined together to form a particular multimodal situation that the teacher would favour. A new *dialogue sequence* follows, with students contemplating on and articulating about the choices the player has made during the dialogues and possible applications in the real-world teaching domain.

10.3.3 Core Game Mechanics

We have designed our core game mechanics to prompt for progressively learning the objectives of each chapter whilst to rapidly comprehend the multimodal aspects that the dialogues convey to the player. The dialogue mechanic drives the multimodality learning process and twins the pedagogical objectives of each scenario with player's chosen response. The dialogue mechanic is part of the *narrative sequence* in which the player responds to questions asked either by colleagues or by students. The player has three options to choose from: one of the dialogue options is the correct, the other is intermediate and the third is not correct (see Fig. 10.1).

When the player selects a dialogue option, this is highlighted with a green frame as a visual representation to denote the choice is correct, with a yellow frame to show that the choice is intermediate and with a red frame to signify that the choice is not correct. The general consensus is to guide players' understandings on how multimodality may be viewed in multiple perspectives that would likely increase student's in-game learning and engagement.

As the player responds to questions, up to ten cards are available separated into different categories such as strategies, activities and locations. The cards need to be combined in order to form a particular multimodal situation.

When the initial engagement is low, the player should select a highly engaging combination. The player selects the combination depending on the objective of the chapter, determined by the initial engagement and learning level of the students. As an example, when the initial engagement is low, the player should select a highly engaging combination (see Fig. 10.2).

Hints about the outcome of each card combination are provided to support the player's choice. Feedback is provided about the effects of designing an activity with students from multiple backgrounds with the purpose of gaining understanding of a

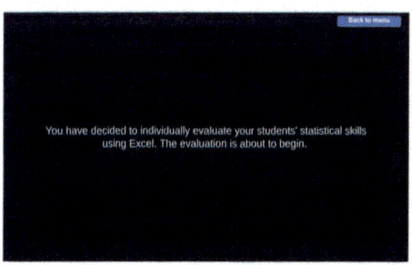

Fig. 10.1 Left chart: the dialogue challenge is set for the player to respond. Right chart: the player has three in-game options to choose from

Fig. 10.2 Left chart: designing a multimodal situation comprised of strategies, activities and location. Right chart: designing a multimodal situation that influences students' engagement levels

multimodal activity involving oral, written, visual and gestural modes of learning and communication. Each card includes information about the type of strategy and modalities that are deployed and the locations that the activity can be implemented. Likewise, for the activity cards, the properties and attributes are highlighted, whereas the location cards visualise the place in which a multimodal situation may be delivered. Based on the card selection, the player decides the engagement level bar increases or decreases thereby affecting the average level's grade.

10.3.4 In-Game Feedback

In-game feedback is augmented in multiple ways for helping players to understand not only ways of conceiving and practicing multimodal teaching but also progress achieved in game play. For example, including the 'engagement bar' and 'the learning bar' indicating engagement of students and their learning level may empower players to monitor progress towards their learning of in-game multimodality. This visual representation type of feedback is displayed during the dialogue sequence with the students for the player to have instant information on his/her progress for quickly adjusting performance. We have integrated this type of visual feedback for the players to be able to comprehend easily the meaning of the feedback received thus to get extrinsic feedback on their performance.

The design of the multimodal card deck library has a dual feedback purpose: firstly, for players to reflect on the combinations already made and assimilate the multimodal features chosen and secondly, to experience and understand how new multimodal card combinations that have not been selected during game play would help to understand different ways and variations of using multimodality. Players may choose any of the card decks from strategies, tools and location categories, and then suggested combinations are provided by the game. For example, if the players select the argumentation debate card from the strategy category, then a suggestion pops up combining a blog tool and a home location (see Fig. 10.3).

10 Experiences of Multimodal Teaching Through a Serious Game: Meanings... 183

Fig. 10.3 Top-left chart: setting a multimodal strategy by using the 'argumentation debate'. Top-right chart: selecting the 'audio' tool. Bottom-left chart: selecting a 'classroom' location card. Bottom-right chart: selecting a museum location card

10.4 Research Design

Fifty-four secondary education teachers were recruited for this study. We have conducted an initial pilot study with 22 secondary school teachers for testing our data collection methods, research instruments and processes of analysis and themes. When we streamlined our methods and devised a set of preliminary themes, we carried out the main study with an additional cohort of 32 teachers, comprising a total sample of 54 ($n = 54$) teachers. This acted as means to achieve variation and commonality among experiences from broad subject topics such as science and technology (e.g. mathematics, physics, chemistry, computing), history, literature and languages. Twenty-six of the teachers were males and 27 were females. All participants were working in schools with varied teaching experience (1–30 years). Twenty participants were playing games, whilst none have interacted with games before as means to develop their teaching practice. However, they all felt familiar with using technology in designing and delivering learning activities and resources. Twenty-two participants had a vague and fragmented view of multimodal teaching, whereas 32 had never came across the term multimodality before commencing this study. Participants were drawn from a wide geographical range from countries such as Germany ($n = 12$), Denmark ($n = 18$) and Finland ($n = 24$). This ensured that a wide range of contexts, practices, beliefs and actions were part of our purposive sampling method for achieving the required variation in the formulation of the experiences.

The data collection process started by involving participants to playtest the game for 40 minutes. Then, they had to complete an online questionnaire with closed and open questions for approximately another 40 minutes. Starting with the playtesting process, we introduced the game to participants, and we elaborated the objectives of the study. All ethical procedures, such as rights to withdraw at any time, data management, handling and storage and their voluntary participation, were made explicit to the participants prior to their engagement with this study. Then, participants started to respond to the semi-structured questions connecting their experiences of in-game multimodality with their own experiences of teaching as a way of constituting a cohesive and structured experience. By asking teachers to provide their own meanings of in-game multimodal teaching would enable us to distil, capture and analyse what felt important to them. Questions related to how the visual representations and interactive nature of the game helped participants to gain an understanding of the elements and properties of multimodal teaching as depicted in game play. The analysis commenced with the premise that a data-driven process will be followed to constitute the themes following an iterative process of familiarising with the data, coding and associating relational inferences and reflecting on the emerging themes. Dedoose, a digital analysis software for organising, associating and reflecting on codings and for constituting the themes, was used in this study. As such, analysis employed an inductive approach that delineated the themes from the data. To achieve consistency, validity and reliability, the analysis was carried out in two stages. During the first stage, the researchers individually identified and coded the data as means to constitute preliminary themes. In the second stage, the researchers worked together to compare, refine and reflect on the codings (consisted of themes description along with interpretations of 'strategies', 'tools' and 'learning spaces' for each theme) and associated quotations to constitute the final datasets. Descriptive (e.g. illuminate themes) and interpretive (e.g. comprehend subsequent meanings) analysis was therefore employed to ensure optimal analysis procedures.

10.5 Results

We present the results of the analysis encompassing teachers' experiences of multimodal teaching and learning through interacting with the STEAM serious game. The themes may be used for rendering how multimodal tools, strategies and locations were experienced by teachers to constitute their conceptions of in-game multimodal teaching and learning and thereby investigating how the game influenced the development of such in-game experiences of multimodality. Table 10.1 presents the four themes emerged and representative quotations. Participant identifiers (P1–P54) were employed to indicate responses from the teachers.

Table 10.1 Themes of in-game experiences of multimodal teaching with associated strategies, tools and spaces and representative quotations

Themes	Strategies, tools, learning spaces	Representative quotations
Learning diversity for engagement and knowledge retention	Discussions knowledge retention, lectures, slideshows, videos, in- class learning	"engaging students in different ways of learning through discussing, debating, and convincing" (P50). "I was looking for choices that increase retention of what was learnt" (P54). [..] it is all about engaging students through various oral and written tools including presentations, videos followed by assignments" (P40). "students were concentrating better in the school" (P12)
Developing senses for attaining deeper understandings of the topic	Increasing attention and focus, visuals, 3D modelling, in-class learning combined with visits from professionals	"multimodality sharpens the senses and enables the student to think more carefully when trying to explain understandings" (P25). "tended to combine a 3D application so students can use their gestural ability to make connections, links, shapes and overall to use their hands with their minds for increasing their understandings" (P5). I wanted to combine tools videos for visual learning followed by a talk from a professional to gain and share insights and observe how they express and use specialist vocabulary to describe a complex topic" (P31).
Involving students into learning design	Learning by design, creativity, video creation and editing, 3D printing, question tool, inquiry, making products, in-class learning combined with fieldtrips, learning in public spaces	"Combining cards that tried to involve students into designing learning activities based on their own learning needs and interests could help them to do and create rather than just listen the topic" (P1). "Using cards with a design-based approach to teaching felt it was working well in co-designing what they wanted to learn" (P42). "I was looking in the cards to find combinations such as a 3D printer or create a game where students can make something as being the designers of their own learning and attempt to apply practically what they know (P52). "I combined the library and information literacy cards for students to search for resources they wanted to use by visiting the library and then discuss how they did their searching in the classroom" (P2).

(continued)

Table 10.1 (continued)

Themes	Strategies, tools, learning spaces	Representative quotations
Supporting student autonomy and self-direction	Establishing teams, developing ideas, gathering requirements, designing, peer-assessment, 3D-printing, question-pool, blogging, online surveys, out-of-class teaching	"I selected a dialogue choice for students to set-up their teams [...], it is just that they [students] need to feel free to choose the peers that they will like to work with... (P11). "I tried to be bold enough to select a design-based learning card, to get them [students] sketch the main project idea and figure out the relations with other sub-ideas" (P18). "Wanted to see if I could make students to start doing some very basic research like learn how to pose questions or collect data from a survey so I combined inquiry-based learning with opinion polling" (P37). "Selecting a problem-based learning card with a 3D printing creation for using their skills to see how they work in practice" (P32). "I thought of multimodality as a more of a self-directing, self-assessment all-self-thing really, so I combined interdisciplinarity and blog cards for preparing collaboratively a blog report for assessing work and identify improvements based on their needs, experiences and backgrounds" (P41). "A game means going wild, and this is what I did as an advocate of context-specific learning though research, problem-solving and inquiry, I wanted to teach out of the classroom, like set a problem-based activity into groups, get them on mobile games to start discover museum-related content for their projects and unleash their real potential" (P41).

10.5.1 In-Game Multimodality as a Way of Stipulating Learning Diversity for Increasing Engagement and Knowledge Retention

In this theme, teachers perceived in-game multimodality as helping students to learn through employing multiple teaching strategies and using an array of learning tools: 'I will try to achieve a more intensive examination of the topic, to increase motivation through the use of modern media' (P29). Teaching strategies such as initiating discussions and debates were prevalent as means of helping students to externalise their interests and for practicing negotiation, argumentation and oral skills. Retention of knowledge was a fundamental purpose achieved via repetition and memorisation of learning content provided by the teacher.

Tools used were predominantly in-class lectures; slideshows and videos prepared are presented by the teacher and writing assignments for recalling subject content. Combining in-game strategies such as choosing dialogues for initiating reciprocal discussions with the teacher for encouraging debates and argumentation was felt central for assimilating and understanding content. This was also a way for students to engage with others via communicating content already retained in memory. 'I tend to think reciprocal discussions about the topic I presented may improve student knowledge retention and engagement' (P48). Teachers felt that students' engagement may be further facilitated by having a free choice in terms of the tools, resources and personal learning strategies they deploy that would likely increase self-regulated learning: 'In the dialogues I tended to select a variety of tools and strategies for enabling interaction and free choice for my students to choose what tools and resources they may choose from to support their learning' (P44).

The classroom is the predominant learning environment, in this theme. It was perceived as the main space for delivering learning but also as a space for introducing and contemplating on extended activities to be completed at home such as quizzes, subject readings and solving exercises from textbook. This was evident by the card game combinations where teachers selected strategies and tools enacted in the class: '...in the card game I chose presenting content in the classroom and then assigning an exercise at home to be presented and discussed in class the next day...' (P8).

10.5.2 In-Game Multimodality as Developing Senses for Attaining Deeper Understanding of the Subject Topic

In this theme, in-game multimodality for teaching is viewed as developing and applying students' senses for gaining an in-depth understanding of the topic: '[..] developing student's senses such as seeing, hearing, feeling, touching and experiencing in detail some of the topics presented...' (P49). Developing senses, therefore, was perceived as means to increase focus and concentration for explaining ideas and understandings. Different types of senses were interestingly correlated with types of learners, meaning that different learners use different senses to enable learning: 'my aim was to choose cards with tools that would allow the use of different senses like for example oral, written, visual or gestural to get to know how a learner learns best [..] I tested different combinations every time' (P30).

Tools that have been used were mainly the ones that promoted different senses for visual learning, 'I chose slides, videos and diagrams for increasing their visual skills' (P21), and for auditory-oriented learning, 'I wanted to combine an audio track with blogging to augment audio with writing skills' (P43).

The classroom is the main space for teaching, as in previous theme, but in conjunction to several informal learning events, such as invitations to people from the industry to come and talk about a subject of interest in class.

10.5.3 In-Game Multimodality as Actively Involving Students into Learning Design

In this theme, in-game multimodality was perceived as collaborating with students for designing multimodal learning activities: 'I saw that some game cards were describing students as the ones who were making choices on how learning could be designed – I tried to play with those cards mostly' (P49). The reasons participants explained approaching game play towards allowing students to participate into the design of learning as a pertinent multimodal activity were for helping students to focus more on learning by doing. It was felt that by giving a 'designer' role to students, it may help them experience different ways of learning by including aspects of learning mostly relevant to them but also developing skills in the design of learning activities: 'game dialogue choices that encouraged students to have a say in the design of activities - and hopefully teaching them the skill of designing learning and its complexities' (P16). Design-based strategies were used to co-develop learning activities with students. As such, design-based strategies were correlated with more applied-based activities rather than focusing only on retention and memorisation as in the first theme: 'we try to co-design the creation of a learning video […] students had to practically engage with the topic and develop something by themselves' (P33).

The prevailing digital tools that were utilised for in-game multimodal teaching were creative tools, such as video creation and editing, 3D modelling and 3D printing. This was perceived as a way to encourage students to develop creative and design-like mindsets in terms of increasing possibilities to apply theory into practice. 'Hands-on' and self-directed learning was key. The use of resources and tools that encouraged this design-like, more applied-oriented learning was in the foreground of teachers' ways of thinking about multimodality during game play.

Classroom was the primary space of learning. However, notably, in this theme, participants increasingly started to select cards that resembled activities in different learning spaces augmenting the classroom space with different spaces. These included, but were not limited to, field trips, visits to other companies, learning in libraries and other public spaces perpetuating learning as a process that is constantly enacted regardless of place and time: 'I looked in the library and I saw an interesting combination so I used this as getting design-based learning, with a location-based play realised on the street […] What an excitement to realise that multimodality is applied regardless of place or time' (P48).

10.5.4 In-Game Multimodality as Supporting Student's Autonomy and Self-Direction

In this theme, teachers perceived in-game multimodality as a way to increase student's autonomy and self-direction: 'the increasingly necessary development towards independent, self-determined learning' (P32). This was practiced through helping students to understand the iterative development cycle of project development: (1) establishing teams for group work, (2) developing ideas, (3) gathering requirements, (4) designing and developing and (5) encouraging/activating peer assessment. The first stage of the cycle felt it was central for students to be guided through the importance of working with peers. Developing an idea collaboratively was a process of debating, visualising, comprehending and relating concepts together. Gathering user requirements seemed to be as an in-game multimodal strategy increasingly correlated with research-related practices: 'I chose this option about getting students to start gathering data for their projects […]' (P22). Designing and developing as a learning process was perceived as putting students' creative skills into practice. Peer assessment was seen as an interdisciplinary process involving students with different skills to assess project's outcomes stemming from multiple perspectives.

Tools that have been selected were mainly for helping students to design, create and self-assess their projects: '3D printing was an interesting card for encouraging students to sit down and discuss what went wrong and what went well and then assess themselves' (P21). Learning how to formulate questions as part of initiating a research inquiry was also a feature of in-game multimodality. Participants increasingly used in-game cards representing tools that helped students collaborate when developing their project ideas and creative mindsets and self-assess final project outputs: 'I stretched my head to find a card-combination that would quickly scribble down their initial ideas, connected the dotted lines and evaluate final project outcomes as a first go' (P15). Blogging was perceived as a tool for practicing reflection on the collaborative project and thinking through both about the process of collaborating on a project and the content of the outputs: 'I saw blogs and I thought why should I not use it for encouraging reflection on what students done and how much they learned' (P24).

Participants were keen on experimenting with employing locations and learning spaces (other than the classroom) to enact multimodal teaching as means to promote a more favourable and context-specific environment for learning: 'I was pondering, if we change the classroom as the primary location and select a "museum" or a "nature" card location, would this increase students' creativity, autonomy and inquiry?' (P43). Being curious on how a learning space, other than a classroom, could be combined with activities and tools for enabling creativity and self-direction was vital in this theme.

10.6 Discussion

Teachers' conceptualisations of in-game multimodal teaching encompass the use of teaching strategies, digital tools and learning environments in developmental modes and at different levels of progression. The four themes that grew out of this study may be seen as an extension to similar experiences supporting the view that multimodality gives emphasis on multiple modes of representation and communication for constituting meaning-making (e.g. Hassett & Curwood, 2009; Jewitt, 2013). To this line, the identified themes resemble a set of conceptualisations of in-game multimodality that were twinned with strategies, tools and learning spaces that represent a set of multiliteracies transcending from monomodality, as a linear, framed and fragmented principle to multimodality and as a non-linear, unframed and cohesive practice (e.g. Kress & Van Leeuwen, 2001).

In an earlier version (Papageorgiou & Lameras, 2017), we revealed an explicit and implicit connection between 'espoused theories' and 'theories in use' in terms of observing contingency and alignment between conceptions of in-game multimodality and the employment of certain strategies and tools for practicing multimodality in specific learning contexts. For example, teachers who perceived in-game multimodality as a process of knowledge memorisation and retention described that their preferred strategies, tools and learning environments supported the materialisation of this specific conception of multimodality. In tandem, conceptions of in-game multimodality that supported a design-based, do-it-yourself culture were consistent with strategies, tools and locations that allowed the instantiation of such conceptions of multimodality. In a broader spectrum of analysis in the first theme, teachers sought to employ more oral/written modes, although there were instances of using visual tools such as slides, alluding to monomodal practices with little emphasis on the semiotic sign (e.g. Kress & Van Leeuwen, 2001).

In the second, third and fourth themes, multimodal conceptualisations and associated strategies, tools and learning environments are employed as a set of 'modes' that connect representational resources with how teachers in the game are using them. Particularly in themes 3 and 4, there is evidence of representations or interactions of more than one mode (e.g. a question tool with a 3D printer for inquiry- and design-based learning) that distribute meaning across a number of modes and not individual modes. Each mode, therefore, has to accomplish a specific purpose, as in the case of deploying a question tool to introduce a research-based endeavour and then designing a model to be produced in the 3D printer. We assert therefore that 'multimodal ensembles' are delimited creating an interplay between modes with explicit goals that each mode is assigned from the teacher to pertain targeted meanings (e.g. Bezemer & Kress, 2008; Jewitt, 2013).

We contextualised the experience of understanding and employing multimodality through a serious game which by itself is a semiotic domain involving symbolic and representational multimodal resources to discern multiple conceptualisations of multimodality. Rich and meaningful representations of multimodality have been communicated and represented to teachers influenced by the rules, mechanics, game play, design and inner logic of the game. Since the STEAM game is an instance of a semiotic domain and visualises multimodal representations as experienced by the teachers, we need to consider the implications of embracing the orchestration of the themes and associated multimodal strategies, tools and location choices in real classrooms. Game design elements such as game and learning mechanics, rules, goals, interfaces, symbols and images used to manifest a multimodal in-game representation are specific to particular in-game situations. This may imply that the way that multimodality was conceived and enacted in the game could be manifested differently in a live classroom. The identified four themes of in-game multimodality may be different to other semiotic domains and specific learning situations. It is a matter of situating the themes and their elements in embodied ways of adapted multimodal manifestations both in terms of a particular learning situation and of a specific learning domain. Building and translating an artificial in-game multimodal meaning to an actual tangible multimodal activity in the classroom is a necessary acclimatisation based on teacher's individual experiences and conditions of a particular classroom domain. This will warrant that the range of meanings attributed to the game's semiotic domain will be consciously and systematically rendered to the classroom's semiotic domain.

Another implication to transferring in-game multimodal experiences to practice is the internal and external structures such the game design influences. The STEAM game was designed with specific content, rules, mechanics, dynamics and aesthetics that may influenced how teachers experienced and understood multimodal learning and teaching. For example, feedback design through multiple visual, textual and numerical instances could regulate alternative conceptions of multimodality due to positive or negative feelings of the feedback received from the game. Another example is core game mechanics influences of the developed multimodal experiences. The dialogue and cards core mechanics likely created multimodal conceptions deemed as transferable, applicable and compatible to be practiced to another semiotic domain with few adaptations or, arguably, as not acceptable practice due to an incompatible internal design grammar (e.g. Gee, 2003). Actively and consciously knowing therefore what counts as multimodal teaching, multimodal strategies, tools and learning spaces and also discerning the roles, goals and identities that are formed in a lived semiotic domain, we could make connections of espoused in-game experiences of multimodality transcended to recognisable, compatible and applicable practice.

10.7 Conclusion

The findings of this exploratory study suggest a number of opportunities for further research. This is important for building on the outcomes of this study and extends interdisciplinary strands of research related to conceptions of multimodality for teaching and learning. It is also central for starting to expand the use of serious games as semiotic domains and artefacts for amplifying learning, teaching and training. For example, it would be sensible to investigate conceptions of in-game multimodality for university teaching or from the student perspective at different levels of study with a different game genre. Another interesting study would be to understand and compare game effects on learning about multimodal teaching in comparison to more conventional forms of teacher professional development programs.

Limitations arise from our study in terms of associating conceptions of in-game multimodality with effects on learning and engagement. We did not aim to develop metrics and criteria that would provide inferences between particular ways of experiencing multimodal teaching with learning performance. However, it would be interesting to investigate whether there is correlation between teachers' conceptions of in-game multimodality with students' learning performance. This would also pave the way in understanding subtly the transferability and applicability of developing in-game multimodal experiences to the classroom's semiotic domain.

Acknowledgements The authors would like to thank the school teachers and our end-user partners that helped us with the data collection process and the EU Erasmus + project with grant agreement n°2016-1-FR01-KA204-024178 which funded the development, design and evaluation of the game.

References

Antonietti, A., & Giorgetti, M. (2006). Teachers' beliefs about learning from multimedia. *Computers in Human Behavior, 22*(2), 267–282. https://doi.org/10.1016/j.chb.2004.06.002

Bellotti, F., Berta, R., De Gloria, A., Lavagnino, E., Dagnino, F., Ott, M., et al. (2012). Designing a course for stimulating entrepreneurship in higher education through serious games. *Procedia Computer Science, 15*, 174–186. https://doi.org/10.1016/j.procs.2012.10.069

Bezemer, J., & Kress, G. (2008). Writing in multimodal texts: A social semiotic account of designs for learning. *Written Communication, 25*(2), 166–195.

Boot, W. R., Kramer, A. F., Simons, D. J., Fabiani, M., & Gratton, G. (2008). The effects of video game playing on attention, memory, and executive control. *Acta Psychologica, 129*(3), 387–398. https://doi.org/10.1016/j.actpsy.2008.09.005

Cope, B., & Kalantzis, M. (2009). "Multiliteracies": New literacies, new learning. *Pedagogies: An International Journal, 4*(3), 164–195.

Cope, B., Kalantzis, M., & Abrams, S. S. (2017). Meaning-making and learning in the era of digital text. In *Remixing multiliteracies: Theory and practice from New London to new times* (pp. 35–49). New York, USA: Teachers College Press.

Cope, B., & Kalantzis, M. (2020). *Making sense: Reference, agency, and structure in a grammar of multimodal meaning*. Cambridge, UK: Cambridge University Press.

Cowan, K. W., & Cipriani, S. (2009). Of water troughs and the sun: Developing inquiry through analogy. *Young Children, 64*(6), 62–67.

Crook, K. M., & Crook, C. K. (2017). Multimodal opportunities with digital tools: The example of narrated photographs. In *Handbook on Digital Learning for K-12 Schools* (pp. 13–29). https://doi.org/10.1007/978-3-319-33808-8_2

Del Blanco, Á., Torrente, J., Marchiori, E. J., Martínez-Ortiz, I., Moreno-Ger, P., & Fernández-Manjón, B. (2012). A framework for simplifying educator tasks related to the integration of games in the learning flow. *Educational Technology & Society, 15*(4), 305–318.

Gee, J. P. (2003). What video games have to teach us about learning and literacy. *Computers in Entertainment CIE, 1*(1), 20. https://doi.org/10.1016/j.vetpar.2013.04.007

Greenhow, C., Robelia, B., & Hughes, J. E. (2009). Learning, teaching, and scholarship in a digital age: Web 2.0 and classroom research: What path should we take now? *Educational Researcher, 38*(4), 246–257. https://doi.org/10.3102/0013189X09336671

Haniya, S., Tzirides, A. O., Montebello, M., Georgiadou, K., Cope, B., & Kalantzis, M. (2019). Maximizing learning potential with multimodality: A case study. *World Journal of Educational Research, 6*(2), 260–269. https://doi.org/10.22158/wjer.v6n2p260

Hassett, D. D., & Curwood, J. S. (2009). Theories and practices of multimodal education: The instructional dynamics of picture books and primary classrooms. *The Reading Teacher, 63*(4), 270–282.

Jewitt, C. (2008). Multimodality and literacy in school classrooms. *Review of Research in Education, 32*(1), 241–267. https://doi.org/10.3102/0091732X07310586

Jewitt, C. (2013). Multimodal methods for researching digital technologies. In *The SAGE handbook of digital technology research* (pp. 250–265). London, UK: SAGE. https://doi.org/10.4135/9781446282229.n18

Kress, G., & Van Leeuwen, T. (2001). *Multimodal discourse: The modes and media of contemporary communication*. London, UK: Edward Arnold.

Lameras, P., Philippe, S., & Oertel, L. (2019). A serious game for amplifying awareness on multimodal teaching: Game design and usability study. Advances in intelligent systems and computing. *The 13th International Conference on Interactive Mobile Communication Technologies and Learning (IMCL2019)*, Thessaloniki, Greece.

Lave, J. (1991). Situating learning in communities of practice. *Perspectives on Socially Shared Cognition, 2*, 63–82.

Lerkkanen, M. K., Kiuru, N., Pakarinen, E., Poikkeus, A. M., Rasku-Puttonen, H., Siekkinen, M., et al. (2016). Child-centered versus teacher-directed teaching practices: Associations with the development of academic skills in the first grade at school. *Early Childhood Research Quarterly, 36*, 145–156.

Mayer, R. E. (2001). *Multimedia learning*. New York, USA: Cambridge University Press.

Miller, S. M., & McVee, M. B. (2013). Multimodal composing in classrooms: Learning and teaching for the digital world. In *Multimodal composing in classrooms: Learning and teaching for the digital world*. London, UK: Routledge. https://doi.org/10.4324/9780203804032

Papageorgiou, V., & Lameras, P. (2017). Multimodal teaching and learning with the use of technology: Meanings, practices and discourses. *14th International Conference on Cognition and Exploratory Learning in the Digital Age, CELDA 2017*.

Picciano, A. G. (2009). Blending with purpose: The multimodal model. *Journal of Asynchronous Learning Networks, 13*(1), 7–18.

Schoorman, F. D., Mayer, R. C., & Davis, J. H. (2007). An integrative model of organizational trust: Past, present, and future. *Academy of Management Review, 32*(2), 344–354.

Shah, P., & Freedman, E. G. (2003). Visuospatial cognition in electronic learning. *Journal of Educational Computing Research, 29*(3), 315–324. https://doi.org/10.2190/QYVJ-Q59L-VE7C-EHUV

Sun, M. (2015). Application of multimodal learning in online English teaching. *International Journal of Emerging Technologies in Learning, 10*(4), 54–58. https://doi.org/10.3991/ijet.v10i4.4697

Thibaut, P., & Curwood, J. S. (2018). Multiliteracies in practice: Integrating multimodal production across the curriculum. *Theory Into Practice, 57*(1), 48–55.

Chapter 11
The Development of Teacher Leadership Inventory in Malaysian Educational Context

Mahaliza Mansor, Jamal Nordin Yunus, and Fanny Kho

11.1 Introduction

Teaching is creative and complex and requires high skills. Hence, teachers must constantly deepen their knowledge, skills, and value to be effective leader throughout their careers. In recent studies, teacher leadership has been defined as it is centered on a vision of a teacher who is able to build influence and interaction, rather than power and authority (Poekert, 2012). According to Fairman and Mackenzie (2012), teacher leadership emerged within many different contexts, such as individual and collective efforts; informal and formal actions; narrowly focused and broader school-wide improvement efforts; a school climate of isolation and mistrust; or one of collegiality, shared vision, and trust. Whereas, Hunzicker (2013) reported that teacher leadership roles and responsibilities are closely related to student-focused concerns. However, their self-efficacy increase when the teacher actively pursued leadership skills and positively influence their self-conceptions of teacher leadership.

Meanwhile, according to Danielson (2006), the leadership of teacher is the activities carried out by individuals who have knowledge and skills to influence other individuals inside and outside the organization. This in line with A. Ghani, Radzi, Marzuki, and Faisol (2014) and Fairman and Mackenzie (2015), where teacher leadership concept refers to teachers who make a difference whether within or outside the organization through knowledge and skill and style that affects colleagues. Therefore, it is shown that teachers use the knowledge, skills, and value to influence colleagues in adopting best practices in school. There are at least three major elements need to be considered in enhancing teacher leadership, which is knowledge,

---

M. Mansor (✉) · J. N. Yunus · F. Kho
Faculty Management and Economics, Sultan Idris Education University,
Tanjung Malim, Perak, Malaysia
e-mail: mahaliza@fpe.upsi.edu.my; jamal@fpe.upsi.edu.my; fannykcy@fpe.upsi.edu.my

© Springer Nature Switzerland AG 2020
P. Isaias et al. (eds.), *Technology Supported Innovations in School Education*, Cognition and Exploratory Learning in the Digital Age,
https://doi.org/10.1007/978-3-030-48194-0_11

skill (Fairman & Mackenzie, 2012; Katzenmeyer & Moller, 2009; Phelps, 2008; York-Barr & Duke, 2004), and value (MOE, 2009), of the teacher, which are going to discussed further below. At present, few instruments exist to measure teacher leadership by using these three elements especially in Malaysian high schools. Meanwhile, most scales were developed in the West such as Katzenmeyer and Moller (2009) and this scale is not designed to tap into the perceptions of teachers, which were reviewed to be meaningful, powerful, and intense in the lives of Malaysians. Therefore, it is a need to develop and validate a good reliable scale which is more suitable to Malaysian educational context.

Hence, the objectives of this study are (1) to develop an initial pool of items for scale to measure the elements of teacher leadership among teachers in terms knowledge, skill, and value; (2) to perform an EFA to assess the factor structure of the scale items; (3) to analyze the initial estimates of reliability indices and construct validity of the TLI scores; and (4) to test the factor structure of the scores obtained from the items determined in EFA, through the use of CFA. These objectives will be answered in two phases of study.

11.1.1 Teachers Knowledge

According to Green (2005); Yusof, Min, Jalil, Noor, and Yusof (2018), knowledge is what teachers know in order to promote the success of all students. Furthermore, with adequate knowledge, they can identify an appropriate and acceptable process for the schools' success. Knowledge in this study refers to teachers' understanding on teacher leadership concept, where teachers tend to use their content knowledge on teachers' leadership and apply it in the school and community in order to strive for schools' excellence. Besides, knowledge in this study also refers to teachers' leadership knowledge, whereby teachers positively influent adults and young learners, formally and informally beyond individual classrooms (Ado, 2016; Carver, 2016; Dehart, 2011). Hence, leadership knowledge requires teachers to have extensive knowledge about students' physical and psychological, as well as theory of pedagogy and andragogy (Darling-Hammond, Flook, Cook-Harvey, Barron, & Osher, 2019; Tamuri, Mahmud, & Bari, 2005).

Leadership knowledge also can be enhanced through practicing teachers' professional learning for continuous improvement (Fairman & Mackenzie, 2014; Lieberman, Campbell, & Yashkina, 2017). In other words, teachers need to collaborate and contribute in the school improvement program by reflecting, collaborating, and engaging in school-wide decision-making based on distinct backgrounds, ethnicities, cultures, and languages in the school community while sharing best practices among colleagues (Bond, 2011; Cherkowski & Schnellert, 2017; Harmon, 2017; Lieberman & Miller, 2005; Spillane, 2005; Teacher Leadership Exploratory Consortium, 2011; Wenner & Campbell, 2017).

In this context, teachers will be able to voice their opinions to achieve the shared vision and mission of the school improvement. Meanwhile, novice teachers who are still lack of knowledge about the school systems and teacher leadership skills (Muijs, Chapman, & Armstrong, 2013) can use this platform to enhance their knowledge. According to Muijs (2015) and Harmon (2017), teacher leadership also provides spaces for teachers to share knowledge through school-to-school collaboration for significant school improvement. Brondyk and Stanulis (2014) and Lieberman et al. (2017), too, claim that teachers' involvement in teacher leadership program at the ministry level would also provide opportunity for teachers to share their views in policy making and best practices as well.

Nonetheless, various empirical studies had proposed that it was crucial to develop the concept of teachers' leadership knowledge during teacher preparation program which will be further practiced throughout their careers (Abidin, Norwani, & Musa, 2016; Bond & Sterrett, 2014; Musa, Yusof, Noor, Mansor, & Abidin, 2019; Neumann, Jones, & Webb, 2012; Padzil, 2016; York-Barr & Duke, 2004). In conclusion, teachers should be exposed with leadership skills since early stage at teacher's training colleges so that they can face the challenges in the process of enhancing instructional practices in the classrooms (Moller & Katzenmeyer, 1996; Ontario Leadership Strategy, 2013; Sawalhi & Chaaban, 2019).

11.1.2 Teachers Skill

Teacher leadership skill is closely related to good teamwork skill. A study conducted by Khan and Ahmad (2012) had also confirmed that good teamwork skill requires effective interpersonal skills. According to Barnett et al. (2018), effective interpersonal skills enable teachers to lead by engaging, inspiring, and motivating others to improve through their actions. They are able to lead by effectively communicate with colleagues and inform them of their goals in ways that can garner support of their vision for the school improvement (Broemmel, Jordan, & Whitsett, 2016; Danielson, 2007; Huang, 2016). However, the teachers can only acquire this leadership skill through a broad range of practice. There are many leadership skills that a teacher must have in order to be successful and effective teacher leader. According to Katzenmeyer and Moller (2009), teachers who have the leadership skills to influence other teachers or students and other school communities can act as facilitators, mentors, counselors, and curriculum specialists toward improved educational practices, student learning, and achievement. Essentially, teachers who are able to lead would shape meaningful systems that contribute to the quality of educational system in the long term (Lieberman et al., 2017; Szeto & Cheng, 2017). In other words, teachers who portray influential skills, formally and informally, beyond individual classrooms would contribute to positive impact in student learning (Dehart, 2011), as well as to create a more enriching classroom environment (Fairman & Mackenzie, 2012). Hence, every teacher should have influential leadership skills and attributes. As a matter of fact, Danielson (2007) had also highlighted other additional skills that individual teachers may adopt. According to Danielson (2007), effective teachers must be open-minded and respect others' views. They also should show confidence, assertive, flexible, and willing to try a different approach if their efforts failed, as well as willing to encounter a variety of risks such as time constraints in their daily job. Meanwhile, De Villiers and Pretorius (2011) and Barnett et al. (2018) emphasize that teacher leadership occurs in four settings which are in the classrooms, working with other teachers outside the classrooms, extracurricular activities, and school development and leadership practices among schools' community. However, their study concluded that most of the leadership practices happen in the classroom, during teaching and learning improvement. Therefore, teachers must learn to lead a group, listen, use the data, and identify other needs to acquire a strong set of skills to be use in the school daily routines (Katzenmeyer & Moller, 2009).

Research done by Angelle, Nixon, Norton, and Niles (2011) showed that teacher leadership skills imposed high impact on school development through shared responsibility among teachers. This can be achieved through collaborative relationship and school culture based on trust. To achieve collaborative relationship and trusted culture, Jackson, Burrus, Bassett, and Roberts (2010) and Lieberman et al. (2017) suggested teachers should learn in groups. In other word, teachers should share best practices among colleagues and engage in school-wide decision-making through teachers' participation with or without position and its positive implication to teachers themselves, students' achievement, and school performance (Teacher Leadership Exploratory Consortium, 2011; Yusof, Vyapuri, Jalil, Mansor, & Noor, 2017). Another study conducted by Frost (2012) also confirmed that teachers who portray leadership skills are able to lead any development projects regardless of whatever positions they hold. Likewise, teachers who do not have any interest in leading colleagues also portray leadership skills informally beyond their classrooms (Leonard, Petta, & Porter, 2012).

In particular, this idea runs parallel with the focus of teachers as leaders who leads other teachers through group learning or commonly known as professional learning community (Wilson, 2016). In group learning, teachers will welcome a group of teachers to join their instructional sessions. According to Roberts and Pruitt (2009) and Olusegun and Bada (2015), group learning refers to the learning process that takes place among teachers to discuss on important issues in schools in identifying students' learning. This professional learning community has led to changes in pedagogy through shared goals, relationships, and trust as well as supports continuous learning which gives a positive impact on student achievement and improve teacher effectiveness (Day, 2017; Harris & Jones, 2010; Sharratt & Fullan, 2009) as an effort to help other colleagues (Ghani & Crow, 2013; Lieberman et al., 2017).

Therefore, Teacher Leadership Exploratory Consortium (2011) suggests that teachers need to understand the family, culture, and society as they give a big impact to the educational process and student learning. Teacher needs to work with colleagues to establish a good continuous relationship with families, communities, and other stakeholders to improve the education system and student learning opportunities. Finally, teachers also can play a vital role as a referral leader to guide students, lead, and guide himself or herself and their colleagues to the shared purposive goals without being autocratic (Idris & Hamzah, 2012). In conclusion, these studies clearly shown that a teacher who poses leadership skills can be the role model and referral leader to students, colleagues, parents, and the community. Indirectly, it showed that leadership skills can be applied in each and every teacher as individual.

11.1.3 Teachers Value

The value is defined as beliefs about what is the right and wrong way for people to behave, and it is also known as moral principles (MOE, 2009). The term value in this study has been defined as a set of beliefs that teachers have toward the school and community and could give a great impact in schools transformation process. The school transformation process requires teachers to be transformative leaders in their respective classrooms. Hence, teachers need to portray at least five core values that shall help them in being outstanding transformative leaders, facilitators, and educators in the classrooms. Firstly, teachers should portray integrity in being instructional leaders in the classrooms. Similarly, they need to be honest in explaining solution to any confusion that the students may encounter. Secondly, teachers should always possess a sense of hope that their students can perform better. In other words, teachers should practice distinct ways of explaining core concepts to students as students have distinct learning styles too. Thirdly, teachers should always possess a sense of urgency in meeting academic as well as nonacademic goals that they had set for their students. Lingering around may not be a good idea as time is valuable, and students have also invested ample time expecting to learn meaningful and important information. Fourthly, teachers should be learners too. Teachers need to stay updated and learn advance technology in preparing students globally. At times, teachers should be accountable in learning distinct culture and beliefs from students as well. Last but not least, teachers also need to have respect and responsibility toward students. In other words, teachers are responsible in developing holistic society via educated and capable manpower. Upon possessing and exhibiting these core values, teachers shall be able to nurture students who will constantly practice good values in their daily lives.

Teachers also need to instill professionalism of teaching practices in them while being a guidance and role model to the students. According to MOE (2009, 2013) and Abdullah, Hassan, and Ying-Leh (2019), the practice of the professionalism will be a platform for teachers to develop good characters to fulfill the function of the school as a place of national establishment to develop human capital and this in line with the Malaysian National Education Philosophy and Philosophy of Teacher Education aspirations. The practice of professionalism in teaching is an initiative to develop a teacher who has a towering personality in becoming an excellent teacher (MOE, 2009).

Teachers also must have a high cognitive skills and a good personality. According Cheng and Zamarro (2016), teachers who have values and high self-esteem should be aware that the dignity of the teaching profession lies in their hands and teachers also should highlight the positive values in them because the students often refer them as the role models. In line with the philosophy of Malaysian Teacher Education, teachers must be honorable, have a progressive and scientific vision, ready to uphold the aspirations of the country, ensuring the development of individuals, as well as preserve the unity, democratic, and progressive community (Mok, 2010). In order to meet the current education challenges, teachers should have a strong values and self-esteem in them. According to Mat Som and Megat Daud (2008) and MOE (2013), the main aspects to be address in promoting the teaching profession are a teacher's own personality. This is because the personal quality of the teacher is a source of knowledge and able to emulate the formation of good character (Abas, 2007; Qomar, 2016). In other words, the teacher is acting as "value developer" (MacBeath, Pedder, & Swaffield, 2007). Therefore, teachers need to show good personal values to the students, schools, and communities. These good personal qualities can guide and educate students to develop their personal character. In conclusion, the core values that a teacher must have are honest, discipline, responsibility, timeliness, and a commitment to work (MOE, 2009).

Thus, according to the literature, teacher leadership can be classified into three dimensions as suggested by Katzenmeyer and Moller (2009), Phelps (2008), Fairman and Mackenzie (2012, 2015), and MOE (2009): knowledge, skills, and values in practice, which are used in our model. However, currently, there are still not many suitable instruments to measure secondary school teachers' perception toward teacher leadership. Most of the previous studies have been carried in Western countries, such as Teacher Leadership Self-Assessment (TLSA) developed by Katzenmeyer and Moller (2009), and the measurement is not really suitable with Malaysian context as well as less has been reviewed by previous researcher. Secondly is the use of suitable statistical procedure in developing and validating items. The exploratory factor analysis has been well suggested by experts if there are less research have been carried out regarding the observe factor structure (Bandalos & Finney, 2018). However, Hair, Black, Babin, Anderson, and Tatham (2018) argued that the exploratory factor analysis (EFA) itself cannot be used as a basis for a final determination regarding an underlying construct, because the analysis is designed to maximize the amount of variance within the current variable set, and subsequent analyses with other data sets may not reproduce the same factor structure. Furthermore, EFA only focuses on statistical and not according to the theory in determining the measurement structure scale as well as not enough to measure error (Byrne, 2016; Morin, Arens, Tran, & Caci, 2016; Schulz et al., 2018). Given these various constraints and limitations of existing instrument reviewed, therefore it was necessary for the researchers to develop an empirically validated Teacher Leadership Inventory (TLI) specifically measuring perceptions, for use in Malaysian educational context. The use of confirmatory factor analysis (CFA) is more suitable in developing and validating items. As the EFA itself, according to Hair et al. (2018), can be used as a basis for a final determination regarding an underlying construct, because this analysis is designed to maximize the amount of variance within the current variable set, and subsequent analyses with other data sets may not reproduce the same factor structure. Furthermore, EFA only focuses on statistical and not according to the theory in determining the measurement structure scale as well as not enough to measure error. However, the use of EFA, confirmatory factor analysis (CFA), content validity, as well as internal consistency are more suitable in developing and validating items. Given these various constraints and limitations of existing instrument reviewed, it was therefore necessary to develop an empirically validated TLI specifically in measuring perceptions of Malaysian secondary school teachers.

Hence, the objectives of this study are (1) to generate an initial pool of items for scale to measure the elements of teacher leadership among teachers; (2) to perform an EFA to assess the factor structure of the scale items; (3) to analyze the initial estimates of reliability indices and construct validity of the TLI scores; and (4) to test the factor structure of the scores obtained from the items determined in EFA, through the use of CFA. The method will be discussed in details below.

11.2 Method and Results

This study was conducted in two phases. The first phase will address the research objectives:

1. To generate an initial pool of items for scale to measure the elements of teacher leadership among teachers
2. To perform an EFA to assess the factor structure of the scale items
3. To analyze the initial estimates of reliability indices and construct validity of the TLI scores
4. Meanwhile, research objective:
5. To test the factor structure of the scores obtained from the items determined in EFA, through the use of CFA
6. Each phase is discussed in details below.

In Malaysia, permission for conducting research and data collection is typically granted by the ministry of education and the school principals. Approval was sought and obtained for the researchers to conduct the research at the schools prior to data collection. The purpose of the data collection was explained to the principals as well as teachers, and consent to participate in the study was obtained from involved teachers. Participation was strictly voluntary, and all responses were confidential. All questionnaires were administered both, in Malay and English.

A multistage cluster sampling technique has been used in this data collection. The first phase of the study has been carried out by using data from 166 teachers from 19 secondary schools in Batang Padang District, Perak. This set of data was used in preliminary study as to perform content validity, criterion validity, and EFA. 15 sets of questionnaires were distributed to each of these 19 regular secondary schools, only 200 questionnaries were return, and 166 valid for analysis. Meanwhile, for the second phase of the study, the confirmatory factor analysis has been carried out toward data of 244 teachers from 19 secondary schools in Perak,

Malaysia. A total of 285 survey forms were circulated, of which 244 surveys were return and valid for analysis.

11.2.1 Phase 1

11.2.1.1 Questionnaire Design

The questionnaire is originally composed of three parts, 18 items including knowledge, skill, and value. The instrument used has been adopted from Niche Research Grant Scheme (NRGS) 2014 Project 4: Teacher Leadership. The questionnaire items were shown in Table 11.5 and answered using a four-point scale anchoring at 1, 2, 3, and 4 (strongly disagree, disagree, agree, strongly agree). The comparative analysis of teacher leadership models such as Katzenmeyer and Moller (2009), Phelps (2008), York-Barr and Duke (2004), Fairman and Mackenzie (2012, 2015), Malaysian Education Development Plan, Malaysian National Policy of Education, and Malaysian Teacher Standard (2009), as well as through key informants and survey of lecturers and teachers from schools and higher learning institutions in Malaysia has been done to develop these items.

11.2.1.2 Exploratory Factor Analysis, Validity, and Reliability

The Cronbach's alpha coefficient is used to measure the internal consistency of these scales (Nunnally & Bernstein, 1994). In this study, the constructs which had Cronbach's alpha coefficients greater than 0.70 have been retained for further analysis (Hair et al., 2018). Furthermore, measures with item-to-total correlation larger than 0.3 are considered to have criterion validity (Hair et al., 2018). The item-to-total correlation of each measure was more than 0.3; therefore we consider the criterion validity of each scale to be satisfactory. The items are reviewed by a panel of Sultan Idris Education University lecturers to ensure the translation of meaning and terminology met the theoretical background as the technique. The panel consists of an assessment and measurement expert, a human resource development expert, and an educational leadership expert.

Then, the questionnaires have been administered to six trained teachers to identify if there were any confusion regarding the items and record it in the space provided for improvements or been dropped out (Gomez-Torres, Batanero, & Miguel, 2016). The purpose was to improve the items and to ensure it was suitable for Malaysian context. Furthermore, it was important to get feedback on quality of each item, as it was easy to understand and used the appropriate language and terminology. The samples were asked to evaluate about the clarity of each items by using the scale given (Kho, Yusof, & Mohamad, 2016). A scale of 1 to 10 is used to determine the validity coefficient for each item. According to Tuckman and Waheed (1981) in Mohd Noah and Ahmad (2005), if the total of the score obtained from the experts is

70% or above, it means that the item has a high score for the content validity aspect. Otherwise, the item will be dropped from the questionnaires. From the experts view, there are 3 items have been dropped from each factor. The items are N2, I model various leadership values and behavior; K5, I coordinate and manage activities with parents and community; and P6, I know the path to go above and beyond prescribed roles. The results of content validity are presented in Table 11.1 below.

Meanwhile, to ensure the instrument has reasonable construct validity, exploratory factor analysis was used. The exploratory factor analysis (EFA) through orthogonal rotation with varimax method had been used on these 15 items. The EFA applied the following rules as suggested by Hair et al. (2018):

- Bartlett's Test of Sphericity had to be significant ($p < 0.05$).
- Kaiser-Meyer-Olkin measure of sampling index ≥ 0.5.
- Eigenvalue >1.
- Items with the factor loading >0.5 were retained.
- Factors building are based on teacher leadership models and previous studies.

The results of exploratory factor analysis are presented in Table 11.2.

11.2.2 Phase 2

The confirmatory factor analysis (CFA) was used to test the stability of this three-factor model, 15 item using AMOS version 21. We analyzed this hypothesized three-factor model with all 15 items as indicators of the variable individually. The parameters were estimated using maximum likelihood. This approach incorporates both observed and latent variables. Multiple indices provided a comprehensive evaluation of model fit (Hu & Bentler, 1999). We examined chi-square per degree of freedom ratio (x^2/df), Comparative Fit Index (CFI), Goodness-of-Fit Index (GFI), and Root Mean Square Error of Approximation (RMSEA). These indices have been

Table 11.1 Content validity scores

Panel	Panel 1	Panel 2	Panel 3	Panel 4	Panel 5	Panel 6	Cum score
Percentage (%)	92.72	91.51	88.48	82.42	82.42	80.00	86.84

Table 11.2 Exploratory factor analysis and internal consistency values for the questionnaires

Construct	Number of Factor	Number of item per construct	Factor loading	% of variance	Cum. percentage	Cronbach's α
Teacher leadership	3	15	0.54–0.84		67.69	0.85
Knowledge		7		46.11		0.91
Value		4		12.85		0.70
Skill		4		8.73		0.66

Table 11.3 The fit indices of CFA model

Fit indices category	Fit indices	Indices value
Absolute fit	RMSEA	0.066
	GFI	0.923
Incremental fit	CFI	0.953
Parsimonious fit	Chisq/df	1.98

Table 11.4 Internal consistency values for the questionnaires after the CFA

Construct	Number of factor	Number of item per construct	Cronbach's α
Teacher leadership	3	13	0.84
Knowledge		4	0.88
Value		5	0.88
Skill		4	0.76

used to evaluate the goodness-of-fit of the model that fit the data. However, given the known dependency of the chi-squared index depends on sample size (Byrne, 2016; Schumacker & Lomax, 2016), it is less suitable to use in determining the fitness of the model (Singh, Junnarkar, & Kaur, 2016). Therefore, indices such as CFI and GFI were also being evaluated. x^2/df ratio value of less than 3 and value of 0.90 for CFI and GFI have been use as a lower cutoff value of the acceptable fit (Nunnally & Bernstein, 1994; Schumacker & Lomax, 2016). In addition, the RMSEA value of less than 0.06 indicate a good fit, while the value as high as 0.80 indicate a reasonable fit (Hu & Bentler, 1999). The convergent indices value of more than 0.3 and less than 0.95, meanwhile for the discriminant indices is ranged more than 0.60 and less than 0.90, also have been used to determine the unidimensionality of the factors (Hair et al., 2018). Therefore, 2 items have been dropped regarding to the cross loading as well as violate discriminant index range. The items are K2, I know the techniques and methods of teaching, students' psychology, and educational environment related to students; and N4, I possess a high level of confidence to implement programs with parents and the community. However, 1 item has been re-specified into the original factor based on the theories and literature. The results of CFA are presented in Table 11.3 below.

Meanwhile, the internal consistency values for each construct after CFA are presented in Table 11.4.

The final items developed are in Table 11.5 below:

11.3 Discussion and Conclusion

The purpose of this study is to develop and validate Teacher Leadership Inventory used to measure secondary teachers' self-assessment in Malaysian educational setting. The study use both theory and statistics to identify items leading to the establishment of the 15 TLI items, consisting of the four-item of knowledge, four-item of

Table 11.5 The TLI items

Teacher leadership construct	Indicator	Item
Knowledge	P1	I understand various teaching theories and practices Saya memahami pelbagai teori dan amalan pengajaran
	P3	I understand the development of the school's capacity for strategic development (vision and mission, professional development, infrastructure, finance, student activities, student achievement) Saya memahami tentang pembangunan kapasiti sekolah untuk pembangunan strategik (visi dan misi, pembangunan professional, infrastruktur, kewangan, aktiviti pelajar, pencapaian pelajar)
	P4	I know the roles of the mentor and coach, to influence others in terms of best practice Saya mengetahui akan peranan sebagai mentor dan jurulatih untuk mempengaruhi rakan setugas dalam mengamalkan amalan terbaik
	P5	I know the important of sharing ideas and practices through interaction with colleagues, communities, and external organization Saya mengetahui akan kepentingan perkongsian idea dan amalan menerusi interaksi dengan rakan setugas, komuniti dan organisasi luar
Value	N1	I value honesty and humbleness in order to build positive interaction with peers and students Saya menghargai kejujuran dan rasa rendah diri dalam membina interaksi positif dengan rakan setugas dan pelajar
	N3	I show willingness to take risks in order to achieve educational goals Saya menunjukkan kesanggupan untuk mengambil risiko dalam mencapai matlamat pendidikan
	N4	I share knowledge and ideas for the best practice Saya berkongsi pengetahuan dan idea untuk amalan terbaik
	N6	I possess high confidence in instructional and management Saya mempunyai keyakinan yang tinggi dalam instruksional dan pengurusan
Skill	K1	I apply various curriculum management skills Saya menggunakan pelbagai kemahiran pengurusan kurikulum.
	K2	I nurture students to apply effective interpersonal and intrapersonal communication skills Saya memupuk pelajar untuk melaksanakan kemahiran komunikasi interpersonal dan intrapersonal
	K3	I practice knowledge sharing to enhance school improvement Saya mengamalkan perkongsian pengetahuan untuk meningkatkan penambah baikan sekolah
	K4	I collaborate and shares responsibility with the others for best practices Saya berusaha bersama-sama dan berkongsi tanggungjawab dengan rakan setugas untuk menghasilkan amalan terbaik
	K6	I provide expert services as directed by the school, district education offices/affiliates, the State Education Department, and the Ministry of Education Malaysia Saya menyediakan perhikmatan kepakaran seperti yang diarahkan oleh sekolah, PPD, JPN dan KPM

value, and five-item of teachers self-assessment subscales. Result across two studies suggested that TLI and its subscales provide reliable scores measuring teachers' self-assessment from perception of secondary school teachers. The obtained scores from the total scale and three factors were found to be internally consistent across the studies with Cronbach's alphas ranging between 0.66 and 0.91. The total content validity scores of the experts are 86.84%, above the cutoff point 70%. This first phase of the study used The EFA to identify 15 items in developing new TLI. The eigenvalues showed that there are three factors which score more than one, and the total cumulative percentage is 67.69%. The factor analysis of 15 items shown that there are 3 major factors have been formed based on the teacher leadership models and previous literatures.

However, the second phase of the study shown that only 13 items have been accepted and pooled to form TLI final version. Results from the second phase of the study also suggested that TLI and its constructs fit with the data, as the fit indices RMSEA is 0.06, GFI is 0.92, CFI is 0.95, and Chisq/df is 1.98. In studying TLI scores for convergent and discriminant validity, we examined the relationships between TLI items in the specific factors and between three major factors. The positive loadings among the TLI items range from 0.51 to 0.92 provide initial evidence of TLI's convergent validity. The relationship between the TLI factors or subscales range from 0.70 to 0.83 provide initial evidence of TLI's discriminant validity. These items also show the good internal consistency values to measure teachers' perception toward teacher leadership. The overall internal consistency value is 0.84, meanwhile the values of each constructs range from 0.76 to 0.88. Therefore, these items are suitable to use in exploratory research.

The emergence of the three factors is consistent with the literature on teacher leadership factors as experienced by the secondary schools' teachers. The factors developed are knowledge, skill, and value, as suggested by previous literatures. As for knowledge and skill factors, both have been highlighted and discussed extensively by Katzenmeyer and Moller (2009), Phelps (2008), York-Barr and Duke (2004), as well as Fairman and Mackenzie (2012, 2015) in their models. Meanwhile as for knowledge, skill, and value, these factors also have been discussed in Malaysian Education Development Plan, Malaysian National Policy of Education, and Malaysian Teacher Standard (2009).

Teachers could apply their content, pedagogical, and leadership knowledge in school and community in order to strive for schools' excellence. By this knowledge, teachers could positively influence colleagues and young learners, either formally or informally beyond individual classrooms. Therefore, teachers should be exposed to leadership knowledge since the preservice training so that they could prepare themselves to cater the education current needs. Meanwhile, every teacher also should have influential leadership skills and attributes. Teachers could use this skill to influence their colleagues, students, and other school communities as facilitators, mentors, counselors, and curriculum specialists in improving educational practices and student achievement. Therefore, teachers who had the leadership skills should able to lead and shape a quality educational system. Lastly, teachers should have a set of beliefs about what is the right and wrong way for them to behave, known as value. As the value developer, teachers could emulate the formation of good character of younger generations and communities. The values teachers should have are honesty, discipline, responsibility, timeliness, and committed to their work. These good personal qualities could guide and educate students as well as communities to develop their personal character. Hence, a set of well-developed items suitable with the Malaysian educational context has been developed, and it is crucial for Malaysian teachers' to know and aware of their leadership elements by using this self-assessment items.

This study has a few weakness, such as the comparison of the values of internal consistency among the studies cannot be done extensively because less of reviewed inventory by previous researchers. Inventory should be statistically reviewed especially been used in different context and culture. Secondly, because the TLI was deliberately restricted in its focus, it was not comprehensive in its coverage of school culture in enhancing teacher leadership. Also, if researchers were interested in developing a more comprehensive measure of teacher leadership in Malaysian teacher populations, it would be necessary to begin with a much broader item bank than was used in this study. Thirdly, the sample only consisted of secondary school's teacher; therefore the future study should be extended to primary school teachers. Similar research could be done on a more diverse sample, so that the validity of the item could be tested across different samples, and the results of the study could be generalized. As suggestion, future studies also need to be conducted on other demographic groups of teachers, for example, age, gender, and year of service, to further validate the obtained scores from TLI. Fourthly, the comparison between research findings cannot be done because this inventory is the newly developed one. Further study also should be explored on the perception of the teachers on the existence of other teacher leadership models as well as using rigorous analysis such as cluster analysis. Notwithstanding the need for additional research, it is hoped that the TLI will become a useful tool for researchers, especially those interested in understanding the role as well as self-assessment inventory of teacher leadership. Moreover, hopefully the findings are also valuable for ministry of education, school-based professional learning developers', teacher educator, school administrators, and teachers references, who are interested more in exploring teacher leadership.

Acknowledgments This research is funded by UPSI University Research Grant (2017-0166-106-01).

References

Abas, I. (2007). Peranan guru membina murid menghadapi cabaran Wawasan 2020. *Jurnal Penyelidikan Pendidikan Institut Perguruan Islam*, Selangor, Jilid, *10*, 82–89.

Abdullah, A. G. K., Hassan, A. A., & Ying-Leh, L. (2019). Kesan nilai kerja guru dan budaya sekolah ke atas spiritualiti di tempat kerja. *Jurnal Kepimpinan Pendidikan, 6*(2), 1–15.

Abidin, M. Z., Norwani, N. M., & Musa, K. (2016). Teacher leadership knowledge to pre-service teachers. *International Journal of Academic Research in Business and Social Sciences, 6*(11), 351–360.

Ado, K. (2016). From pre-service to teacher leader: The early development of teacher leaders. *Issues in Teacher Education, 25*(1), 3–21.

Angelle, P. S., Nixon, T. J., Norton, E. M., & Niles, C. A. (2011). *Increasing organizational effectiveness: An examination of teacher leadership, collective efficacy, and trust in schools.* Paper presented at the annual meeting of the University Council for Educational Administration, Pittsburgh, 19 Nov 2011.

Bandalos, D. L., & Finney, S. J. (2018). Factor analysis: Exploratory and confirmatory. In G. R. Hancock & R. O. Mueller (Eds.), *The reviewer's guide to quantitative methods in the social sciences* (pp. 93–108). New York, NY, USA: Routledge.

Barnett, J., Diaz, M., Merz, S., Redfield, C., Wawro, T., & West, B. (2018). *The teacher leadership competencies.* National Education Association, National Board for Professional Teaching Standards, and the Center for Teaching Quality.

Bond, N. (2011). Preparing preservice teachers to become teacher leaders preparing preservice teachers to become teacher leaders. The Educational Forum, 1725.

Bond, N., & Sterrett, W. (2014). Developing teacher leaders through honorary professional organizations in education: Focus on the college student officers. *Education, 135*(1), 25–38.

Broemmel, A. D., Jordan, J., & Whitsett, B. M. (2016). *Learning to be teacher leaders: A framework for assessment, planning, and instruction.* New York: Routledge.

Brondyk, S., & Stanulis, R. (2014). Teacher leadership for change. *Kappa Delta Pi Record, 50*(1), 13–17.

Byrne, B. M. (2016). *Structural equation modelling with AMOS: Basic concepts, applications, and programming* (3rd ed.). New York: Routledge.

Carver, C. L. (2016). Transforming identities: The transition from teacher to leader during teacher leader preparation. *Journal of Research on Leadership Education, 11*(2), 158–180.

Cheng, A., & Zamarro, G. (2016). *Measuring teacher conscientiousness and its impact on students: insight from the measures of effective teaching longitudinal database.* EDRE working paper no. 2016-05. Available at: http://ssrn.com/abstract=2768970

Cherkowski, S., & Schnellert, L. (2017). Exploring teacher leadership in a rural, secondary school: Reciprocal learning teams as a catalyst for emergent leadership. *International Journal of Teacher Leadership, 8*(1), 6–25.

Danielson, C. (2006). *Teacher leadership that strengthens professional practice.* Alexandria, VA: Association for Supervision and Curriculum Development.

Danielson, C. (2007). The many faces of leadership. *Educational Leadership, 65*(1), 14–19.

Darling-Hammond, L., Flook, L., Cook-Harvey, C., Barron, B., & Osher, D. (2019). Implications for educational practice of the science of learning and development. *Applied Developmental Science*, 1–44. https://doi.org/10.1080/10888691.2018.1537791.

Day, C. (2017). *Teachers' worlds and work: Understanding complexity, building quality.* New York: Routledge.

Dehart, C. A. (2011). A comparison of four frameworks of teacher leadership for model fit. University of Tennessee. Retrieved from http://trace.tennessee.edu/utk_graddiss/1072.

De Villiers, E., & Pretorius, S. G. (2011). Democracy in schools: are educators ready for teacher leadership? *South African Journal of Education, 31*(4), 574–589.

Fairman, J. C., & Mackenzie, S. V. (2012). Spheres of teacher leadership action for learning. *Professional Development in Education, 38*(2), 267–286.

Fairman, J. C., & Mackenzie, S. V. (2015). How teacher leaders influence others and understand their leadership, *International Journal of Leadership in Education, 18*(1), 61–87. https://doi.org/10.1080/13603124.2014.904002

Frost, D. (2012). From professional development to system change: Teacher leadership and innovation. *Professional Development in Education, 38*(2), 205–227.

Ghani, M. F. A., & Crow, G. M. (2013). Amalan komuniti pembelajaran profesional: Perspektif pemimpin sekolah cemerlang negara maju. *Jurnal Kurikulum dan Pengajaran Asia Pasific, 1*(3), 10–27.

Ghani, M. F. A., Radzi, N. M., Marzuki, S., & Faisol, E. (2014). Pengenalan kepada amalan kepimpinan guru di Malaysia: Cabaran dan cadangan. *Management Research Journal, 3*, 71–92.

Gomez-Torres, E., Batanero, C., & Miguel, C. J. C. (2016). Developing a questionnaire to assess the probability content knowledge of prospective primary school teachers. *Statistics Education Research Journal, 15*(2), 197–215.

Green, R. L. (2005). *Practicing the art of leadership: A problem-based approach to implementing the ISLLC standards*. Ohio: Pearson.

Hair, J. F., Black, W. C., Babin, B. J., Anderson, R. E., & Tatham, R. L. (2018). *Multivariate data analysis*. New Jersey: Pearson Prentice Hall.

Harmon, H. L. (2017). Collaboration: A partnership solution in rural education. *The Rural Educator, 38*(1), 1–5.

Harris, A., & Jones, M. (2010). Professional learning communities and system improvement. *Improving Schools, 13*(2), 172–181.

Hu, L., & Bentler, P. M. (1999). Cutoff criteria for fit indexes in covariance structure analysis: Conventional criteria versus new alternatives. *Structural Equation Modeling: A Multidisciplinary Journal, 6*(1), 1–55. https://doi.org/10.1080/10705519909540118

Huang, T. (2016). Linking the private and public: Teacher leadership and teacher education in the reflexive modernity. *European Journal of Teacher Education, 39*(2), 222–237.

Hunzicker, J. (2013). Attitude has a lot to do with it: Dispositions of emerging teacher leadership. *Teacher Development, 17*(4), 538–561. https://doi.org/10.1080/13664530.2013.849614

Idris, N. H., & Hamzah, R. (2012). *Nilai profesionalisme bakal guru berteraskan indikator Standard Guru Malaysia (SGM)*.

Jackson, T., Burrus, J., Bassett, K., & Roberts, R. D. (2010). Teacher leadership: An assessment framework for an emerging area of professional practice. ETS research report series, 2010: i–41. https://doi.org/10.1002/j.2333-8504.2010.tb02234.x.

Katzenmeyer, M., & Moller, G. (2009). *Awakening the sleeping giant: Helping teachers develop as leaders*. Thousand Oaks, CA: Corwin Press.

Khan, A., & Ahmad, W. (2012). Leader's interpersonal skills and its effectiveness at different levels of management. *International Journal of Business and Social Science, 3*(4), 296–305.

Kho, F. C. Y., Yusof, H., & Mohamad, S. I. S. (2016). Development and validation of the teacher leadership competency scale. *Malaysian Journal of Learning and Instruction, 13*(2), 43–69.

Leonard, J., Petta, K., & Porter, C. (2012). A fresh look at graduate programs in teacher leadership in the United States. *Professional Development in Education, 38*(2), 189–204.

Lieberman, A., Campbell, C., & Yashkina, A. (2017). *Teacher learning and leadership: Of, by, and for teachers*. New York: Routledge.

Lieberman, A., & Miller, L. (2005). Teachers as leaders. *The Educational Forum, 69*, 151–162.

MacBeath, J., Pedder, D., & Swaffield, S. (2007). *Improving learning how to learn: Classroom, schools and networks*. New York: Routledge.

Mat Som, H., & Megat Daud, M. A. K. (2008). Globalisasi dan cabaran pendidikan di Malaysia [Globalization Educational Challenges in Malaysia]. *Masalah Pendidikan, 31*(1), 91–101.

Ministry of Education. (2009). *Malaysia teacher standard*. Putrajaya: Ministry of Education Malaysia.

Ministry of Education. (2013). *Malaysian education development plan 2013–2025*. Putrajaya: Ministry of Education Malaysia.

Mohd Noah, S., & Ahmad, J. (2005). *Pembinaan modul: Bagaimana membina modul latihan dan modul akademik*. Serdang: Penerbit UPM.

Mok, S. S. (2010). *Psikologi Pendidikan dan Pedagogi Murid dan Alam Belajar*. Kuala Lumpur: Penerbitan Multimedia Sdn. Bhd.

Moller, G., & Katzenmeyer, M. (1996). *Every teacher as a leader*. San Farancisco: Jossey-Bass.

Morin, A. J. S., Arens, A. K., Tran, A., & Caci, H. (2016). Exploring sources of construct-relevant multidimensionality in psychiatric measurement: A tutorial and illustration using the Composite Scale of Morningness. *International Journal of Methods in Psychiatric Research, 25*(4), 277–288.

Muijs, D. (2015). Improving schools through collaboration: A mixed methods study of school-to-school partnerships in the primary sector. *Oxford Review of Education*, 1–24. https://doi.org/10.1080/03054985.2015.1047824.

Muijs, D., Chapman, C., & Armstrong, P. (2013). Can early careers teachers be teacher leaders? A study of second-year trainees in the teach first alternative certification programme. *Educational Management Administration & Leadership, 41*(6), 767–781.

Musa, K., Yusof, H., Noor, M. A. M., Mansor, M., & Abidin, M. Z. (2019). The influence of preservice teacher's self-efficacy on teacher leadership readiness. *International Journal of Academic Research in Progressive Education and Development, 8*(4), 66–76. https://doi.org/10.6007/IJARPED/v8-i4/6436

Neumann, M. D., Jones, L. C. S., & Webb, P. T. (2012). Claiming the political: The forgotten terrain of teacher leadership knowledge. *Action in Teacher Education, 34*(1), 2–13.

Nunnally, J. C., & Bernstein, I. H. (1994). *Psychometric theory*. New York: McGraw-Hill.

Olusegun, S., & Bada, S. O. (2015). Constructivism learning theory: A paradigm for teaching and learning. *IOSR Journal of Research & Method in Education, 5*(6), 66–70.

Ontario Leadership Strategy. (2013). Exploring five core leadership capacities-promoting collaborative learning cultures: Putting the promise into practice. *Bulletin, 3*, 1–23.

Padzil, F. D. A. (2016). Domains of teachers' leadership knowledge: Comparison between models. *International Journal of Academic Research in Business and Social Sciences, 6*(12), 99–112.

Phelps, P. H. (2008). Helping teachers become leaders. *The Clearing House: A Journal of Educational Strategies, Issues and Ideas, 81*(3), 119–122.

Poekert, P. (2012). Teacher leadership and professional development: Examining links between two concepts central to school improvement. *Professional Development in Education, 38*(2), 169–188.

Qomar, M. (2016). Profesionalisme guru berbasis nilai-nilai religius dan akhlak mulia. *Jurnal MPI, 1*(2), 194–205.

Roberts, S. M., & Pruitt, E. Z. (2009). *Schools as professional learning communities: Collaborative activities and strategies for professional development*. Thousand Oaks: Corwin Press.

Sawalhi, R., & Chaaban, Y. (2019). Student teachers' perspectives towards teacher leadership. *International Journal of Leadership in Education*, 1–17. https://doi.org/10.1080/13603124.2019.1666430.

Schulz, A., Muller, P., Schemer, C., Stefanie, D. W., Wettstein, M., & Wirth, W. (2018). Measuring populist attitudes on three dimensions. *International Journal of Public Opinion Research, 30*(2), 316–326.

Schumacker, R. E., & Lomax, R. G. (2016). *Review of a beginner's guide to structural equation modeling* (4th ed.). New York: Routledge.

Sharratt, L., & Fullan, M. (2009). *Realization-the change imperative for deepening district-wide reform*. California: Corwin Press.

Singh, K., Junnarkar, M., & Kaur, J. (2016). *Measures of positive psychology, development and validation*. Berlin: Springer.

Spillane, J. P. (2005). Distributed leadership. *The Educational Forum, 69*(2), 143–150.

Szeto, E., & Cheng, A. Y. N. (2017). Principal–teacher interactions and teacher leadership development: Beginning teachers' perspectives. *International Journal of Leadership in Education, 21*(3), 363–379. https://doi.org/10.1080/13603124.2016.1274785

Tamuri, A. H., Mahmud, Z., & Bari, S. (2005). Permasalahan pelajar-pelajar fakir miskin di daerah Sabak Bernam. *Jurnal Pendidikan Malaysia, 30*, 21–33.

Teacher Leadership Exploratory Consortium. (2011). *Teacher leader model standards* [online]. Available from: http://www.teacherleaderstandards.org. Accessed 10 Feb 2012.

Tuckman, B. W., & Waheed, M. A. (1981). Evaluation an individualized science programme for community college students. *Journal of Research in Science Teaching, 18,* 489–495.

Wenner, J. A., & Campbell, T. (2017). The theoretical and empirical basis of teacher leadership: A review of the literature. *Review of Educational Research, 87*(1), 134–171.

Wilson, A. (2016). From professional practice to practical leader: Teacher leadership in professional learning communities. *International Journal of Teacher Leadership, 7*(2), 45–62.

York-Barr, J., & Duke, K. (2004). What do we know about teacher leadership? Findings from two decades of scholarship. *Review of Educational Research, 74,* 255–316.

Yusof, H., Min, Z. M., Jalil, N. A., Noor, M. A. M., & Yusof, R. (2018). Teacher leadership and its relationship with students' academic achievement. *International Journal of Academic Research in Business and Social Sciences, 8*(9), 1551–1562.

Yusof, H., Vyapuri, L., Jalil, N. A., Mansor, M., & Noor, M. A. M. (2017). The factors affecting teacher leadership in Malaysian Primary Schools. *International Journal of Academic Research in Business and Social Sciences, 7*(6), 620–631.

Index

A
Acceleration, 53, 58, 61, 67
Adjusted Rand Index (ARI), 59
Advanced computing environment (ACE), 120, 125
Algorithms, 51
Amusement equipment, 45
Animation movies, 51
Arduino
    autonomous system, 94
    description, 94
    learning activities (*see* Learning activities)
    microcontrollers, 94
    microprocessors, 94
    sensors, 94
    teaching approach, 108
Arduino board
    microprocessors and microcontrollers, 94
    as a power source, 96
    user test, 105
Automatic assessment
    adaptive teaching, 121
    digital testing, 120
    E;learning objects/technologies (*see* E-learning)
    learning habits, 116, 117
    microlearning, 122
    questuioning, 121
Automatic assessment system (AAS), 120, 124
Automatic methods, 51
Autonomous
    computer literacy, 40
    and ideological models, 33
    language literacy, 37
    literacy, defined, 34
Autonomous model of literacy, 34, 35
Average Silhouette Score (ASS), 58

B
Bee Bot® (floor robot), 93

C
Cell phones, 36
Children's programming language, 91
Clustering, 130
Clustering algorithms, 52
Clustering techniques
    analysis of motions, 55–57
    ARI, 59
    automatic analysis block, 56
    automatic analysis of motions, 64
    ball throwing experiment, 63
    bottle flip challenge experiment, 60
    cluster homogeneity, 58
    GUI, 68
    IT environment, 56
    kinematic descriptors, 52, 64
    k-means algorithm, 56, 58
    motion learning, 52
    random cluster assignment, 61
    separation quality, 58
Coding
    and CT, 92 (*see also* Computational thinking (CT))
    description, 91

Coding (cont.)
  education, 92
  PNSD, 109
  problem-solving, 94
  use of robots, 92
Community-based learning, 162
Comparative Fit Index (CFI), 203
Computational thinking (CT)
  algorithm skills, 107, 108
  and coding, 92
  and programming, 92
  Arduino (see Arduino)
  description, 92
  educative activities, 92
  Google, 92
  importance, 91
  interdisciplinary skills, 92
  learning path, 92
  non-human agent, 91
  skills, 91, 92
  tools and resources, 93–94
Computer behaviour, 4
Computer chip-based electronic technology, 46
Computer literacy
  amusement equipment, 45
  buying a personal computer, 45
  children's acquisition, 42
  definitions, 40
  digital culture, 41
  digital literacy, 36
  evolution, 34
  ICT, 37
  playing games, 45
  regular and power users, 39
  school policy, 45
Computers, 5
Confirmatory factor analysis (CFA), 200, 203
Content knowledge, 160, 161, 165, 166, 170
Cooperation across schools, 162
Cubetto, 93
Cyber effect, 4

D
Data labeling, 54
Data processing, 51
Desktop-based VR applications, 18
Digital citizens, 36
Digital communication, 5
Digital communication technologies, 3
Digital competence of teachers
  digital transformation, 161
  instructional level, 169
  interventions, 169
  media skills, 160
  online environments, 162
  in online PLC, 168–169
  professional competence, 161
  professional knowledge, 160, 161
  professional teaching competence, 160
  questionnaire, 170
  sample questions, 165
  school level, 169
  teacher training, 160
  TML, 161
  vocational education and training, 161
Digital competences, 109
Digital ethnicity, 4
Digital ethnicity model, 3
Digital ethnicity scale (DES), 5
  development process, 7
  digital ethnic profiles, 9–12
  digital ethnicity, 7
  factor analysis, 7
  intellectual mode, 7
  Likert-type items, 7
  orientation mode, 7
  semantic differentials, 7–9
  social value pattern, 7
Digital literacy, 36
Digital media, 159
Digital transformation, 159, 161, 164
Distance, 65
Domain model, 115
Dynamic time warping (DTW) algorithm, 53, 68

E
Educational robot, 92
E-learning (EL), 71
  automatic assessment items, 122, 123
  learning objects, 123
  metadata, 123, 124
Electronic devices, 39
Ethnic groups, 5
Ethnicity
  digital environments, 5
  digital ethnicity, 7
  gender, 7
  intellectual mode, 6
  national, 7
  nonverbal communication, 6
  orientation mode, 6
  patterns, 5
  race, 5
  social value patterns, 6
  sociobiological definition, 5
  verbal communication, 6

Index   215

Ethnographies, 3, 41
Expert motions, 53, 66
Exploratory factor analysis (EFA), 200, 203

F
Facebook, 3
Face-to-face (F2F) mode, 73
   descriptives, 80
   explanatory data analyses, 79
   hypothese tested, 81
   online instruction, 73
Face-to-face instruction
   research (*see* Research method)
Face-to-face meeting, 163
Feedback system, 68
Field experiment, 24
Formal concept analysis (FCA), 131, 134
Fully immersive VR system, 31

G
Gaming experience, 29
Gender distribution, 24, 25
Gender ethnicity, 7
Gestures, 51
Girls school, 33
Goodness-of-Fit Index (GFI), 203
Google, 92
Graphical user interface (GUI), 68

H
Handwriting, 38, 39, 42, 46
Head-mounted displays (HMD), 18
Hour of Code, 93
Human development, 6
Human learning motion, 52
Human motion
   analysis, 51
   Chinese culture, 53
   cognitive effort, 54
   DTW algorithm, 68
   extreme machine learning, 54
   MLS system, 56
   quality, 53, 54
   skeleton model, 53
   visualization, 54
Human-computer interface (HCI), 51

I
ICT literacy, 41
Ideological model of literacy, 34, 36

Ideology
   ideological model of literacy, 34
Importance-performance map analysis
     (IPMA), 164, 166, 167
Information and Communications Technology
     (ICT), 117, 118
   capability, 40
   computer literacy skills, 41
   digital culture, 41
   ethnographic quantitative approach, 41
   handwriting, 38
   home/school environment, 44
   language literacy skills, 37
   literacy, 41
   multidimensional-related literacies, 40
   self-efficacy, 43
   skills, 43
   teaching and learning practices, 36
   tools and environments, 35
   use of computers, 37
Information system (IS), 71
Information systems success model (ISSM)
   defining, 71
   e-learning context, 72
   empirical research endeavors, 72
   experimental approach, 84
   feedback loops, 71
   IT service, 71
   OL systems
     contribution, 83
     findings, 82, 85
     implications, 83, 84
Infrared camera system, 61
Intellectual modes, 6–8, 11, 12
Internet, 36, 40
Internet access, 4
Internet of Things (IoT), 3
iPads, 36
iPods, 36

K
Kinect sensor, 53

L
Language literacy
   awareness of phonemes, 37
   children's acquisition, 42
   handwriting, 38–39
   interaction, 37
   Internet, 40
   read and write, 37
   skills, 42, 44

Learner model, 115
Learner motions, 52, 53, 56, 64–66
Learning activities
   AND logic operator, 99
   blinking LED, 97, 98
   design and implementation, 95
   learning by doing and tinkering
      approaches, 94
   LED controlled by a switch, 96
   OR operator, 100
   rail crossing, 102, 103
   traffic lights, 100, 101
   turn on and off, LED, 98
Learning communities, 160
Learning management systems (LMSs), 120
   AAS, 124
   ACE, 125
   FCA, 134
   integrating online communities, 135
   recommender systems, 126
   retrieval systems, 125, 126
   teaching and assessment, 135
   VLCs, 124, 135
Learning maps, 128
   clustering, 130
   MLP, 130
   NLP, 129
   ontology, 128
   semantic analysis, 129
Learning success
   field experiment, VR, 24
   hypothesis, VR learning unit, 26–28
   pre- and post-tests, 24
   pre-test and post-test, 25
   P-value, 25
   statistical test, 24
LEGO® Mindstorms, 94
Levene test, 28
Literacy
   autonomous model, 34
   definitions, 34
   ideological model, 34
   as knowledge acquisition, 35
   Street's theory, 36
Literacy practices, 36
LOGO, 91
Lower secondary schools, 15, 19, 22, 24, 31

M
Machine learning techniques, 51
Malaysian educational context, 196
Mathematical knowledge management
   (MKM), 134

Mathematical language processing
   (MLP), 130
Microlearning, 122
Microplastics, 20, 21, 23, 25, 30
Missing Completely At Random (MCAR)
   test, 166
Mobile learning, 143
Mobile phones, 43
Monitoring learner activities, 51
Motion capture, 51
Motion Learning Analytics (MLA)
   system, 56, 64
Motivation, 23
Multimodal teaching and learning, 176, 184
Multimodality
   for active and student-centred
      learning, 178–179
   in-game
      classroom, 187
      design of learning, 188
      in-depth understanding, 187
      prevailing digital tools, 188
      strategies, 186
      as student's autonomy and self-
         direction, 188–189
      teaching strategies, 186
   learning and teaching strategy, 176
   learning context, 180
   multiliteracy/multimodal literacy, 176
   serious games, 175
   STEAM, 176, 178, 179
   teacher-directed approaches, 178
   teaching and learning, 175

N
National Assessment Program– Literacy and
   Numeracy (NAPLAN), 37
National ethnicity, 7
Natural language processing (NLP),
   129, 131
Negative attitudes, 167
Niche Research Grant Scheme (NRGS), 202
Nonverbal communication, 6

O
Online PLCs
   challenges, 163
   competence requirements, 162
   cooperation across schools, 162
   development and validation of
      instruments, 166
   discriminant validity, 167

effectiveness, 162
face-to-face meeting, 163
instructor/moderator, 163
learning communities, 162
online environments, 162
online setting, 163
professional development of teachers, 162
purpose of measurement, 164
specific tasks, 163
structural equation models, 167
teacher education and training, 162
teacher training, 162
teachers digital competences, 168–169
teachers motivation, 163
technical issues, 163
Ontology-based retrieval systems, 134
Orientation mode, 6, 7
Osmo, 93
Outdoor learning
adaption/flexibility/intervention, 151
Avastusrada and SmartZoos apps, 146, 148, 153, 154
awareness/assessment, 152, 155
design/planning, 150
learning through creating, 145
methods, 146–148
mobile learning, 143
orchestration, 144, 145
regulation/management, 151
results, 149
teachers role, 152–154

P
Papert's Logo project, 93
Partial least squares (PLS) modeling approach, 79
Pedagogical content knowledge, 160, 161, 165, 166, 170
Pedagogical knowledge, 160, 161, 164, 165, 167
Physical technology, 92
Problem-solving skill, 91, 92, 94, 108
Professional competence, 161
Professional knowledge, 160, 161
Professional learning communities (PLCs)
description, 162
online (*see* Online PLCs)
success factors, 162

Q
Questionnaire, 106

R
Reliability, 202, 203
Research method
applied data analytics, 79
factoral experiment, 73
hypothesis, 75, 77, 78
measurement, 78, 79
participants, 74
procedure, 75
proposed structural model, 77
research design, 73, 74
Robotic education, 93
Robots, 92
Root Mean Square Error of Approximation (RMSEA), 203
Route Planner, 115
Route planning, 127
learning maps, 128
self placed learning, 127
students remediation, 130, 131

S
Scholastic ethnicity, 7
School transformation process, 199
Science, technology, engineering, and mathematics (STEM), 115
Scratch, 93
Scratch4Arduino, 94
Secondary education (K-12), 19
Self-assessments, 164, 167, 168, 170
Self-correction, 65
Semantic web, 133
Serious games
as semiotic domains, 190, 191
in-game learning goals, 175
multimodality, 176
STEAM (*see* STEAM game)
technology and tools, 179
Shapiro test, 27
Situational learning, 17
Skeleton model, 53
Snapchat, 3
Social interaction, 6
Social media
and computer, 4
sites, 3
use, 4
Social networking sites, 36
Social value patterns, 6, 7
Sports motion learning, 53
Statistical test, 24

STEAM game
   core game mechanics, 181
   description, 180
   design and usability study, 180
   goals and outcomes, 180
   in-game feedback, 182
   in-game scenarios, 180–181
   school teachers, 183
   serious game, 175, 179
Superimposition, 53
Supervised learning, 51
Supervised learning algorithms, 55
Supervised machine learning algorithms, 54

T
Teacher education, 161–165, 167, 168
Teacher Leadership Exploratory Consortium (2011), 198
Teacher Leadership Inventory (TLI)
   activities, 195
   CFA, 203
   chi-squared index, 204
   cluster analysis, 207
   contexts, 195
   convergent and discriminant validity, 206
   convergent indices value, 204
   definition, 195
   demographic groups, 207
   elements, 195
   exploratory factor analysis, 202, 203
   factor analysis, 206
   fit indices, 204
   internal consistency values, 204, 206
   inventory, 207
   items, 205
   Malaysian educational setting, 204
   multistage cluster sampling technique, 201
   parameters, 203
   preparation program, 197
   questionnaire design, 202
   reliability, 202, 203
   research and data collection, 201
   school and community, 196, 206
   school culture, 207
   school systems, 197
   school-wide decision-making, 196
   secondary school teachers, 206, 207
   self-assessment items, 207
   self-efficacy, 195
   skills, 197, 198, 206
   students' physical and psychological, 196
   validity, 202, 203
   value, 199–201
   violate discriminant index range, 204
Teacher Leadership Self-Assessment (TLSA), 200
Teacher training, 160
Teachers skill, 197, 198
Teachers value, 199–201
Teaching strategies, 186
Team-based learning, 162
Technology, 92
Technology-enhanced learning (TEL)
   children learning specific motions, 53
   clustering techniques, 52
   dance motions, 53
   environment, 52
   motion learning, 53
   scientific and technic challenges, 52
   targeted motion, 64
Technology-mediated learning (TML), 161
Telepresence, 17
Theory-driven research model, 83
Throwing motion, 52, 53, 58, 62, 66
Twitter, 3

U
Unsupervised machine learning algorithms, 55

V
Validity, 202, 203
Value developer, 200
Verbal communication, 6
Video-game, 51
Virtual communities
   e-learning systems, framework, 117, 118
   examples, 120
   fundamental processes, 118, 119
   integration technologies, 117
   instructors, 116
   learning targets
      educational references, 132
      mastery levels, 132
      ontologies, STEM, 134
      ontology based educational system, 133
      semantically structured, 132
      teaching, 132
   VLCs, 118
   potential problem, 116
Virtual learning communities (VLCs), 118
Virtual reality (VR), 51
   benefits for education, 17
   challenges for education, 18

characteristics, 16, 19
controllers, 16
desktop-based applications, 18
egocentric and exocentric perspectives, 17
field experiment, 24
HMD, 18
in training sector, 18
learning environments, 15
learning unit
   analysis, 17
   features, 19, 20
   immersion, 22–23
   implementation, 29
   interaction, 23
   learning environment, 23
   micro world, 20
   motivation, 23
   underwater landscape, 19
   video games, 22
secondary research objective, 16
situational learning, 17
telepresence, 17
training benefits, 17
Vocational education and training, 160, 161, 168–170
VR learning environment, 23

W
Writing skills, 34, 37, 38

Y
YouTube, 3

Printed by Printforce, the Netherlands